The Long Tide To Silence

Julian Cowan Hill

The Long Tide To Silence

First Edition

First published by Kindle 2018

Other books published by Julian Cowan Hill

A Positive Tinnitus Story: How I Let Go of Tinnitus the Natural Way
Published by Kindle 2014

Tinnitus, From Tyrant to Friend: How to Let Go of the Ringing in your Ears
Published by Kindle 2010

Foreword

This is the story of how I managed to turn off extremely bad tinnitus after many years of symptoms. I made a complete recovery and have lived a tinnitus-free life for many years now.

If you have tinnitus please read this book with care. The last thing I would like to do is to activate your tinnitus. If you are feeling vulnerable or afraid, I recommend reading my other books first on how to get better with tinnitus. They are full of positi constructive advice.

My aim is to help people with tinnitus and to improve the often appalling way tinnitus is managed. Getting help to release nervous activation with calming body-based therapies like Craniosacral Therapy, settling the nervous system with Yoga, Tai Chi, and understanding how tinnitus works and what helps switch it off, all help tinnitus get better.

The medical profession would save a lot of money by signposting tinnitus people towards calming therapeutic support. Saying it will never go away and that you have to learn to live with it can harm people, sometimes with devastating consequences. This is not true. This is my story to show why I say this.

Please note that, apart from my family, I have changed the names of people I have known in real life to protect their identities. All references to people I have worked with have been changed to form composite characters that generally reflect various tendencies in tinnitus people rather than referring to any one specific person.

Chapter 1 The Sound of Silence

Riyadh, Saudi Arabia, 1979

"Suppose in the beginning there is an open plain without any mountains or trees, completely open land, a simple desert without any particular characteristics. That is how we are, what we are. We are very simple and basic. And yet there is a sun shining, a moon shining, and there will be lights and colours, the texture of the desert. There will be some feeling of the energy, which plays between heaven and earth. This goes on and on.
Then, strangely, there is suddenly someone to notice all this. It is as if one of the grains of sand had stuck its neck out and begun to look around. We are that grain of sand, coming to the conclusion of our separateness."

Chogyam Trungpa Rinpoche - Cutting Through Spiritual Materialism, p125

This story starts in 1979, driving through the dusty streets of Riyadh in Saudi Arabia. It was the end of April and the sun was baking the bone-dry air to 120 degrees. I was 13 years old, and the proud owner of a brand-new Seiko watch. I was timing how long I could hold my breath for on the digital stopwatch. My father was at the wheel. He was singing along to a tape of Dudley Moore, Joni Mitchell, and Stan Getz. He was happy, fit and strong. He was at his peak then.

Dad was a pilot. He wanted to show me something. From the air he had seen a new road being built from the capital city running eastwards to the coast. Down below, the small line or tarmac stretched out into the vast empty desert like a line traced across a piece of slightly crumpled brown paper.

4

This line filled him with curiosity. What would it be like to drive to the end of the road? The idea flashed through my father's head for a couple of seconds. A couple of days later, there we both were, setting out on a journey with our own heart-beating lives towards the road which ran out into the baking oven-hot wilderness.

"It just stops in the middle of nowhere," he said.
I tried to look enthusiastic.

I don't know what compelled Dad to leave the relative safety of the city behind and head off into the unknown? Maybe it was that male energy that simply likes to penetrate space, explore and then conquer it. Maybe it was something deeper, acting through him, wanting to challenge both of us. Whatever it was, I was in, and it was in this pioneering light that Dad and I found ourselves about to be the first father and son to drive down this virgin road.

We drove past the ubiquitous lines of water trucks that marched into town from all corners of the Arabian Peninsular and sloshed into line like over-watered camels. Out of the large, apparently open lids, their life-giving elixir would splash and spatter all over the dusty street below. Every minute or so each truck would let out a sudden spit of air, making you jump out of your skin. The thirsty city pulled in so many trucks that, wherever you went the sound of spitting and ticking filled the city roads with sound.

Lines of date palms and vibrant green grass lay waiting to guzzle up the water. The battle was on to stop being swallowed up by the silent, engulfing sand or to be evaporated into thin air by a blazing and savagely hot sun. Empty space was a constant threat to civilisation here.

So there I was, driving off to the vast furnace of a Saudi Arabian desert, with no help for miles around. Should we run into trouble, a thirteen-year-old boy was still perfectly capable of placing his life entirely into the hands of Dad without giving it a second thought. Any problem and he would deal with it. I would just sit back and enjoy the ride. I didn't have to worry about a thing. Seems such a luxury now. For years, Dad successfully managed to keep the stresses of the world off my shoulders. I am deeply grateful to him for that. Of course I took it for granted at the time. That's just how it works.

First we had to get across Riyadh, a sprawling, half-modern, half-ancient city that was sprouting shopping malls and buildings wherever the oil and water landed. This place was built on the tenacity and will-power of tribal families of the dessert who, despite the ferocious climate, determined to settle here.

We were driving along in a battered white car that one of Dad's students had given him. He worked for the Saudi Air Force as a fighter-pilot instructor. Every week he would get back to his room in the officer's mess to find yet another generous present left for him by appreciative students. Sometimes he would find a suitcase crammed full of coffee and incense burners. Sometimes there would be a parcel with a beautiful, curved Arabian Dagger or a framed picture of King Khalid.

His students were handsome, with big black moustaches and warm handshakes. They behaved like adoring sons with a never-ending respect for the ex-Vulcan-bomber pilot.

Sometimes, when we met, they would be dressed in the crisp, white thobe and red headdress. This traditional dress looked formal and intimidating and commanded respect. In the hair-dryer hot air, the white cotton was cool and reflected the sun, and allowed the lower body to be as free as could be. Black clothes absorb the sun and are the hottest hell. They are reserved for the women. But most of the time Dad's students would appear in flying suits with a dark line of sweat running down both sides of the zipper. To cool down after a flight they would undo the zip down to the gold medallion and jet-black chest hair.

Above the pilot sunglasses a tight helmet mark would still be visible across the top of their foreheads. In their hands they would be carrying a navigation map, or a helmet with a long, black, curly wire dangling down with a gold prong sticking out of the end. Every day Dad and a student would climb into a two-seater Strike-Master that would be waiting in the sun at 55 degrees centigrade inside. One of them would ram the throttle forward, and then in a thunderous, chest-rattling roar, they would both hurtle down the runway and tear into the sky. In seconds the sprawling building sites would fall away to reveal patches of bare desert that skirted around the airport. Patterns of squares and rectangles appeared with walled-in housing complexes and their swimming pools, linking together along green avenues to the narrow mud-streets of the old parts of town.

The fighter jet would steam past the striking, black and white vertical stripes of the funnel-shaped water tower, over the ancient adobe citadel, the mud-walled men's souk, the camel market, reaching the south side of town in just a few minutes. Then, tugging aggressively upwards against gravity, the plane would pull away from the outskirts of the city before suddenly petering out into dust, reaching the big, nothing.

Nothing.

Soon there was just nothing. An expanse of nothing would open up and fill the entire horizon with its hard, unforgiving emptiness, and they would disappear into it like a tiny dot on a page.

Astride the rocket, Dad would magic each student off into a pilot's paradise of endless sky and desert. He would find his favourite ridge of rock and follow it up, as it serpented back and forth, higher and higher out of the sand, chasing the spine of a giant reptile of rock, before reaching the massive plateau of sand and rock at the top.

Then, suddenly he would plunge his students over the edge of a huge canyon opening up in front of them. As if on a supersonic switchback ride, he would tear down at a terrifying angle down towards the valley floor, sending the blood bulging into his student's cheeks. Then, down even further he would fly them, closer and closer to the ground with dizzying speed, until they were so low that pairs of rocky pinnacles would tower above either side of the tiny cockpit like orange skyscrapers, that flashed past in a blink of an eye.
He would carry on flying deliberately low until Yussuf or Abdul's forehead broke into a sweat. Dad dared to push lower than they ever would have dreamed of until single tamarisk bushes could be seen flying past in a blur along the wadi floor. Dad held his breath and then,

"Saiyr, you are going veri low!" The student's nerve snapped.

At that moment, Dad would suddenly pull hard back on the stick till his biceps shook, sending the jet rocketing back up into the sky. The earth would fall away, the gravity gauge would shoot to 4.5Gs plunging the student's entrails to the back of his body, forcing his back hard into the curve of the ejector seat, cheeks squeezing against his teeth, chest squashed and blood draining from his head to the verge of blacking out. His eyes, if still open at this stage, would be filled with nothing but a pale blue sky spiralling round and round.

Then, breathing out slowly, Dad would gently push the stick away forcing the plain gently forward, sending the colour flooding back into the Saudi's, cheeks going slack, and returning his stomach back to its normal position. As the plane levelled out and the student regained his composure, Dad would ease the plane forward until a map he left on the dashboard lifted up and started floating in air right before the astonished face. Grinning from cheek to cheek, Dad would turn to them and say calmly, "Now it's your turn. Over to you."

Then the plane would head south east, off to the Rub' al Khali or Empty Quarter, a vast ocean of sand larger than the whole of France and with more sand than the whole of the Sahara. There they were free to do whatever their wanted in the empty sky, as long as their fuel-tank would extend them to. Together they would discover intricate formations of dunes sculptured by invisible artists hidden in the wind, seen for the first time by a chosen few, for just a few minutes.

Together Dad and his students would learn to fly free, darting round giant dust-bowls the size of small cities, hanging in the sky, rotating slowly in silence. Sometimes they would chase dust-devils, the tall thin tornados of sand, whipped up into a frenzied vortex by columns of rising heat. They clearly had a ball. In this pilot's paradise of empty airspace his students slowly turned into fighter pilots and their minds took on the shape that slots neatly into a war machine.
Once back on the ground his students would greet me with a hand on their heart, eyes still wide open and a beaming smile. They had been on the mother of all fairground rides, thanks to my father. As much as I wished I could join Dad, I made do with sometimes watching them from the hut at the end of the runway and loved hearing these stories which made me feel really proud of him.

For a thirteen-year-old boy Saudi Arabia was a wild and exciting adventure. I loved driving through the streets of Riyadh. We were on an adventure. The burning sunlight made the dusty walls glow like a crazed giant toaster, heating the air in between to an almost unbearable degree. Demons of heat spiralled off the road surface into every opening, scavenging the alleys and porches for any remaining moisture or coolness that dared to lurk at this time of day, and quickly sucking the life out of them.

If I sniffed in with any force, the air burnt up the insides of my nostrils. If I didn't keep sipping from a bottle of water my mouth would dry up and quickly start tasting of dust and my throat would start burning. And yet people were carrying on life as normal, showing only a minimal frown or sometimes shading their faces from the sun with their hands.

We drove past rotisseries of chicken and rice shops and then hit a wall of pungent blue smoke billowing out of the coffee roasters. When the car drew still, a huddle of women in black shuffled past giving off a powerful scent of rose oil. There was never any eye-contact with them, unlike the men, who stared right at you curiously.

On my lap was a large sack of lemon cashew nuts. We crunched through whole handfuls at a time. I pulled out a long, thin tamarind pod and sucked on its sharp yet delicious flavour.

The road was full of aggressive white Toyota trucks hooting and overtaking yellow taxis forcefully. Fast cars revved in a show of testosterone and speed and from time to time my father had to suddenly swerve to avoid a huge hole in the road or an angry driver pulling in front of us far too close. It was like the Wild West, but with red headdresses and white thobes on.

Then, out of nowhere an ear-splitting "Allahu Akbar!" started up. Almost immediately the traffic started to slow down. Then another long, slow rising crescendo of "Allaaaaaahuuu," followed by a sudden release of "Akbar!" In the supermarkets the checkout assistants sighed and immediately started to shut down the tills. The merchants in the gold souks and people working in the banks obediently started finishing off what they were doing. The midday Salah or prayer-time had started.

Down the street another voice started up across the tannoy, "Allahu Akbar!" and soon other voices joined from other parts of the city filling the streets of Riyadh with a solemn sound of men singing perfectly out of tune to a western ear. At first it sounds wrong, but quickly the more mathematically correct Arabian scale becomes hauntingly beautiful.

Each muezzin would sing the call to prayer or "adhan" at a slightly different pitch to the one at the following street corner, setting up a dissonance that caused the air to wobble. It was discordant, chaotic and yet mesmerising. This strange, male happenchance choir that appeared out of nowhere pervaded everything with an eerie force. It gave me goose pimples.

The age-old message of "God is Great" was being brought to life and reawakened by the hearts of men in the same way that it had been across the centuries. The sky was filling with this powerful call to prayer that was flowing into every space in the city, giving each person a stark reminder to reflect on the seriousness of life's spiritual purpose and struggle.

Quite literally normal life was being interrupted and shaken out of its stupor. Something deeper and more meaningful was being called upon. Everyone was to stop what they were doing and get ready to turn their focus inwards and start accessing something that can only be reached through contemplation and prayer.

"Oh Christ, we are going to get Salah-ed," shouted Dad, as he put his foot down and aimed for the crossing up ahead. Men were now praying everywhere, on the pavements, in front of cafes and at the back of supermarkets. Everything was grinding to a halt.
"Gosh look! There's a guy over there rolling out his prayer mat in the street!"
"Yup!" my father said with a can-you-believe-it tone of voice.

"Do you think they have any choice?" I asked.

"What, with Islam you mean?" Dad replied.

"Yes. I didn't absolutely everyone seems to be getting ready for prayer. Are they forced to? "

"Oh probably."

"But that means some of them are just going through the motions without their hearts being in it."

"So what?" Dad asked. He needed to concentrate hard on driving around the slowing traffic clogging up in the narrow streets.

"Well if their hearts are not in it, then they might as well not be there."

"If you say so, Sonny Jim. If you say so..."

Everywhere we looked men were kneeling down and reciting the Qur'an under their breath. The mood was changing, becoming serious, and faces filled with heartfelt feeling. The city was slowing down like a cine film running slowly enough to see the gaps in between each frame. Something else was appearing in between the normal actions.

I thought about British towns at midday and they seemed a bit flabby by comparison. After a couple of hours of work, midday is the time to undo the belt a bit and enjoy lunch, have a pint, a chat and a bit of a burp.

But Riyadh showed me disciplined spirituality for the first time and it commanded respect. Something was causing these men to stop their cars, get out their prayer-mats and start praying in the middle of the street. This was not about pleasure or fun. People here were expected to struggle a bit and show a spiritual commitment. Peace-loving Muslims refer to this struggle as jihad.

"I find it a bit scary. Don't you?"

"Not really. You get used to it after a while. Mind you, I didn't like seeing that guy's hand being cut off in Chop Square."

"You didn't really see it, did you?"
"Yes I did, but... it was a long way off," Dad admitted. He slowed down to make his way carefully around a couple of men in prayer.

"Do you remember when Fiona was beaten in the men's souk?"

"Yes, Fiona was a very naughty girl. She shouldn't have exposed her wrists and ankles in that way. We should have known better. When in Riyadh do as the Mutaween do."

"Indeed." We both laughed. "Fancy showing a wrist. How outrageous of her.."

The road ahead was clear. Suddenly Dad was able to accelerate ahead, and shortly we found ourselves cruising along a dual carriageway with lamp-posts and date palms stretching ahead to the outer limits of the city. Blocks of flats either side turned into solitary buildings with gardens of rubble around them. Every so often there would be a brilliant patch of green grass.

Then, large empty spaces of desert opened up on either side of the road. In places, sand-drifts started to reach over the hard-shoulder. Sometimes the sand engulfed the foot of a lamppost or a wall completely.

Then all signs of civilisation fell away. After a few abandoned bull-dozers on the side of the road, the car passed through empty spaces. No trees, no lampposts, no signs, no rubble, or even road markings, just a jet-black, newly tarmacked road stretching straight ahead to the horizon. Above there was a yellowish-blue sky, below was an endless flat desert of rock and rubble. The only thing that filled the entire visible world was the single line of the road running for miles and miles ahead, drawing up thinner and thinner to the horizon until it disappeared into a tiny point.

My father turned off the music. Even though the engine was running at quite a speed, this sudden lack of sound felt like a crutch had been pulled away exposing us to the big nothing that was opening up around us.

I had never seen a vast expanse of nothing before. In Britain there is always a church, or over the other side of the moor, a pub. Even in the most spectacular and remote parts of Scotland, if you walk for a few hours you will sooner or later come across a letter box or a Bed and Breakfast.

Here, on the other hand, a great big void was opening up to us and extended for hundreds and hundreds of miles in all directions. The light was so bright I had to squint through the sunglasses. We were entering a place where you die quickly without water.

The searing heat made the light swarm and flutter in the desert either side of the road as if there were a million invisible birds flying frantically around us. Up ahead, a finger of wavering blue mirage touched down onto the road like a hallucination. It was the hottest air I had ever experienced, burning in through the windows like a cigarette lighter. My face felt tight like a grilled sausage, and I had to hold my breath to cool down my throat and nostrils.
If I stopped sipping the water, within a minute my throat started drying up uncomfortably. The temperature was going up in the giant oven outside and it was starting to scare me. How much hotter would it get? My heart quickened.

"Meep meep!" my father cried, and blew a raspberry like Road Runner. The road did look like one of those in the cartoon. He laughed and I tried to laugh back. He seemed really happy to be here sharing this with me. This cheered me up a little and I released my tight grip on the hot door handle. Immediately I felt a cool flash up my forearm from the sweat, which quickly evaporated and went hot again.

"Where are we going?" I asked nervously.
"Just wait and see." He replied, staring straight ahead. He had a wry smile on his face.

The car accelerated and slowly the tiny speck of movement the car brought into the empty hemisphere edged out into the endless, flat frying pan, getting further and further away from human life and help. My eyes started to fixate on the monotonous road ahead. There wasn't anything else for them to react to. Even though we were moving fast across the sand and rock, at times it seemed like we weren't moving at all. I imagined that our wheels had left the ground and that we were actually flying along on a layer of fiery air.

"What happens if we break down?" I asked. Dad's dishevelled car had survived the daily gauntlet of Riyadh's mad driving and massive pot holes, but it didn't fill me with confidence. I craned my neck to look out of the side rear-view mirror. All I could see behind was exactly the same yellow-blue sky above and yellow-beige desert below, and the same black line running all the way to the horizon behind. The view was identical in front and behind. All there was in the whole world was Dad, me and a black line.

We were going somewhere, and yet were going nowhere at all. For a moment I imagined that all the civilisation and life that I had experienced had just been a strange dream, and that Dad and I had driven into a strange loop, and this world of unbearable, nostril-burning, lung drying heat would carry on and on for ever and ever.

"Don't worry. We've got enough food and water to keep us going for a few hours. When they start the tarmacking the road again, they'll be back. They'll find us…"

I looked at Dad and gave him a filthy stare.

Then Dad started singing, "Mad dogs and English men go out in the midday sun…"

"Oh shut up."

We sped on, and on, and the heat continued to build like some sadistic furnace. The sand and rock all around was glowing incandescent and looked like it was about melt. My bottom was starting to burn on the hot black leather of the chair. My shorts were wet with sweat underneath. Every time I shifted position my legs burnt and I had to sit on my hands for a moment.

Then it appeared, barely noticeably at first. Up ahead, just in front of the shimmering horizon, a tiny point opened up at the end of the long black line. The end of the road. There it was. A small gap appeared and stayed immobile for a while, getting barely any larger. Then a beige dot of desert started to be clearly distinguishable between the horizon and the end of the road, the point where our journey would rapidly come to an end.

We both stared ahead and started to notice the end of the road approaching us very slowly in the distance. It was creeping up on us. The jet-black line, that we had been fixated upon for the last hour, as if it was the backbone of the entire world, our raison d'etre for being here, there it was, a far off ending.

Beyond the end there was just nothing. Our eyes that had been mesmerised by the black line, following its powerful mark across space, bewitching us with its clarity, suddenly gave way to nothing. Not having anything to rest our gaze on was a bit shocking. The view just fell away into an indistinct dusty colour. There was no clear delineation between the yellowy sky and beige sand and rock below. There was nothing to break the view. The closer we got, the more of the end of the line started accelerating towards us.

Dad was clearly as mesmerised by the monotonous and unreal view as I was, because the end of the line suddenly flew past underneath the car at great speed. The wheels jumped and darted noisily on the uneven surface, slipping and sliding, and flying into a deafening, scrunching of gravel and dust. We skidded and swerved, juddered and jolted, and hit a bump and took to the air for a horrifying moment before coming to a sudden, crunching, screeching, deafening stop. Momentarily my body felt like it was still carrying on for a few metres before being jolted back into the seatbelt. The engine stalled. A cloud of dazzling white dust towered all around us like giant curtains as our senses hit a wall of silence.

The silence was deafening.

We both stared ahead, speechless, shaken, and watched as the dust slowly cleared like giant curtains opening out onto a celestial theatre. As the veils melted away, they revealed an emptiness that I had never felt before. We sat there and felt a stillness descend upon us. It took a few moments to come to and meet the full glory of terrifying emptiness, and its vast landscape around us. It met us and, in return, we dared to meet it.

This soundless Theatre of God for two was overwhelming. It seemed to mass all around with its endless silence and I felt like I was going to disappear. I took a deep breath and deliberately took a noisy swig of water, anything to stop the silence from swallowing me up into its vacuum. My heart was racing.

"God!" I said to break the silence. Dad turned to me and smiled and did one of his terribly amused chuckles. His face was bright red and sweaty.

"Let's synchronise watches. What time do you make it?"

"What?!"

I took a moment and then refocused, made sense of his words, and looked down at my Seiko watch.

"Twelve forty-eight," I replied.

"Same as me. Have a last swig of water and put your hat on."

"Oh my God, what now." I groaned.

"Now I want you to get out and stand on the opposite side of the car to me. Face the desert and don't say a thing for 12 minutes. Listen to this silence. Do you think you can do that?"

"Oh.. kay?" I said in semi-agreement.

"Come on!" he said in his chivvying-me-along tone of voice.

"Oh God! Alright." I replied begrudgingly.

"Not a peep until one o'clock."

"OK!"
With that, I stepped out into the eye-ball smarting bright light and walked round to the boot end of the car.

The car felt like a comforting mooring as I slowly moved my gaze out across the bare desert which blazed back at me like a sea of molten glass. There was no longer any car window protecting me from the vastness outside. I was in the vastness now. It was insanely hot. The only refuge from this inescapable furnace was a thin, cool line of sweat caught beneath the rim of my hat. Everywhere else the bone-dry air felt like it was sucking the moisture out of me like a vampire.

I looked for something to fixate my eyes onto, telescoping closer into beige dust and then panning out further away onto beige dust. I had so sense of how far anything was from me.

Then it hit me. Something I had never experienced before. The sound of pure silence. It was so alien at first that I couldn't quite take it in. But there it was, a vast, primordial void of sound.

It intimidated me so I breathed deliberately to create a bit of noise. But the instant I stopped I just felt a deafening silence build connecting me to hundreds of miles of silence in all directions. I felt so small. Thank God Dad was there. I could never tolerate this by myself.

This deep silence seemed to mass in the stillness like some great presence. It seemed to press in against my temples, and push inside my brain. The silence was there. I was in the silence. I was somehow part of the silence. Just let go and feel it. Let go. Go on… Something vast rushed inwards and overtook me. And yet, at the same time, something in me seemed to spill out and rush back out and fill the overwhelming space. I felt a bit shaken, like every molecule of my body was opening up and letting the whole desert in.

I swear there was something conscious out there that was aware of me and my father standing there. It was palpable. It was like there were eyes in the air watching us and seeing through everything. There seemed to be something there that was responding very gently. The silence was present and went right through everything. The air was in the silence. The world was hanging in the silence. The light was in the silence. The two bodies with beating hearts were there in the silence. The whole shimmering experience felt diaphanous and light as if it could be blown away with one puff, and yet this was grounded by a calm, underlying silence that was strong and still.

For my ears, thirteen years of sound stopped for the first time. It was arresting. There was nothing for my ears to latch onto. I found myself holding my breath so that I could notice the silence more clearly.

Then I looked down at my watch and distracted myself with the three knobs that controlled the digital display. I cleared my throat. I took another deep breath, and listened out at the desert and the total lack of sound again, worlding out in all directions.

My ears reached out further and further like extending antennae, trying to detect something to monitor or some background noise to rest on. They were used to detecting noise and had been quietly pottering along my whole life but now there was nothing for them to grasp onto and they were floundering.

I found myself thinking about what it will be like as we are dying, when the body falls away and we find ourselves in space with none of the usual bearings to interact with or come up against. No body, no breath, no sight, no sound, nothing to bump into or rub up against, nothing of substance to effect anything with. For the first time I felt a deep and frightening sense of how one day I was going to die.

I didn't like this feeling at all and wanted to crawl back into an air-conditioned, music and Coke-filled house again. I wanted to step back into ordinary everyday life instead of being thrust into this ultra-reality, exposed and open, with no control buttons to play with. This deafening silence was starting to freak me out.

There were seven minutes to go. The challenge Dad had set me was much harder than I thought it would be.

Out of nowhere a very feint rushing sound started up in my ears. It came as a bit of relief. I thought it was air molecules beating up against my eardrums. I found myself being distracted. Clearly the silence was so strong that I could now hear something that I had never noticed before. Little did I know how this feint rushing sound in my ears was going to be a seminal moment in my life with consequences for decades to come. I can't believe my first experience of ringing in the ears was such a comforting one.

All around the air was dancing with such intense heat that that I was not sure I was going to be able to last the full twelve minutes. I felt slightly panicky again and I felt pressure starting to push into my temples.

I can't stand it. I'm not going to last. I need to make a noise. I felt myself weaken. I needed to see my father. Breaking the agreement, I turned around and looked across the car. I felt like I was cheating. I locked my gaze onto him standing there with his back to me. He was staring motionless out into the desert ahead. I couldn't see his face but I could see his chest rising and falling. It was slow and deep and he seemed really still. This comforted me.

I could hear him breathing. Even though it was three metres away, the gentle rush of air was clearly audible. I felt such relief in that that I found my body starting to relax, my breathing settling and quickly I felt able to stay the course. I made my mind up to stick to the challenge. I wasn't going to give up that easily. I turned round and faced the desert, this time standing away from the car.

With renewed determination I was able to settle enough to hear more of the silence. The calmer I felt, the more I could dare open to the magnificence of this place and the extraordinary experience that was opening up before me. The more I relaxed the more I could just let the great emptiness sweep in like the desert was introducing itself to me properly.

A single grain of sand would be here long after we had both expired.
I felt so small again. This smallness was putting me in direct contact with something that was unfolding in that silence. It wasn't a void. There was something there, something important, just out of reach. I could sense it somehow, but I couldn't quite put my finger on it.
It was like a vast awareness hanging quietly in the air. It was powerful in its emptiness. It didn't respond in any way that I could directly fathom but I sensed that, whatever it was, it was aware of Dad and I. Our thoughts and feelings were being logged by something. I felt something melt inside like a space was being cleared that let the outside in more and more. Inside and outside started interacting with each other like the desert was realigning me. It was utterly terrifying and yet, at the same time, deeply comforting. I felt a rushing sensation all

around like something was exploding outwards and at the same time was crashing in.

When one o'clock arrived, Dad and I turned to look at each other at exactly the same moment and smiled. We got back into the car but didn't say anything. We didn't need to. The reason why we had come all this way had made itself very clear. We'd got to the end of the road and there was nowhere to go. And then stopping in the stillness for a moment with nowhere to go, we went somewhere, somewhere big and awe-inspiring that was both inside and out. I was very grateful to Dad for daring to share this with me.

Whatever it was that stirred inside on that day had a deep impact on me. It would be a couple of decades before I met such a strong sense of presence again.

Chapter 2 The Sound of Boys Becoming Men

Lancing College, on the South Downs, West Sussex, 1982

"I will take the sun in my mouth
and leap into the ripe air
Alive
with closed eyes
to dash against darkness"

E E Cummings
Poems

It started when I was sixteen. I was sitting in the houseroom, in my cubbyhole-cum-desk, known as an "alley," trying to finish an essay, when, out of nowhere, an almost imperceptible hiss started up. It was like a leaking gas-pipe that seemed to be coming from the corner of the room.

It was a warm summer afternoon. Normally this room was filled to bursting with a never-ending symphony of sound created by male adolescents. First there is the upper-wind section, that is, the show-off burping, throaty belching, falsetto sneezing, panting, coughing, hoicking up of phlegm and spitting, with the lower-wind adding forced farts, the gentle, long melodious breaking of wind, an occasional trump in the pants and the accidental, occasional shart. This would be accompanied by the vocal section with whispering, chatting, laughing, sniggering, guffawing, whistling, humming, singing, hollering, crying, yelling, screaming, shouting, pleading, begging, or panting out of breath.

Then external percussion of slamming cupboards, balls bouncing off walls, doors banging, books snapping shut, heavy doors closing with their squeaky hinges, creaking for ages before juddering, and then yammering shut, scratching the head, scratching one's balls, scratching the desk, tapping the desk, rapping and drumming the desk, banging one's pen on the desk, flicking elastic bands across the room, squirting ink across the room, dropping a rubber into the tea. All this cacophony of sound would then meet the main melody of man on man contact percussion with sounds of thumping the chest, spanking, slapping, stamping, kicking, punching, and screaming out in pain, with the background fillers of creaking floorboards, papers rustling, pens scratching on notebooks, hands flicking underpants free, books thudding to the ground, the rustle of illegal porn mags and consequent body rubs. One afternoon, all of this male din just stopped. Everyone was out. Except me.

A beam of sunlight flooded in through the warm stuffy air, lighting up millions of particles of dust, which were gently oscillating backwards and forwards in the eerie stillness.

I couldn't concentrate, and looked up from my books. Where was everyone? Have I missed something? For a second I imagined the whole school sitting together in an important chapel service or assembly that I didn't know about.

The houseroom continued on in its undisturbed state. No noise echoed up and down the corridors. Nothing stirred. It seemed like the whole of Chapel House had been unplugged. Everything was quiet, except for a high-pitched hiss, which was filling the air. Tsssssssss. I looked around. Where was it coming from?

I looked around the other alleys with knotted ties thrown across Sony Walkmans that were still warm. What on earth was this sound that was piercing through the silence like a mosquito?

The houseroom was the place where twenty men tried to focus on getting an education while our bodies flooded with hormones and exploded with maleness in all directions. Together we put on brave faces and did our best to memorise Chemistry tables and read Chaucer while hair sprouted all over our faces, our jaws started jutting out and trousers tightened in new places. We set out on a marathon journey of collecting as many O and A levels as we could, astride a powerful motorbike of testosterone, which sometimes sped out of control.

We all knew whose voices had broken, and whose manhood had grown more respectable in size. For two years we ripened together like cheeses in the houseroom that smelt of polish, mouldy cake and the ferment of teen-aged men.

In between classes, this space became the strutting ground for music where we were all took turns to dominate the room with our own favourite mix of songs. There was a secret pecking order to this invisible, giant-juke box that we all lived in, and every moment that there was no study being enforced, a guy would push the play button and would dare to take over our minds, vibrating the insides of our heads with their taste in music. Goodman would blast us with Peter Gabriel's "Games Without Frontiers." Then from the other side of the room Buckley would rival him back with a trendy blast of Spandau Ballet's "Don't Need This Pressure On." Dan Reuter would then challenge back with ABCs "Poisoned Arrows Through Your Heart," then Chisholm would get his extra loud ghetto blaster and smash the others to pieces with "Go Wild in The Country," by Bow Wow Wow.

This juke-box connected us together, often sending us onto the tops of tables, singing along at the top of our voices, strumming air-guitars like crazy to zeitgeist messages of the times: "Boys, now the times are changing, The going could get rough…"

The houseroom was where secret initiation ceremonies took place that earned our place in the male hierarchy enforcing a sense of fraternity.

A crucifixion meant you found yourself being held down by many strong arms as a broomstick was rammed through your shirtsleeves across your back. Then a lot of muscle power and panting and tensing stomach muscles would send you flying up into the air with legs pointing to the ceiling, arms outstretched, turned upside down, and then dropped headfirst into the bin and its stench of sour milk, pencil shavings and putrid gunk at the bottom.

The houseroom was like a jungle where we were sussed each other out and tested each other's strength and ingenuity. The warrior training took place effortlessly and automatically. We all knew this was necessary and respectfully went through each initiation so that we could settle and fit in. Here we learnt to become a man amongst men. This secret and most important education that all fathers understand, affected us all deeply, and at the time mattered far more than an A grade in History.

So, for me, to find that the tribe had gone, and to be suddenly surrounded with a silence was a rare, and somewhat disturbing event. Tssssssssss. Where the hell was it coming from? I chucked my pen down, got up and walked over to the corner of the room to examine the school tannoy system. I could hear the usual feint buzz of feedback coming out of the speaker, but it wasn't the same noise. I walked out of the houseroom into the small kitchen that smelt of burnt toast and off milk. Perhaps someone had left the gas rings on. I looked under the pans stained brown with burnt on food and was disappointed to find the rings were switched off. But the Tssssssssss was still there. What was going on?

Irritated, I walked down the stone spiral staircase into cool of the "groves" alias toilets. Normally this place of varying bodily release would be fully occupied, and sometimes had a queue to boot. But now the toilets were empty, and all I could hear was a feint trickle from the urinal and the scurrying, swilling sound of the faulty toilet cistern. There is always one.

Through the open window a warm sweet smell blew in from the privet bush heating up in the sun just on the other side. The hiss wasn't coming from out there. It did, however, follow me up round three complete spirals of the stone stairwell into the dormitory. All the beds were immaculately made having passed matron's rumple test. The "presses" or chests of draws were neatly closed. I walked along the line of fourteen beds or so to the large window at the end. From this vantage point I could see past the massive chapel, down to the playing fields, where cricketers in white were playing a match. Beyond that ran the river Adour with its sulphury, muddy flats exposed in the low tide, then the green of the Downs rising up behind Shoreham village. I could hear that intoxicating mid-summer sound of distant lawn-mowers and the drone of a small plane coming into land at the airfield. But the Tssssssssss was still there.

I walked back down to the ground floor and out into the lower quadrangle. Around the large lawn tall flintstone walls stood proudly upright beneath a deep blue sky. Instead of the usual drab grey that was so depressing and austere in winter, today the bright sun made the stones sparkle brown, white and black. I could hear a few masters and boys talking on their way to tutorials.

I made my way around the corner of the quad to the to the tuckbox room. Long before I got there I could smell that strangely comforting smell of cake and biscuits that lingers no matter how often the room is scrubbed down. Opening the door I found three large shelves crammed full of different coloured, small trunks. Each one was embossed with a surname, followed by "Chapel House," printed in white, across the front of it. Underneath the name, a large padlock protected the precious booty put together by one's mother, normally. I didn't see my mother much during my boarding school years, so, for me my tuckbox reminded me of dad and the life beyond school I had left behind.

I climbed up onto the third shelf where I found the small navy-blue trunk marked "J C HILL CHAPEL" and unlocked it. I knew exactly where I had left each packet of crisps, biscuits and chocolate. Opening the tuckbox and seeing everything was still there was reassuring. It was delicious connection with home full of warm memories that slowly ran out like an egg-timer the more you ate. I sat back against the opaque yellow windows that created a gingery light and felt down beneath the various biscuit packets until I felt the reassuring crackle of something special that I had been saving it up for weeks. I tore open the top of the packet and a tangy burst of orange peel and roasted cocoa hit my nostrils. I remembered the small shop Charbonnel Et Walker in London where dad and I had bought it.
The woman had been lovely. She had lipstick red lips and laughed in a devilishly collusive way each time Dad and I decided to taste yet another chocolate. She knew we had already decided which ones we wanted to buy, but let us pretend we had no idea as we tried yet another one before plumping for the Parma Violet for Dad and the Dark Cocoa Dipped Orange Peel for me.

"How do you cope working here?" my father asked.
"I don't," she answered back coquettishly. She looked around mischievously, and then quickly and illegally popped a Rose Fondant Cream into her mouth. Dad and I laughed.

"Thank you gentlemen! That was fun," she whispered under her breath.

I took another piece of plain chocolate dipped orange peel out of the packet and placed it on my knee, and then forced the packet against my will back down to the bottom of the tuckbox to be safeguarded for next time. I had to make everything last for a couple more weeks until exeat, when were let out and could restock again.

Slowly, I chewed into the dark, voluptuousness and let my tongue revel in the pleasurable feeling that comes with providing juice that forces the slightly dry pasty texture to open up and release its treasure. For a minute or so I allowed myself to get wrapped up in the pleasure. Then, as the last traces of delicious flavours slowly melted away in my mouth, the happy memories faded too, until I was left with a sense of emptiness, just sitting in the tuckbox room, alone. Its funny how, if we just sit somewhere alone with no stimulation, everything fades away to nothing. Its all seeps effortlessly away anyway. Either we can just accept this or we need to keep inflating our minds with more distractions and more distractions to stop the nothingness from flooding back in.

That afternoon, as loneliness flooded back in, it was not silence that greeted me, but Tsssssssssss, which, annoyingly, I could hear in the tuckbox room too. It was really starting to irritate me. I felt homesick. My tuck was running out and, along with it, the small attempt to sweeten the challenges of fending for oneself alone at school. It was always a bleak moment indeed when the biscuits ran out and we had to deal with the unspoken, brutal realisation that we were in exile from our families and had been emotionally cauterised from home life.

Nobody ever talked about this. It was the great boarding school taboo. Yes, we were most definitely privileged, with fantastic facilities and quality teaching. We could all smile off any sense of elitism or preferential treatment with a slightly awkward and contrived modesty. But behind this we were living out a Victorian dream, sent away like colonialists setting up in a foreign land. We were expected not only to survive this rupture from home and family by ourselves, but also to succeed and do very well indeed. The expectations and payback for privilege were great.

I felt this exile from my family very keenly as my family home had fallen apart. I couldn't pretend to be a darling of society that everyone looked up to, arriving for chapel in a helicopter. For me, Lancing was actually a bit of a sanctuary. Beyond the school walls my family life was in turmoil. Of course I longed to be with my family like anyone else, but my family had collapsed and along with it a sense of support and identity.

My mother, father, sister and I were now exposed to bleak winds of change and the agendas of total strangers. New relationships moved in. My parents fell prey to the predators of jealousy, wounded pride and rage, and my sister and I became lost in a quagmire of confusion. School became a refuge from a life filling with step-families, strange houses and alien rules. For a few years I was tossed about in divorce warfare like a plastic bottle in a storm. I didn't see my mother for long periods of time. My father was winning the parental tug of war.

I found myself embarking on a fight for the right to have my own opinion. This would last decades, culminating in a landmark right to say "No" which would be won with devastating consequences later on. Home was overwhelming. I shut the tuckbox.

Instead I had this infuriating sound of Tssssssssss to contend with. Where the Dickens was it coming from? As I sat there that afternoon I suddenly realised that there was no point pretending anymore. After two weeks of looking high and low for a source of the noise I eventually gave in and realised that it was coming from my own head. It was coming from my ears. Had I damaged a nerve? The thought of this freaked me out. Had something gone wrong? I imagined that my ears had broken somehow. Would I need surgery to fix it? Oh God. I missed my family. Wait a minute. Where is my family? I remembered, once again, that my family was still in tatters. Was it my imagination, or was the noise getting slightly louder?

I suddenly find myself back in the car. Dad is driving. My sister is in the front seat. I'm sitting with my face pressed against the back window. We are pulling away from our family home. I hear the tyres crunching on the gravel. I'm starring blankly at the small shape of my mother standing alone on the side of the driveway next to the bungalow. She looks crumpled. She is disconsolate. She cannot fathom what is happening. She is crying. I feel sick. My father has won custody. I'm off to live with him and his wife.

The immediate world is turning a bit floaty. It feels like we are made of water and we are trying to make our way away from our family home through a slow-moving river flowing slowly against us. The car moves down the drive and the part of me that doesn't want to go, stops moving, stops pulsing, stops in mid-air, goes cold and rigid and disappears. Something is extinguished inside me. I don't want to leave this place. I don't want to go to bloody Colindale. I like Sussex. I don't want to live with my step-family. They are good people but they are still aliens.

The village greens, cottages, pubs, churches and woods of the beautiful, open, bluebell-covered countryside accelerate past the window, faster and faster as if a giant blender has been stuck into my world and is sending everything flying round and round into a blur. Horizontal lines of green, yellow and purple streak across the windows. Slowly they darken into grey as streamers of rain race across the glass. Then that harsh, sodium-orange street lights flicker in from suburbia as we hit the never ending-line of soulless, semi-detatched houses welcoming us into London like a homeless person would welcome you into his sleeping bag. The journey passed in silence. Our family, as we knew it, had gone forever.

"Julian," my mother called out, "The custody officer is here." A very forgettable man with glasses, a quiet voice and bad breath lurched forward and offered me a cold handshake. His arm felt wooden and hinged as I shook it. He perched on the edge of a chair opposite me. It was time for my interview. We had rehearsed it many times. He put the questions to me. I knew what to say. The words came out. I felt empty. There was no real choice. The sentence was delivered. I found myself condemning my mother and singing the praises of my father. Whose words were they? Just say them. They are the path of least resistence.
Where am I? Where is home? What on earth am I doing in bloody Colindale? Who are these strange people in the same house as me?

While home life was being turned upside down Lancing College was a haven of positive energy, bursting with colourful, dynamic minds that challenged us all to think for ourselves. The school had more than its fair share of strapping, well-heeled, strong lads and enough sexy six-formers girls to keep us all moist and on our toes and ready for anything. As we all went about our studies, moving closer and closer to A-levels, the quiet teaching, the thing that people really pay for, which has little to do with getting a run of straight As, started to slip in without us realising. While we are conjugating Latin, puzzling out maths dilemmas, debating politics and divinity classes, while we were firing up bunsen burners and learning how to cook, act, and play rugby, the golden learning, what people really pay for was quietly being instilled in us. All the while we were being instilled with a sense of can-do dynamism in a world as a place we can succeed in. We became so steeped in optimism and confidence with our beautiful theatre, swimming pool, and great halls to dine in, that the sense of being capable and ready to take on the world sent us all off into life with a turbo-boost rocket of advantage.

It took me a good decade before I came back down to earth. The so-called "best days of your life" really were spectacular and protected me in part from the difficulty of my family. Down beneath the Great Chapel, buried deep within the crypt, I took refuge in the pottery room. For months and months I found focus centring clay and turning out pots.

I could do it the first time I sat at the wheel. I don't know where this ability came from. I just sat down, picked up a heavy slab of cold, damp clay, whacked it onto the spinning wheel, wet it, put my hands on it. Within seconds, a balanced, slippery, neat column emerged. It felt deeply satisfying.

I loved the way the turbulence of the un-centred clay wobbled and shook against my hands, sometimes in a highly unstable way, forcing me to breathe firmly and use all my strength and focus to meet the resistance. With the whole of my upper body held tense for a few seconds, I would feel the clay buck against my arms. Steadying my hands around the shaking mass I would maintain a calm, clear focus, squeezing steadily, and would wait, not giving into the chaos. Staying there firmly and resolutely the shaking mass would meet my firm, balanced centre. Then, all of a sudden, the trembling and vibrating clay would give up its fight and yield. In its place would be a neatly formed, predictable, calm and centred mass with its own sense of internal order and structure. Even though spinning at high speed, the wet column of glistening clay would look still and displayed a strength and effortless balance of its own.

From this place of order the most intricate forms could be thrown, and moulded into beautiful shapes. Once formed, the fire of the kiln would then transform the ordered mud into a permanent shape that would emerge shining and immaculate and could last longer than a string of human lifetimes. If we are lucky enough to have a good birth and upbringing, we can be centred by our families, shaped by an education system, then, with our own sense of inner balance, we can go out into the world, and form enduring patterns that set us up for life.

Yet, if there are any internal inconsistencies, or imbalances, the whole process of forming a self gradually wobbles more and more, losing touch with its centre until it starts juddering and shaking uncontrollably, losing its grip with the wheel and then flies out of orbit and is sent thumper-splatting into a wall.

In this way, while many guys at school were being moulded and shaped from their place of balance, I was one of a small group whose life was already wobbling out of kilter and about to have my centre uprooted and sent crashing into, well, Colindale.
To find my own balance, I found myself addicted to centring clay in the silence of the crypt. Instead of tugging on shorts of other men and shoving with all my might into the backsides of a rugby scrum, or swotting up on physics books to ensure entry into the top Universities, I found solace in learning to centre clay. It taught me to establish a focus and then to keep a sustained attention on this focus. The skill of being able to sustain one's attention was to turn out to be the very bedrock that would help me survive a journey to hell and back over the next couple of decades. It would be through my hands and an ability to centre that I would find a way into a new profession and way of being.

I loved the silence of the crypt, and spend many months submersed in its cool, monastic stillness. The hiss in my ears accompanied me down there, but having a relaxing activity to focus on made it easier to manage.

Back above ground, where the grass was kept neat and the school honours were fought over, Lancing held us all proudly together within its grey flint walls on the hillside of the Downs. But beyond these limits the family weather was darkening further and the hearts were starting to gather force, sending out violent squalls of rage that rattled through and shook us like dried up sheds being battered about in the wind.

When the going really got tough the alarm bells started to ring more loudly in my ears. The gentle shushing hiss ramped up into a more of two-note whistle blasting through my head. Fortunately school was so hectic that I barely had a moment to focus on it, except at night time where sometimes it sounded like high-pressure air escaping from a valve about to blow. It started to keep me awake.

What was I doing on the platform in my pyjamas? The concrete floor started shaking, and felt icy beneath my feet. I turned round and saw a giant building-sized steam-train tearing at top speed towards me. Its whistle was sounding, and all the people on the platform were moving out of the way. My feet were glued to the concrete so I couldn't move. The train screamed as it passed in a flash nearly sucking me into its wake. Something awful was about to happen. Just down the line there was… Oh my God, no…

Coming round from various nightmares I would first notice my body covered in a cold sweat, then I would hear some guy snoring and notice the turgid smell of the dormitory air. The whistle was still sounding in my ears and I couldn't shrug it off. The sound was locked inside my head. It was starting to really annoy me. I only fell asleep because I was exhausted.

When the sound was up I found it hard to focus on classes and I felt irritable. I didn't realise that the noise in my head reacted to stress, even though it was blatantly obvious looking back. I just didn't want to deal with it and brushed it aside and did my best to try and ignore it for months.
But one day, I went to the school doctor. I told him about the ringing. He gave me a thorough examination and then, in that critical moment, when a minute of feedback can potentially change your life, he said, "Its just one of those things. Try not to worry about it. It'll probably back off and go away all by itself."

This was the first message I received from the medical profession about tinnitus, and was without doubt, the best one. I believed him and it did back off a bit when I managed to stop thinking about the family dramas and focus on school life. But neither the dramas nor the tinnitus went away.

The Headmaster, known as "Budge," made me cry one day when he summonsed me down to his house. What the hell did he want, I thought as I walked nervously down the hill past the "the Grubber," alias tuck shop, to the old cottage with its neat garden on the lower slops of the college grounds.

"Come in young man," he boomed with his deep, yet welcoming voice. He was a well-built rugby player of a man and wore a grey suit with a black teacher's gown across his shoulders. A large warm hand grabbed me off the lane and into the sitting room, and before I knew it, plonked a cup of tea onto the table in front of me. I took a sip wondering what on earth I had done wrong.

"I heard what happened the other day…" he ventured.
Oh God. I felt my stomach lurch.
"Yes. This is a difficult situation." He looked at me and frowned. I felt the base of my spine starting to go cold.
"Your step-father came to the school the day before yesterday. He came straight into my office and started making demands at my secretary. Something about your mother wanting to have more access to you at school…"

"Really?" I said, and felt a sudden sense of embarrassment and yet relief. It wasn't me. I hadn't done anything wrong. I sat for a moment, and then pictured the secretary staring blankly over the top of her half-moon spectacles at my step-father ranting with his red face and red beard. When he stopped to draw a breath, I could see her calmly asking, "And who are you?" feigning a smile.
I felt my face flush bright red.
"I'm really sorry he disturbed you, Sir. My housemaster told me about it yesterday," I added.

We both looked at each other awkwardly.

"I know. It's a dreadful business…" Budge looked sternly at the floor and furrowed his brow. He was thinking carefully about what to say.

"Listen, Hill, I want to give you a piece of advice…"

I looked at him in surprise. The last time I had spoken to him for any length of time was a couple of years ago when I first came to visit the school. This man was our leader, the positive role-model at the helm, who addressed the whole school from afar, and was a paragon of the strong and successful man that we all aspired to becoming. There he was, talking to me as if we were close friends.

"I know what its like to go through periods of great stress like this. It can be hell." He looked at me with a frankness that took me off guard.
"I want you to promise me something…"
"What Sir?"
"Don't let this family business be an excuse for you not to succeed in life. Do you understand?"

"Yes Sir," I answered, not really understanding at all. I heard the words and put them in the to-be-remembered part of my brain and would take them away and think about them. I looked back at him a bit blankly.

"It is precisely because of this challenge that you need to focus and be strong. Don't let this be an excuse, will you? When the hell begins again, just get on with your life and don't let it drag you down. Do you understand me, Hill?"
"Yes Sir," I said obediently, starting to get his drift a little more.
"I think you will be fine, Hill, do you hear? You've got a lot to offer but you're going to need to take care of yourself. I'm sorry you are going through all of this." With that he put his hand on my shoulder.

Suddenly, as if a tight bag had been slit open down the front of my chest, I burst into tears. I found myself sobbing out loud. His reassuring kindness was totally unexpected and unlocked months and months of tightness, loneliness and fear I had been holding inside.

He stood there firmly, reassuring me like a great scrum of support. He had that expression that showed me he understood and that it was fine for me to cry. I stood there crying for a while, and a pain in my chest started to free up. The sense of relief was palpable. He continued to stand there with his hand on my shoulder and I could feel his strength. It was deeply comforting. We were open and connected, man to man, heart to heart. Time stood still for a couple of seconds, and yet, this moment also turned out to last a lifetime. Somewhere, something inside me stood back up again. I have a sense that he could feel this.

"Gosh," I said with tears still streaming from my eyes. "I don't know what to say. Thank you." I laughed a bit. We looked each other in the eye.

"Good man," he said, and smiled.

"Good man," he said again, patting me reassuringly on my back.

Then he offered me a hearty handshake and I found myself back on the lane.

"Thank you," I said again, and started walking back up to the main school building. "Thank you," I still say sometimes, even today.

Sure enough, the hell recommenced shortly after that meeting with Budge. It was exactly the night before my English A-level when my father called.

"You broke all the rules. I told you strictly not to see your mother."

"Oh my God, I'm sorry Dad. I just wanted to see her."

"Because you disobeyed me this is going to cost me £2000 in court fees."

"Oh God, I'm sorry. I didn't mean to cause you any hassle."

"I've had it with you, Sonny Jim. Do you hear? You are on your own now. You disobeyed me. So, as I can see that you are big enough and ugly enough to make your own decisions from now on, so be it."

"What?"

He slammed down the phone in a fury. I stood there with my hand pressing the 50p piece hard into the slot. But instead of beeping to invite more money, the line went dead. My mouth was wide open. "What?"

I felt like a criminal. The crime I had committed was seeing my mother. My body started shaking and I felt a surge at the bottom of my stomach, like I was going to throw up. In a panic, I picked up the phone to my mother. Oh shit. What have I done? The phone started ringing. Come on. Come on. Answer. Come on.

"Hello?" came a feeble voice.

I could tell by the way she answered that she had been crying.

"Mum, what's happened?" I asked, bracing myself against the answer.

"Oh its you, Darling, hello…" She sounded really patchy.

"What's going on? Are you alright?" I asked.

"I can't cope with this any more."

"Can't cope with what?" I felt a sense of dread clutch at the pit of my stomach.

"Listen, you are just going to have to get on with your education by yourself, and contact me again when you have finished university. I can't cope with this stress anymore. I'm really sorry. Lots of love to you darling."

"What do you mean? What on earth are you talking about?"

"I'm afraid it's all too much for me now. Contact me when you've finished university. "

"But that's years away!"

"I'm sorry darling. I can't talk about this now. Lot's of love."

"No don't hang up. Wait!"

"Good-bye."

With that the line went dead again.

"I don't believe it." My head started swimming. I stepped out from the telephone space under the main stairs and stood in the hall. I felt a bit dizzy. I couldn't move. I couldn't think.

A floaty feeling started telescoping around me and I felt like my moorings had been pulled away, and the future that I had been working towards for the last couple of years was suddenly slipping quickly over the edge of the horizon. All I could see were rising waves of dread.

At that moment my Housemaster came out. He looked flustered. His eye-brows were slanting upwards strongly, almost reaching the top of his head. A crisis was erupting somewhere in the House. Maybe a guy had been thrown into a bath in his pyjamas or turned up at 90 degrees in his bed. He tried not to make eye contact with me.

"Hi," I said, embarrassedly. Clearly this was not the moment to talk. He hesitated for a moment. Over the last year he had been the most tremendous support for me. He knew exactly what had been going on.

"Are you ok?" he asked, without wanting to, and moved towards the stairs, glancing upwards to see what was going on.
"No actually. I've just had two bad conversations with my parents."
"Listen Hill, I haven't got time for this just now." He breathed in sharply and hesitated. Some screams and laughter exploded out onto the upper landing. Then there was a sudden loud thump and a yelp of pain.
"Look, I've had just about as much as I can take!" he snapped, and tore off up the stairs.

My feet gripped onto the floor, which started to hover and float, and then sank down about six feet or so. A wave of icy cold passed through me. Something gave way, and started to come loose. I found myself floating outwards from my body into a strange, calm space. All around me boys rushed upstairs with washbags and pyjamas. They seemed to be speeding up. I felt like I was slowing down.
"You're on your own now Sonny Jim..." The voice knocked about in my head like a giant cannon ball and gripped my chest with fear. I walked outside to the quadrangle. £2000 in court fees! How come? What's going on? I felt crushed and started to run down the steps. My legs were numb. Walking felt more like hovering. I needed to just sit somewhere quiet. I bee-lined for the pottery room.

"Sorry darling. Lot's of love." As I walked towards the chapel I felt like I was falling further into the thorny spines of my rosebush-like family. I wanted to find a place to settle but every time I moved or reacted sharp thorns would tighten their piercing grip on me. How was I going to get through the next couple of years without parents? Where would I live?

The gravel crunching underfoot and mild drizzle on my face brought me to my senses. Ahead the great Chapel loomed up in silence like a giant monk meditating. I pressed against the door to find it was locked. "Oh no, not now."
I pushed against the door harder, but it refused to let me in. All I wanted was to go into that beautiful, quiet place and just sit quietly.

"Oh Fucking hell!" I yelled at the top of my voice, and hammered against the doors. "Even the fucking Chapel is pushing me out now!" I hit the doors again and again, feeling utterly rejected. And then I stopped.

Nearby there was a bench. I went over and slumped down onto the wet wood. Across the valley a lone scud cloud appeared out of the gloomy night sky cloaking the sea and glowed orange as it fled over the lights of Shoreham. Then it skirted off into the darkness over the downs. "You're on your own now Sonny Jim." My stomach and chest tightened and kept flooding with a sense of dread.

I felt a cold wet patch soak gently in through my trousers. The mild night wind buffeted the drizzle against me and was the only comforting thing in my world just then. The air smelt sweet and salty with that familiar pong from the river-bank.

I felt lost and intensely alone. I wanted to cry, but I couldn't. The noise in my head had picked up and sounded like two ferocious cats screeching. It was not just a noise. It started to feel like it was buzzing too and was starting to pierce its way into my head. I winced slightly.

"Contact me when you've finished university." My chest tightened. What did she mean? My feet were pressing into the ground as if they were trying to find something solid. My clothes we becoming cold, wet and heavy and I could feel my chest pushing into the damp shirt. But I couldn't face seeing anyone just then, so I waited out in the wet long enough to ensure that I'd miss most of the pre-lights-out banter. I was not in the mood for joking or pillow fights or rolling underneath all the beds while matron was there in the room checking up on us and not understanding why we were all laughing.

A while later I sneaked back into the dorm without being seen, dried off and settled into the safety of my bed. As the chorus of snoring started up, I lay there listening to the noise in my head. It had backed off a tiny bit and now sounded a bit like a loud, hissing kettle. It didn't bother me too much because I was far more worried about the following morning. It was the day of my English A-level exam and I needed to focus on that. I also needed to sleep, but couldn't. My mind became entangled in arguments that wrapped themselves round me like sheets of fear. I turned over and over again and then stared at my watch. I'm really sorry. I didn't know it was going to cause you so much difficulty. Oh God I'm sorry. I turned onto the other side. Please don't do that. What have I done wrong?

I opened my eyes. 3.30am. Its my bloody A-level in six hours time.

"Couldn't you have said all of this on another day? I'm damned if I don't get into St Andrews University because of all this crap," I thought to myself.

I looked across the pillow and stared at all the guys sleeping soundly. The snoring had died down. I turned onto my front and as my eyes closed, felt my bed starting to get lighter and lighter until it floated up into the air and out the window, back out to the bench on the hill overlooking the night sky over Shoreham, and then out to sea into the darkness.
When I opened my eyes it was 9.31. My English A level exam had started a minute ago. I nearly threw up. "Fuuuuckkkk!"

I leapt out of bed and got dressed at top speed. I ran to the examination room where a hundred or so guys were sitting in neat rows with their heads down and pens scratching away furiously on the paper. I found an invigilator. He raised his eyebrows at me and shook his head. It was 9.45am. He quickly ushered me to a desk. I sat down with a thundering heart and started to look at the words on the page. I ran my eyes over them again and again, but they didn't talk back at me like they normally do. In fact they just danced around slightly before my eyes and looked like a foreign language. I hadn't a clue what the questions were saying. Oh my God. I'm going to fail my English A level.

"Read the following extract and answer questions 1 to 10 beneath." A feeling of dread gripped my stomach. I tried to focus. "The wandering airs they faint on the dark, the silent stream, -- The champak odors fall like sweet thoughts in a dream." What?

The text stayed on the page and refused to reveal its meaning to me. I needed to pee. I wanted to cry. My breathing was restricted as if I had a belt strapped tightly around my chest.

I decided to start writing. It was a pure nonsense, but it didn't matter. I had to do something and it helped me focus. Ten minutes later I threw a full piece of A-4 paper into the bin, but it paid off. My mind was starting to crank back into gear and the words were started to mean something again. Slowly associations were triggered and I started to weave together some kind of a response. In the end I managed to answer two-thirds of the questions. Would it be good enough?

Fortunately the rest of the A-levels flowed through without too much disturbance coming in from the outside world and I found myself being swept along into a river of frantic activity carrying us through to the end of term, and the end of school life. Before we knew it, the final chapel service had arrived, ready to cut us off from the best days of our lives like a giant guillotine. Seven hundred young men and a few dozen women found ourselves standing smartly in our suits, upright, strong and proud, singing to the great organ bellowing out in the great perpendicular building of the largest school chapel in the world.

Twenty brilliant rays of summer sun streamed in through the huge, south-facing windows, illuminating us from above like a God-like send off.

We all looked great, had bodies and minds that were in tip-top condition and were brimming with positive energy, like a great dam waiting to burst its banks and send its treasure surging out into the world beyond. For four years we had steeped in a dynamic, can-do enthusiasm, and most of us felt sure to become great directors and people of influence.

The great organ sent vibrations deep down into the crypt, out across the rolling open green Downs, and shook us all to the core. "I will not cease from mental fight, nor shall my sword sleep in my hand: till we have built Jerusalem, in England's green and pleasant land."

As the last hymn came to an end and the Chaplain blessed us with the final prayer, many faces filled with tears. Even the coolest he-men melted and hugged each other. We were being catapulted on to the next level, on into the next chapter of our lives.

Chapter 3 The Sound of my Twenties

Colindale, London, 1984

Waiheke

You yearn so much
you could be a yacht.
Your mind has already
set sail. It takes a few days
to arrive…

James Brown

I failed to get the grades. The D for English A-level sent St Andrews University scurrying over the horizon, out of reach. My escape plan and gateway to the future had been snatched away. I felt crushed.

At the bottom of a cul-de-sac in North London, I found myself locked inside a house with a strange, new step-family. For several weeks we fitted together like tuna fish and chocolate, or ketchup and ice-cream. Individually we were fine, but there are some combinations that just don't go together. My step-brother had never met someone like me before, and I had never met someone like him. He towered over me, he was street-wise and had grown up in South London. My step-mother was kind and did her best, but she didn't understand why I wanted to study literature, and, apart from being overly tolerant, I felt I had absolutely nothing in common with her at all.

Overnight I had turned into a horridly posh, over-indulged twit who read the wrong papers and was interested in boring things. Each day we made our way through another family hotchpotch trying our best to smile at the gentle curdling together of different mannerisms, ways of speaking, house rules and dress sense. More pineapple and gravy? Would you like some tomato soup with marshmallows? We couldn't really say, "No thanks." Quickly this indigestible life experience would bloat and sit in the stomach for days. But unlike food, the clash of two families could not be vomited out.

The awkwardness and discomfort weighed down more and more heavily until one morning, I woke up in a body that didn't want to move and that felt very heavy on the mattress, like a lump of meat. There was no spark or purpose. I just felt like a lump of meaninglessness plonked on a bed, cheeks rammed into the pillow, staring eyes that looked straight ahead at the window without really seeing it. I felt so heavy that I was on the verge of giving up and rolling over the edge into a pit of despair. I could feel myself being pulled down, lower and lower, slowly being taken over by thoughts of awful futures, tawdry places, mind-numbing jobs, and a life of pretending to be happy. There was nothing much to get out of bed for.

The station was dark and the empty platforms and kiosks were blackened in a thick layer of soot. I could hear a few people walking about but I couldn't see them. There were footprints everywhere but I looked down and saw my bare feet on the cold ground and realised I was standing in my pyjamas. A rumble started up and suddenly an enormous steam train thundered into the station. Each carriage was like a mini-cinema playing out different memories of being on holiday in Ibiza with friends, smoking at the five bar gate with the lads, winning the night exercise army cadet challenge, having sex in the long field of wheat at the top of the hill, and so on. The train was full of light and so I jumped onto it. I walked straight into a carriage where I was taking my English exam and watched myself sweating. I saw how my exams had been swamped by my family stuff. I didn't fail. I just wasn't allowed to complete what I was supposed to do. Bloody hell. It was not my fault. I started to feel anger erupt in my heart, and my throat and face felt hot. Behind me was a trail of black foot-prints. Why the hell should I fail because of that?

I woke up and was breathing heavily. "Fuck this. I'm not going to give in," I said to myself as I went down to breakfast. My step-brother had already disappeared round to the next-door neighbours. The American couple served as his escape route and coping strategy. My step-mother was washing up and asked me if I wanted any eggs with my toast.

"Um, Yes please," I smiled back politely.

I was deep in thought, already planning a letter to St Andrews. The moment I finished eating I raced back upstairs and found myself writing an impassioned letter to the admissions officer. "Dear Sir/Madam, I am writing to say that I am unable to accept being turned down for a place in the Faculty of Arts, as it was not my fault I failed my English A-level. I had a family crisis during the week of my exams. I am ideally suited as an Undergraduate in French and Spanish literature because…," and a longish list ensued. I needed to be there. I needed to get as far away from my family as possible, but I didn't write that in my letter.

A couple of weeks later I got on to a coach nervously. Maybe this was taking things a bit too far, but I was determined that the Admissions Office knew just how seriously I meant what I had written in my letter. Half-way up to Scotland the coach stopped off at a motorway café and I called my father.

"I'm glad you called," he said in a concerned voice. "I have a letter from St Andrews in my hand. Do you want me to open it?"

"You're joking! Oh God. Um. Yes please." I held my breath and closed my eyes. I heard my dad rustling the paper down the phone. There was a pregnant pause. I couldn't bear the thought of being turned down again.

Then he started laughing.
"What's happened? What does it say?" I asked impatiently.

"Oh that's good. Yes, its good news." He continued reading. "Well done. You've got in."

"Really? Yes!" I yelled out lifting a clenched fist up victoriously. "Yes, yes, yes!"

"It looks like you were right to complain about the family situation. You always land on your feet, Sonny Jim. Sometimes I think you were born with a silver spoon in your mouth…"

"Dad, must go. I'll see you on Monday."

With that, St Andrews came flying back over the horizon and settled back into place in my life again. My escape route was open. My future was back. I got onto the coach and sat with my mouth wide open all the way to Newcastle, and then grinned all the way up to Fife.

When I got there I bee-lined for the admissions office to double-check that I really did have a place. "Ah, Mr Cowan Hill, yes I remember reading your case. I'm so glad you got in. Well done!"

Then I checked in at a guesthouse on the road running along the north side of town facing out to sea called the Scores.

"Will you be having black pudding with your breakfast?" asked a sturdy yet friendly woman showing me to my room.

"Er, Yes please."

Then I walked quickly down the incline, past the Martyrs Monument, the rock pools and car park, and then onto the vast open West Sands. I broke into a sprint and ran as fast as I could. Along the left hand side sand dunes with tufts of marram grass ran northwards towards the hills beyond Dundee. To the right a great expanse of sand and emerald-green water stretched out to the horizon, chopping and sparkling in the cold, salty wind.

Bright white clouds coursed overhead through the blue sky like racehorses. I found myself running at top speed across a huge expanse of wet sand, which acted as a giant mirror reflecting the clouds and patches of blue both a bove and beneath me as well, creating a great sense of space. Sky above, sky below, I was half-running, half-flying through space, splashing cold water into my shoes. Happiness was surging through me, filling me with energy. A new sense of freedom stretched ahead of me in all directions. Everything was ok. I had made it.

A mile or so down the beach I came to a stop near the water's edge. My chest still puffed frantically for a minute, my breathing gradually getting slower and slower until all I was left with was the sound of the wind whistling in my ears, and the rapid lapping of tiny waves trying to make it ashore against the wind.

I could make out a feint ringing in my ears, but I didn't care. It didn't matter at all. I turned back and stared at the proud line of town houses and steeples that stood on top of the cliffs. St Andrews was to be the backbone of my life for the next four years. Thank God.

The first couple of months of Uni was a long, enjoyable party, finding my way to endless new people in lecture rooms, cafés, dinner parties, pubs, tutorials, libraries and halls of residence bedrooms. I found myself learning about the Picaresque Novel, translating ridiculous French words like "Vasistas" into English, or being moved by Shostakovich's Piano Concerto in C minor sipping tea with friends looking out to sea, or shagging passionately to Joe Jackson's "Will You Be My Number Two." It was all a steep and exciting learning curve.

My room at the top of Hamilton Hall felt like a penthouse suite in the best location in town. This bold red building looked straight down to the 12th hole on the most famous golf course in the world on one side, and out across the sea on the other.
Us young lads on the top floor made no effort to be grown up or responsible like those on the lower floors. We were determined to make the most of our last teen-aged years, and, in retrospect, thank God. We had the best coffee, the coolest music and turned the living up loud.

Sometimes our ghetto blasters echoed down the internal well of the building, causing the more serious undergraduates to yell up in a rage. Sorry Hazel. Sorry Callum. Life was about dancing as coolly as possible to pull as many as possible, and trying to outdo the sound of fun going through each other's walls.

Studies only formed a loose background thread at first. What was far more important was what had been stirred up in you at the Debating Soc, or who you had been chatting to climbing up the side of Ben More and Stobinian in the Mountaineering soc, or how much Morey St Denis you had tasted in the Bacchus Soc, or who you got away with squeezing in the Hug Soc. Life was all about discovering where the all-night bakery was and how those hot, delicious pies were great for sobering up in the middle of a cold, blustery night.

We all donned our bright red pyjama-like gowns, at least once, and walked to the end of the pier with icy green waves crashing at the wall beneath. Then we would stare out to sea as intelligently as possible in that undergraduate kind of way. Then, upon our return to Hall, we would hide the ghastly red things at the back of the wardrobe, never to be seen again. From then on, the red-gown walk fell squarely on the shoulders of the Wee Marys and Alastairs that resolutely carried on this tradition every Sunday.

We got to know reeky Kerrachers that had the best kippers in town, the humid smell of hot chips and battered Mars bars that blasted out of the droning fan of P&Ms at the end of Market St, and the finest seeded batch loaves and vanilla slices from Fisher & Donaldson, the best baker in Fife.

I loved the Spanish department. Castlecliffe was a sturdy, stand-alone manor house next to the ruined Castle and had its own gardens and views across the sea. There was plenty of space, a lovely library, and three of the sweetest men holding the faculty together, Bernard, Alan and Douglas.
These scholars of the Hispanic world would flock to Douglas' study next to the grand-piano room, every day at 11am and grind up fresh coffee. We would clamber onto a stool or a cushion and drink from wonky clay pots and mugs while Bernard got overly enthusiastic about Quevedo with his slightly French accent, and Alan would fight back chesty laughter after some joke or two. And Douglas would exude, well just such a sense of warmth, and generosity of heart.

We all enjoyed trying out our spoken Spanish with Pilar, the Spanish assistant, or Santi the Argentinian exchange student. It was the perfect place to fumble our way towards fluency in the warm, fun and lively department that Castlecliffe was. This was a thousand miles away from the brilliant, brainy and somewhat icy French and German department, where precision meant everything.

But the high point of the week was the Friday night Bop at the Student's Union. Being a good dancer was hot currency and this was the place to find a partner for the night or for life. Indeed some couples formed in the first year, are still living together today in holy matrimony. My penthouse neighbour Andy, was a bit shy during the first few weeks. But having been let out of an all-boys, Welsh boarding-school, seeing so many available women around left him with a permanent grin on his mouth, and raised the eyebrows off the edge of his face.

We would arrive reasonably early at the Bop and stand next to the speakers, which were so loud that the rhythmic bass-line of "Ghost Busters" would make the pints of beer pulsate in the glass and clear the phlegm on my chest.

It wouldn't be long before every square inch of the huge room was heaving, and "Walking on Sunshine" would bring on a frenzied wave of dancing that left us all sweating and happy. By the time U2's "Pride," came on, we were hoarse from singing so loudly and usually knew who we were going home with. Stella looked stunning. She had danced so well to: "That's the way, uh huh, uh huh, I like it."

Two by two we would leave behind the hot, smoky air, and ashtrays stuffed to the brim, the half-drunk glasses of Pernod and Black, and bottles of Newcastle Brown. We found our way back out into the cool fresh North Sea air of the cobbled streets and made our way back to the privacy of our rooms. Lively chatter and raucous laughter echoed down each lane as we all streamed back to Hall. My head would still be humming with the aftermath of the music, and then back in bed, once we had enjoyed each other's bodies, the room would fall into silence.

All that would be left, before dropping off to sleep, would be the feint intermittent flash on my wall from the lonely light house shining in from far out to sea, and the ringing in the ears. The sound was often quite loud at first, and my head felt like it was buzzing a bit. For a while the songs would keep playing inside my head over and over again, but soon I would be fast asleep. There was so much distraction and fun during those days at University that the tinnitus rarely took over.

Upon waking, the sound would be much quieter and I would be far more interested in who to chat to at breakfast and finding a good view of the stormy sea outside, or the fog being blown in off the North Sea by the Haar wind.

It took me half a year to realise that nobody else was going to make sure I got my degree other than myself. Nobody cared if I missed lectures or didn't read the books. Not doing the work just meant tutorials would be embarrassing, and a waste of everyone's time. So slowly I found my favourite cubbyholes and quiet desks at various libraries around town where I would force myself to read the huge pile of books at the end of my desk. This did not come naturally to me at all. I frequently woke up with my face pressed against the book cover and could tell you more about how it smelt than what the words were expressing inside.

In second year I shared a flat in the middle of Tentsmuir Forest, about 20 minutes drive north of St Andrews. We lived in a mini Arc de Triomphe-shaped gatehouse to a castle. It was remote and bohemian and smelt musty.
I enjoyed opening the kitchen window and throwing out cabbage leaves to the highland cow trying to poke its head in through the window. Its horns meant it couldn't reach in far enough, but I was still able to stroke the thick brown, shaggy fur.

I hated getting into the bath with my jumper on. This terrifyingly cold room was on the ground floor and seemed designed to draw in the frigid north wind as much as possible. The air was literally freezing, and the walls would often sparkle with frost on the inside. Scalding hot water would fill the whole room with steam and no matter how many times you dunked your head under, the wet hair would turn icy cold far too quickly.

My flatmates were great fun and had a sanguine air of confidence and wit that attracted a hearty social life into the gatehouse. Frequent dinner parties filled the place with laughter and funny stories. Afterwards we would all huddle around the fire warming ourselves with a good glass of Aberlour or Bunnahabhain. One of my flatmates, Jessica had an MG. I used to love riding into town with her, singing "Barbarella Psychodella" at the top of our voices, the roof down, and the freezing Fife air turning our cigarettes into blazing red dots.

Back at home in Sussex, a new step-family came into roost at my mother's home, with a whole new set of overwhelming changes and rules. So holidays became doubly awkward with, albeit, nice people, but still strangers nonetheless living in both parent's houses. Our family really had been replaced now. Sometimes, when I was in favour with my step-father and was considered the "number one son," we could pretend that we got on and had loads in common. At best, when family styles clashed, we could smile politely and move on. Other times, when I had fallen from grace, I would hide away at the bottom of the garden in my shed, or spend my whole time trying to get away, on my clapped out moped, working in pubs, brickworks, and hotels.

One day my step-father was standing ginger-bearded and red-faced in the kitchen and yelled:

"As far as me and my wife are concerned, you are nothing but a fly on the wall."

I had been caught in the fall-out when my father complained about him going to my school. This escalated into an inter-step-family row, which passed through me necessarily as the most natural point of contact. So I got a job even further away, working as an usher in London, at the National Theatre. This meant I could get seats to most plays and musicals there and save up money for my year off where I could get as far away from my family as I could.

One winter term at Uni, I came back a few days early to try and catch up on some essays. The train from London had raced through hours of heavy snowfall, which rubbed out much of countryside leaving just a sketchy outline of the odd hedgerow or wood. Even the towns seemed to be taken over by clouds descending down into the streets and filling them with their grey-brown, icy magic.

I got off the train at Leuchars. A welcome patch of blue sky let the sun stream through. Thick snowdrifts were lit with millions of sparkles and lay round the grey Fife stone and pub windows like luxuriant, glittering scarves.

I jumped into the warmth of the taxi.

"Cold enough for yer?"
"Bloody freezing," I answered. "Can you take me to Earlshall Gatehouse?"
"That's not far," the driver said, looking a bit disappointed.

There was a brief pause, then he tutted. "Och well, we'll guv it a go."

With that we skidded off across the small town and reached the top of the lane only to find that it had not been cleared. Instead there was a giant pile of bulldozed snow blocking the entrance.

"I'm afraid that's yer lot pal. Good luck."

I put the money in his hand and he drove off with a wheel-spinning skid. As the sound of the engine faded, I found myself immersed in a wintery silence. Across the fields there were no lights to be seen at RAF hangars. Not a bird stirred in the hedgerows. The world was deep in hibernation.

I clambered over the heavy compressed snow and set off down the lane, boots squeaking into the undisturbed, pristine white powder. The surface of the snow was really light and glided away easily with each stride. It breathed a chill up to my knees and deep into my bones.
A few fiery clouds overhead sent an orange hue across the purple snowscape. Daylight was plummeting quickly over the horizon leaving the long, dark Scottish night to freeze everything through to the core.

Up ahead the dark points of the pine trees rose up like sentinels heralding the change from open fields to the gloom of the thick, dark forest. In places the snow drifts were so deep I had to lift my legs quite high to make headway. But fortunately it was too cold for the snow to melt into my trousers.

The black silhouette of trees thickened like a silent army all around and cast their darkness over the lane turning it into night. The air had that lovely mineral, rocky snow smell mixed with the scent of pine-needles. Soon I would be in front of the fireplace burrowing into books to get more of a handle on Don Quixote and Baudelaire.

Presently the arch of the gatehouse loomed out of the dark. There were no visible tracks in the snow anywhere. Clearly nobody had been here for days, possibly weeks.

I groped around in my pocket for the keys and put them into the lock. The door didn't want to open. With a bit of push it suddenly gave way and released a foul smell that hit my nostrils. Something wasn't right. I flicked the light on. A dozen little shapes darted out of sight.

"Oh no." My heart sank.

I looked at the normally white work surfaces. They weren't white. There were hundreds of small droppings everywhere, on the bread-bin, the sink, the cooker, the spice rack, the fridge, the floor. The smell of mouse was so pungent that, for a moment, I had to breath into a hanky to adjust. I stepped into the icy, humid room and watched my breath form a small cloud that hung in the air for a long time before evaporating. The stone walls of the kitchen were sparkling with frost.

I opened the door to the living-room and the carpet pattern suddenly changed as a dozen or so mice shot behind the book shelf, the log basket, and the curtains. There were so many droppings that my boots felt tacky.

I grabbed the broom and started sweeping a path through to the fire and managed to amass a couple of centimetres of mouse-droppings in a couple of minutes. I scraped them into the bin.

"Oh God." I groaned. "This is all I need." I said the words out loud because it was so quiet. It felt comforting to break the silence.

I went over to the log pile and picked up some kindling. A couple of mice darted out from between the pieces of wood and shot across the floor. I jumped and yelled out in shock.

I was feeling really cold now and quickly tore off some newspaper and piled some kindling on top with frozen hands. My non-responsive fingers fumbled with a match and after a few attempts managed to strike it alight. The flame took and slowly started to grow, spreading a welcome ball of warmth onto my face and onto the snow that was still powdering my trousers. The fire made me feel less alone. The warm glow and occasional spit and crackle was really reassuring.

I piled on several small logs into a vertical position and a couple of minutes later the fire started to blaze, and heat tentatively started to reach out into the icy-cold room and turn it from a forgotten winter burrow back into a students' home. With the fire alight, I could face the kitchen again.

I turned round and three mice darted across the floor in front of my feet. I jumped out of my skin and yelled again.

"Christ Julian. Pull yourself together. They are just mice, for God's sake!" I said, trying to reassure myself, but my heart was beating strongly.

I pushed open the kitchen door slowly and, up ahead, I could see a couple of dark-brown faces sitting on the sideboard next to the kettle, twitching away, just where I wanted to make some tea. I walked in. At that moment every corner of the room moved and little spots of black turned white as the mice cleared off with a sudden scamper. They were everywhere.

I put the kettle on and reached up to a packet of Earl Grey tea. Droppings fell off the top of the packet and bounced off the surface in front of me and then onto the floor. I pulled down a mug. I looked inside. It was clean. If I stopped moving for a moment, out of the corner of my eye, little movements crept back in. The whole place was creeping either slowly or suddenly with mice like live wall-paper.

The kettle element started popping and thumping enthusiastically bringing a promise of something hot. My body was shivering slightly and I put my purple fingers onto the hot metal. Until that day I always thought mice were sweet little things, but en masse, there was something a bit spooky about them.

I didn't want to turn around because I knew they would be there, back on the living-room carpet. My movement would make them dart off again, and that, in turn, would make me jump yet again, unavoidably.

The kettle started to hiss and bang as it heated up a bit more. It felt too hot now and I had to rub my hands together to distribute the warmth without burning them. I had never considered how loud a kettle was before. This one was starting to fill the silence with a harsh rushing sound, getting louder and louder, ticking and exploding with water about to boil. I waited for another minute and listened to it build up in crescendo banging and spluttering with sound that reverberated off the empty kitchen surfaces before falling away back into the deathly winter silence. But then the fire crackled again.

I popped a tea-bag into the mug and walked back through to the fire, stamping as I went to scare the mice away. That felt better. I didn't jump. I pulled out an armchair and sat drinking the steaming tea, feeling the warmth dropping inside my chest and stomach and starting to soak through my clothes from the bright yellow dance of fire. I let the flames captivate me for a few minutes and started to settle.

I thought I had better go up and turn the electric radiators on. My bedroom was directly over the living room. After opening the heavy oak door, the spiral staircase up looked pretty clear. Compared to the living room floor, there were only a couple of droppings here and there, all the way up to my room. I pushed open my door and the smell was fresher, definitely less mousy.

I switched on the tall radiator and noticed that the windows were covered in intricate patterns of frost which reflected the light with intricate swirls and eddies. I scraped a peep-hole in the frost with my fingernails and looked out towards the castle. The snow was cobalt blue in what was a dark, moonless night.

My high bed with its copper knobs and thick mattress looked really inviting, but I had to get the room above freezing before I could even consider the thought of braving the frigid sheets with pyjamas and a hot-water-bottle. The end of my nose was freezing cold and wet.

I grabbed a blanket and went back downstairs. Before I went back into the living room I hit the door loudly to scatter the smelly, shitting vermin that I knew would be on the other side. I could just make out a feint sound of scratchy sharp feet dashing off in all directions.

I opened the door and the air was warmer and felt a bit more inhabitable, even if the increasing humidity had made the smell more rancid. I fetched a hot-water-bottle, another mug of tea and huddled into the arm-chair and wrapped myself up in a thick blanket and stared at the now blazing fire.

For a while I managed to enjoy watching the flames leaping about. The warmth was really comforting, but to my horror, out of the corner of my eyes, the brazen invaders would re-emerge and start twitching and scurrying about the place as if I didn't exist.

If I clapped my hands, they would dart off with such speed that it made me jump again. The choice was to either do nothing and let the cringy scurrying recommence, coming close to my shoes, sniffing, running, stopping, running, stopping, creeping, changing direction, scratching, twitching, darting, constantly on the go. Or I could banish them with a sudden clap, jump at the sudden speed, only to face imminent invasion all over again within seconds.

I tried putting some music on, but they seemed to like it. If anything more mice came out to enjoy the party. In the end I plumped for the sound of quiet and the crackling fire. I tried closing my eyes and pretended that they weren't there. But they were. I had only to open my eyes again and I would guarantee being able to see at least one or two mice between me and the fire, without moving my head.

I felt alone, and I had to admit it to myself that I was scared. The nearest person was a good twenty-minute walk through the freezing winter night.

Sitting there my ears had readjusted to the relative quiet and now I could hear the feint scratchy sounds of constant scurrying in the background, the whole time. I didn't like it. I wanted it to stop.

I thought about going to the chippy or looking for a pub or a bed and breakfast somewhere to spend the night. I couldn't really afford it, but at least I would get a good night's sleep and be able to do some studying the following day. But the thought of leaving the fire and walking back out into the thick snow in the freezing cold and walking all that way was too much. It must have been minus 8 degrees outside already. It had been a long journey from London and I was exhausted.

The flames were jumping about, flickering red and yellow against my eye-lids. Under a thick blanket I felt warm and comfortable. The hot-water bottle, which I was now clutching against my stomach and chest, was sending a stream of warmth all the way down into my shoes and to the end of my nose. My mind turned to an essay I had to do over the next couple of days on the development of the Picaresque novel. I sat there looking at the mesmerising flames doing their quantum dance between here and not here, flickering, moving, white, orange, red, with an occasional burst of blue. The warm bright light took me back to a summer beach in Ibiza, smelling that happy, resinous smell of hot Stone Pines with a million sparkles on the sea dancing under the late-afternoon sun.

I look down to my feet standing on the warm sand. I can feel the cool Mediterranean water gently lapping up between my toes and sloshing around my ankles. The water comes up and then pulls back, comes up and then pulls back. The sparkles are countless. Each one is dancing on and off, on and off to its own unique rhythm. A couple of tiny crabs come out of the water and start scurrying over the sand and across my feet. They don't bite me, but I don't want them to run across my feet. I watch as their red backs and white pincers sidle their way along the sand. The water feels a little bit colder now. I look down. There are a dozen mice there, running across my feet with their little scratchy little claws, across my feet, how disgusting.

I opened my eyes and looked down to find a mouse sitting on top of the blanket on my feet. "Yuck!" I yelled, kicking out in surprise. It flew off and at the same time the whole carpet scarpered. I shuddered in disgust. The fire had turned to red embers, and the room was already cooling down.

There was no way I was going to sleep there. That room made my flesh creep. So I grabbed my hottie and ran up the stairs into to my room.

The radiator had bought the temperature well above freezing, but my bed was still ice cold. I put my pyjamas on, and then a thick jumper, and finally a pair of skiing socks and climbed inside. The mattress seemed to crunch a bit. I turned off the bedside lamp and pulled the blankets over my head. Under the covers it was pitch black and the combination of the cold air of the bed, my breath and hot-water-bottle made everything fee damp.

I lay there in the dark. I thought I could hear scratching, so I held my breath so that I could listen more carefully. Yes. There was a scratching sound right over my head. Oh my God. What the hell is that? Out of the silence there came more and more scratchings and scurryings. I lay there as my eyes started adjusting to the dark and the ghostly shadows of the room furniture started to emerge. I felt so tired. Where is that bloody noise coming from? I pulled the covers back and looked around. The light from the stars and reflecting snow outside was enough for me to make out the beams on the ceiling above.

It sounded like there were mice running along right there. Maybe they were in the cavities between the roof and ceiling above my bed. I held my breath and listened out more acutely. I could hear scratching and little frantic movements. I couldn't face getting out of bed and investigating. I was exhausted. I closed my eyes.

I tried to get back into my dream of Ibiza, the sparkling water, sleeping on the top of the house, laughing with Tasha as we looked up at the stars. But it didn't work. The noise felt close by. For the second time that night came that ominous feeling. My back started shivering. There was something not quite right. The scratching and scampering were really close by. I lay extra still and realised that there was a feeling of movement below me. I felt more fully through my legs and to my horror, noticed movements were coming from within the mattress.

There was a moment of silence between realising there were mice in the very mattress I was sleeping on, and yelling out where I opened my eyes and saw it, sitting there, on the pillow, in front of my eyes. A mouse. My mouth opened and I let out a blood-curdling scream. The mouse shot off into the ether.

Still yelling at the top of my voice I reached down and turned on the light. Sure enough there was a mouse poo right in front of where my face was on the pillow. There was also a wet patch of mouse piss around it. It must have had a great shock too.

I shuddered as I put my trousers and socks on over my pyjamas. I could literally feel my flesh creeping all the way down my back. I pulled off the bed covers and found a hole in the bottom of the mattress. I didn't wait to watch any mice come out. Before I knew it I was off up to the top landing that went over the arch. I couldn't face going back down to the living room. I couldn't stand these mice. Anything to get away.

I turned on the light in the upper bedroom. There were mice droppings there too. I ran down over the other side of the arch and turned the lights on. Droppings. The bedroom on the ground floor on the far side of the house was my last resort. I flicked the switch. A dozen black shapes darted in all directions. There was a whole other infestation going on down there.

There was nowhere to go, except back to the living room. The fire was the only sanctuary on this freezing cold night. So I walked like a zombie back over the arch flicking off the lights as I went, and down to the door of the living room. I turned on the light and watched half-a-dozen mice shoot out of sight.

I didn't yell this time. I was just to tired. In fact I felt numb and a bit floaty. I found myself building up the fire almost calmly. It was good to start hearing that crackling again. I waited until it was burning really brightly and then walked solemnly into the kitchen.

The mice scattered in all directions but I didn't jump. I felt a bit heavy and calmly made a cup of tea, and a freshly filled hot-water-bottle. I grabbed a couple of blankets and sat back in the armchair. This time I put my feet on a footstool. There was no way out of this. I would have to spend the night with the mice the best way I could. There were lots of them, so many of them. Gosh, I didn't know there could be so many at once. I had to just give in and accept the whole room twitching around me with its endless creep all around me, alone, in the middle of a frozen forest in Scotland.

I heard an alarm go off. It was like a police whistle. I was too tired to move. Sleep was starting to push down on me like an overwhelming drug. I thought the sound was coming from an alarm outside for a moment or two but I calmly realised it would be the ringing in my ears. It was really loud. I had never heard it like this before. It seemed like the policeman was blowing his whistle right by my head. It was almost unbearable. I lay there at half-mast in the armchair, trembling inside. I didn't know it could get this bad. Whatever next? I started crying. I stared at the fire and let myself cry. The whistle carried on and on and was unbearable. Thoughts started to speed up inside my head.

What if mice start crawling all over my body while I'm asleep? What if this noise gets worse and doesn't go away? The tinnitus seemed to get louder. I don't know how, but, eventually I gave in to exhaustion and let the full weight of unconscious sleep bear down on me, snuffing out the horrific events of the evening and steeling me away for a few hours of rest.

The brilliant sunlight streamed through the window onto my face. I opened my eyes and remembered where I was. I had managed to sleep for hours propped up in the chair. I looked down and found a few mouse droppings that had been deposited all over the blanket covering my body during the night. My body was aching, I had a stiff neck, but the sound had dropped off quite a lot. It was more like a hissing kettle next door, which was irritating, but not deafening like it had been a few hours before.

There was a lot to do. So I spurred myself into action and chucked out the mattress, made a new bed up with a spare mattress I found in the out-house. I hoovered my room and swept up what seemed like an ocean of droppings on the ground floor. I disinfected and wiped the kitchen down returning it to a gleaming white surface.

Outside there was a fresh layer of snow and the sky was a bright, limpid blue. I wrapped up warmly and managed to enjoy the walk into Leuchars. I found a hardware-shop selling mouse-traps and poison, and bought enough food to last me all week-end. I resolved to stay on track with my studies and essay-writing. It would just have to be interspersed with a massive mouse slaughter.

I felt frazzled but being in my early twenties I had enough strength to bounce back quickly.

The gatehouse warmed up. I put the poison down. The mousetraps snapped shut about once every ten minutes at first, but then rapidly petered out by the following day. I quickly learnt that trying to empty the traps straightaway was the wrong thing to do. Seeing the little bodies writhing around in pain was ghastly. So I got used to doing something else for ten minutes or so before going to empty it. When the squeaking was bad I had to shut the door and go fetch some more logs in. Once the mouse had gone, I would chuck the innocent creature's remains onto the fire.

57

In a moment of drowsiness I found myself watching in morbid fascination at the eyes popping and the tail shrivelling amongst the burning logs. The whole experience was disgusting and disturbing, but what else was I to do? I hate killing animals, but either I let them take over and get behind with my essay writing or I just got on with it and do what I had to.

Fortunately the poison kicked in quite quickly, and the gatehouse became silent again. Unfortunately this meant that the place stank for a few weeks as bodies decomposed just out of reach. But I managed to get the work done. When the others returned the weather warmed up enough for us all to fling the windows open and clear the bad smell.

For a few weeks after mouse night, my tinnitus remained at constant hissing kettle level, and followed me into tutorials. I felt its pressure during quiet periods in the library, where it would try and distract me from my studies. At night, when I was alone in bed, I would lie there trying to get into more comfortable positions believing this would ease the noise, but the only way round it was to fall asleep. Slowly over a few weeks the kettle gradually faded back until it sounded like it was one or two rooms away, which I was able to easily ignore.

Chapter 4 Latin Sounds

Agua Amarga, Almería, Spain 1987

La Monja Gitana

Silencio de cal y mirto.
Malvas en las hierbas finas.
La monja borda alhelíes
sobre una tela pajiza.
The Gypsy Nun

The Gypsy Nun

Silence of white lime and myrtle
Mallows in the meadow grass.
The gypsy nun embroiders wallflowers
Onto a straw-coloured cloth.

Federico García Lorca
Romancero Gitano

My father bought a house in a white-washed, flat-roofed Andalucian fishing-village called Agua Amarga. "Bitter Water" was named after the salt-water found in its wells.

I loved it there. During the holidays, at the height of the afternoon, I would take the short-cut over the wall, down through the sun-bleached grass and scraggly fennel plants, releasing a sweet herb-cupboard smell with every step.

Often I would have to unpick a spiny bush that got caught on my shoulders or clawed against my scalp, and then walk over the thick black hose-pipe that ran through the thyme. It looked exactly like one of the large black snakes that lived behind the dustbins. No matter how many times I walked over that pipe, and told myself it wasn't a snake at all, I still felt a rush of fear and had to tap it quickly with my toe to make doubly sure.

Then over the mound of tom-cat and scorpion rubble, the path ran down into a freshly-mopped, narrow white street that blazed so bright that I had to squint my eyes.

Even though there was never anyone in sight during siesta, doorways were left wide-open with metal fly-curtains dangling gently in the breeze. The sound of TVs echoed out onto the street with the afternoon soap that sent everyone off to sleep. Warm currents of frying fish and garlic still hung in the air. Sometimes a cooler current of air would descend down from a bedroom above, gracing the street with a Catholic whiff of mothballs.

Between doors, bougainvillea hung down brazenly in day-glow red, and fluorescent orange like colourful panties. Sometimes a woman's voice would shout out across the village in that blown out voice-box kind of way that you only hear in Spain, causing a dozen neighbours to float up from their dreams but not quite touch the surface. Normal Spanish is usually delivered at machine-gun speed. But in the deep south of Spain, this is given more local colour in its delivery, for the consonants never touch the sides of the mouth. Andaluz Spanish literally flies out of the mouth like slurry. So "Los Andaluces hablan así" sounds more like: "loh ana loo hey ala a hi." But to sound like a local you have to make this as nasal and quick as possible.

At the bar in the small circular square there was always one wilting drunk with gazpacho breath, dozing into his horribly warm beer. And then, finally, at the end of the dazzling white lane, stretched the dark blue, sparkling sea.

I would walk past sunbathers bronzing in coconut oil before following a small rubbly track up the side of the small mountain. Rising up, a view of the entire stretch of beach quickly appeared with its restaurants, chiringuitos (glorious summer eating shacks) and banks of tall green reeds.

With a bit more height, I could see across to the coves that looked like large white bites taken out of the sandy coloured mountains running all the way down to the two camel-hump peaks of Cabo de Gata in the distance.

The path edged along precipitous drops down to the blue and turquoise water with shoals of fish darting out of view behind occasional clumps of weed. The light in the water was made doubly bright by the reflection off the white tufa cliffs turning the sea into a giant and unusually bright turquoise swimming pool.

At the high of the afternoon the turquoise was so intense, it seemed to blaze inside with each in-breath and penetrate deep into your lungs and glow there for hours, long into the night while the houses were still releasing their heat like storage heaters.

At siesta time, while locals fled from the heat of the sun to cool off in their air-conditioned bedrooms, I would walk across the cliff-tops to an empty cove on the other side. I would arrive like a piece of rotisseried pork with eyes smarting in salty sweat. As my feet hit the sand of the tiny beach I would run and then dive with full force into the cool, frothing waves, feeling the bubbles sparkling and crackling around my shoulders in delight.

Once, when I was 20, I went to visit my father just after he had bought a red speed-boat. Early one morning we got up just after dawn and went down to the beach. The sea was as still as a pond. The whole village was still asleep. Even the wind was dormant. The only sign of life came from a few fishing boats making a distant hum far out in the bay.

We jumped into the warm, clear water and swam out to the mooring and clambered on board. While he tinkered about, I sat there listening to the water lapping against the boat, feeling it rock from side to side. It was really peaceful and my father seemed excited to be showing off his new pride and joy.

He turned the key which sent a loud thudding, spluttering sound across the whole beach, and the engine started vibrated powerfully, shaking me more awake. A tiny move of the throttle sent us shooting across the smooth water, leaving a bright white wake behind us and bringing up a cool salty breeze. Then a fair way off from the beach the engine dropped, and we were plunged back into a lapping silence again.

Dad threw the skis into the water and handed me a life-jacket.
"Go on, in you get," he said.
I looked down into the dark, blue-green water. I could see the fine ripples in the sand about two houses down below the surface. There were a few small fish darting about.

I jumped in and slid my feet into the cool slippery straps and fasted them to the skis. My heart was thumping.

"Just point the skis straight up out of the water and when you feel the line go taught, hold on tight and keep straight. OK?"

"Ok," I replied excitedly.

The engine started up and I watched Dad move the boat gently away. The rope started to race across the surface of the water. I watched it tighten, then engage, then start tugging me through the full weight of the heavy water. Eddies and whirlpools started to spiral off around my shoulders.

Suddenly he rammed the throttle forward and I came flying up out of the water, and for a few glorious moments I felt the smooth slippery surface of the water gliding under the skis. I was up. I could feel the length of the skis slipping into the long shiny groove of the water and felt them clattering about. I looked back to the village. Wrong move. The tip of the ski caught the water and I went flying like a canon-ball into the water and received a hefty face-spank. A litre of salt water shot down my nose and throat into my stomach. My skis came off instantly.

"Try again," shouted my father. "You'll get it soon enough."
My heart was really thumping now. I knew how powerful the boat was and how hard the water felt hitting it at speed.

Slowly the line went taut, and then I was yanked up onto the skis. This time I found a more comfortable groove in the wake. On either side the sea was like glass, and I was literally flying over rocks, banks of dark seaweed, and small shoals of fish underneath.

Then the boat accelerated up to top speed and the wake became really smooth. It was glorious. We careened across the bay, and the village receded back into a horizontal white line gliding past the dark blue water. White cliffs were approaching up ahead and so Dad slowed just a bit. He turned slightly. Instantly I found myself accelerating round in a broad arc, accelerating like a missile, and had to hold on with all my muscle-shaking strength to stop being catapulted off the line into the rocks. I managed to stay upright as I came surging round at formula one speed in a great pendulum almost catching up with the boat. Dad signalled thumbs up in approval. I took one hand off the bar and signalled thumbs up back to him.

At that moment, the tip of one ski dipped under the water and, in a split second, vanished from my foot. For a second I was airbourne, flying horizontally over the water. Then the other ski, at cross-angles to directing of travel, landed like a violent brake. As it locked into the surface of the water my lower body was yanked to a standstill. The upper body meanwhile was still travelling at great speed. The consequence of this was a colossal force that sent the side of my head thunder-splatting against the rock hard water.

Suddenly everything went quiet. A rush of bubbles was rising up. The body was there somewhere. My head felt like it was flashing and smarting. It took a few moments before I could tip my mouth out of the water and breathe again.
Dad turned the boat round and manoeuvred back and forth and eventually bobbed noisily up against me. I managed to gather the skis and clamber on board.

"Are you alright?"

"Uh yeah," I said, in a complete daze.

"Do you want to try again?"

"Uh no."

Dad stopped for a moment.

"Are you okay enough to drive the boat for me a bit?"

"Um, I'm not sure… Probably better not."

"Ne'ermind then."

Dad turned back to the throttle and took us for a gentle cruise south past the village over to Cala de Enmedio, my favourite beach. He dropped anchor and switched off the engine. After the loud noise of the boat stopped, the sudden silence seemed uncomfortable.

The beach water was a light emerald green colour. There was nobody there except majestic white cliffs rising up like giant, vertical waves frozen in time with curved shaped crests. Behind, mountains rose up revealing a barren and desolate countryside.

An alarm sounded. I looked at the boat to see if there was a flashing light.

"Its great, isn't it?"

"What?"

"The boat. This place."

"Um, yes," I said distractedly. I felt a rush of pressure inside my head. The alarm got louder.

"What's that noise?" I asked.

"What noise?" Dad replied.

"Can you hear that sound?"

"What sound?" He turned round to see if he could hear something. "I can't hear anything."

"I can hear an alarm. Can't you hear it? It sounds just like someone is playing two notes a semi-tone apart on some high-pitched organ. It is really loud."

"No."

"That's so weird."

Dad listened out again.
"Nope. Can't hear a thing."

I got off the boat and waded onto the white, sandy beach. I walked along for a few metres. The alarm was still ringing. I walked a bit further. Same sound.

Where the hell was this sound coming from?

On this idyllic summer morning, at the most beautiful beach around, my heart sank as I realised, once again, that the sound was coming from my head.

"Oh God no."

I sat down on the sand. How could I keep on missing the obvious again and again? I pushed my hands down into the cold wet sand and started sifting it through my fingers nervously, trying to distract myself from the noise. I stared back across to the boat where Dad was tinkering.

"You know, I can't believe you sometimes Sonny Jim..."
I looked up at my father. He seemed angry. Why was he starting to raise his voice at me? Why did he sound like a Dalek? I felt a rush of butterflies hit my stomach.

"You are just so bloody indifferent sometimes."

I wasn't listening to the words. His voice sounded like a bloody Dalek. It sounded like I was listening to a recording and someone had superimposed two slightly different pitches together, but badly. His voice was coming out as if he was speaking through a Dalek amplifier.

"My ears have broken," I muttered to myself. Hitting the water at high speed must have broken my ear nerves. I felt a wave of panic come over me. Then I felt a painful twinge in my ear and a dull pain set in.

"Couldn't you just for once show some bloody appreciation?" My father was going into a rant, but all I could focus on was his voice. He still sounded like a bloody Dalek.

Oh my God. I'm going to be like this for the rest of my life. I've damaged my ears. Oh fuck!

I looked at Dad's red freckly face and watched his finger starting to point. The Dalek voice sounded like it was being funnelled down a tube from somewhere else. Why did it sound like Dad was talking down a long, plastic tube? What the hell is going on? This made me feel a bit dizzy. I felt really disorientated all of a sudden. I also felt a bit queasy and was breathing heavily. The sun seemed suddenly a bit too bright so I buried my face in my hands and tried to anchor into the feeling of sand under my bum.

"Oh there's no use feeling sorry for yourself now." The Dalek sounded up again, sounding tinny, almost laughable.
"Come on. Pull yourself together. We're going back to Agua."

There it was again. Exterminate! Exterminate! I was kind of waiting for someone to burst out onto the beach and say, "Surprise surprise!" and tell the camera-men and sound teak to take the speakers down. But nobody came. The special effects resulting from my broken ears remained.

I coughed. There it was, I had found my inner Dalek! My own voice reverberated back to me in two tones. A sudden shooting pain went across the side of my head sending a surge through my tinnitus. "Oh that's all I bloody need." My head started to vibrate painfully. I cleared my throat. The noise turned up into a really loud siren.

I can't fucking believe it? Now I have a frigging Dalek's voice. I've broken my ears. I'm never going to hear properly again. Oh my God.

I felt my heart quicken, my chest tighten and the top of my head squeeze tight like a tennis ball.

"Let's go then," I said.

Getting back onto the boat I had to shut my eyes against the light that seemed unbearably harsh.

"What an ungrateful sod!" the Dalek said, as we started to bound across the water back to the village. The engine sounded distorted. The bouncing waves sounded strange. The whole world seemed different and I couldn't handle it.

We tied the boat up and swam back to the shore. On the way back up to the house my father went into one of his foul moods and stopped talking. I didn't care. I didn't want to talk because the sound of my own Dalek voice was too disturbing.

We got back to the cool of the house. I asked my step-mother for some pain-killers and said I had a migraine. She was an incredibly tolerant woman and could see straight away that Dad and I were having one of our "situations."

She raised her eye-brows knowingly, took a deep sigh and wandered off to the kitchen cupboard. "I hope you feel better soon," she said, placing two pills into my hand. I went downstairs to my room and closed the curtains and lay in the dark cool space. For a while I worried, but thankfully I fell asleep.

When I woke up it was siesta time and the house was quiet. I felt much calmer and more together, and because there was no sound anywhere, things felt normal again.

I went to the bathroom to have a pee. Normally I like humming to find the right note that makes the whole room reverberate, so out of habit I hummed a couple of notes. Daleks hummed back at me. Like a robot in a cartoon when it bashes its and all the wires fly out and get into a tangle, I imagined broken ear nerves inside my head. I walked into the sitting room and hummed a long note. Daleks. Out loud I said, "Hello Dalek one, Dalek number two here." The Daleks were still here. I hummed a note and put one finger in my left ear, and then put it in the other ear and to my horror it came out a different pitch. I had discovered a new trick.

I turned on the radio on and put one finger in one ear and then put it in the other and the music slid down a pitch. One ear heard the world sharp, and the other ear heard the world flat. This was weird. I then started oscillating between both ears, making the music go up and down like I was twiddling a knob on some kiddies' synthesizer.

I felt trapped and paced around a bit. I tried to read, but I couldn't focus at all. I couldn't get out of this. The only thing that seemed to help was having a shower.

Supper-time came round and it was time to go and re-join the mood upstairs.

"Feeling better?" my step-mother asked.
"No. Not really. I've got this weird thing going on with my ears."
"What do you mean?" she asked.
"As you are talking to me now it sounds a bit distorted. It's like there are two voices sounding at the same time. Its really weird."
My father pricked up his ears. "Oh. I had that."
"What?" I asked in surprise.
"You can hear two notes at the same time?" he confirmed.
"Yes." I was surprised at dad's sudden interest.
"I had that too." He went on. "I dived into a deep pool once and went down to the bottom too quickly and burst my eardrum. For the next few weeks I had diplocusis."
"You had what?"
"DIPLOCUSIS is what it is called," he said to me in that just-shut-up-and-listen-to-me kind of voice.
"What, like a Dalek?"
"Yes," he laughed. "I couldn't play jazz the whole time. You know how I can't stand hearing two different pieces of music at the same time. Couldn't bear it. But then it just kind of died away."
"Oh, so it didn't last for long then?"
"No, but I've had tinnitus ever since."
"I didn't know you had tinnitus?"
"There are lots of things you don't know about me…."

I felt a wave of relief sweep through me. Maybe this thing wouldn't go on forever, after all. Maybe it would eventually sort itself out. I felt myself relax a little bit.

"Yes, I've had the passing jet plane sound that appears out of the blue." He suddenly imitated an engine sound that suddenly got louder and then went down several pitches, like an American freight train whizzing past.

"God! That happens to me too… I've had tinnitus for years."

"Really, I didn't know that," my father said raising his eyebrows.

"There are lots of things you don't know about me either."

"Don't push you luck!" he snapped.

I looked towards the kitchen where my step-mother was doing the washing up, and saw her eyeballs roll and her mouth imitating Dad under her breath.

Completely ignoring Dad's fractiousness, I started to feel more relaxed and optimistic about things. There was some strange comfort in knowing someone else in the family had experienced the same thing. Maybe my ears weren't broken after all. This was probably quite common and probably ran in families. I wasn't in the mood for an argument. Nor could I be bothered to tiptoe on egg-shells either, so I went back downstairs to my room and turned in early.

Over the next few weeks the strange Dalek sounds started to subside. For a few days I became a bit obsessed with sticking a finger in and out of each ear making the sounds of the world go up and down a semi-tone. My tinnitus remained at quite high pitch, like a hissing kettle, but because it was constant, it was more ignorable. Anything was better than the maddening Diplocusis Daleks. Or so I thought.

Back at St Andrews, over the next few weeks I had to decide where I was going for my year out. I had to learn to speak Spanish fluently, and everybody's fingers pointed to Spain, except my own. The professors encouraged me to consider Salamanca, one of the best Universities around but, because my father now had a base in Andalucia, it would always be easy to go to Spain. So I felt this was a chance to explore further afield, and be more adventurous and push across to South America.

This was not just about learning Spanish, this would be about discovering a new continent, a new climate, history and a new way of thinking. This was a chance to see the New World.

In the end I was left with a choice of either Buenos Aires or Caracas. I only had a few months to save money working as a barman in the National Theatre so I eventually chose Venezuela because it had a later start date, therefore more time to save money. Besides, Caracas sounded great with its 26 degrees every day of the year climate, and a nearby Caribbean coastline to explore.

I was twenty years old, and the thought of jungles, table-top mountains, cowboys galloping across plains, the highest cable-car in the world, and a population where 75% were under 30 years old seemed more exciting than studying Spanish literature in an erudite University where everyone lith-ped like a Cath-stillian.

So towards the end of the summer off I headed to the New World with not much money in my pocket. After a long flight I found myself stuffed inside a collective taxi listening to loud salsa, breathing air that was so hot and soupy it glued my clothes immediately to my body. Welcome to the tropics.

The road from the airport snaked its way up through long dark tunnels with jet-engine ventilators fanning four lanes of American-style cars. We stopped and started in a semi-permanent traffic jam. In front a young handsome man with sunglasses was hooting flirtatiously at a car full of pretty chicas in front. They were bouncing coquettishly around to merengue blaring out of the speakers. He kept on climbing up and blowing kisses at them and they screamed back at him, flattering him about his body.
Another car honked and someone shouted '¡Que pases por encima, huevón!' Pass over the top then, you big dickhead. A few seconds later another long beeeeeeep, and then another angry voice answering back, "Perdóname pendejo, no encuentro el botón de helicóptero!" Pardon me tosser, I can't find my helicopter button!

As we edged past sun-beaten faces of all shapes and sizes, we came within earshot of different salsa songs, which everyone in my taxi started singing along to. It was like an impromptu game of name that tune, taking just a few seconds before someone started singing and then everybody else joined in with a laugh of recognition. Then a merengue blared in through the window and the taxi chorus changed once again, and then a classic bolero started up converting our driver into passionate crooner. Through the hot choking fumes we crawled, until an hour or later so we emerged out of the final tunnel of the steep motorway that connects the Caribbean to the city in the mountains. Caracas.

The first view opens up onto a shantytown clinging to the side of a steep hillside. The first smell is of sewage, raw sewage that hits you in the face with a punch. The makeshift houses or ranchitos with their corrugated iron-roofs touch their toes into the slimy, brown river of "cloacas" gushing at the bottom of the valley. Then, thankfully, the peppery smell of hot vegetation clears the nose again.

Then the road veers round a corner and opens out into a breath-taking valley of Caracas, a tropical city with high mountains all around cloaked in shantytowns as far as the eye could see. Hot sun, bright blue sky, brilliant white clouds and brilliant green bursting out everywhere.

I was dropped off at the address of my host family. They were lovely, and greeted me warmly, but having spent two years reading Lope de Vega, Cervantes and Quevedo, and having studied the art of translation, I realised that I couldn't understand a word anyone was saying. Two years of language study suddenly reduced to a measly, "Er Hóla. Um No entiendo.."

Feeling a bit stupid, I was shown to my room where I was to live for a year, just around from the school where I was to be an English teacher for a year. I had never taught before in my life. The room, it turned out, was on the top of the roof. It stood in between TV aerials and a water-tank and looked like it was built out of lego. There were two other lego rooms built on the roof too. One had a 9-year-old boy in it with a big smile, a couple of teeth missing and a green parrot that would occasionally let out a piercing screech, making me jump out of my skin.

In the other room, lived a middle-aged man with a permanent fag in his mouth, and a slightly browning white T-shirt pulled permanently above his sweating belly.

I put my bags down and watched my new housemates talking to me. I imagined they were saying things like, "So where do you come from then? We hear you are going to be an English teacher." I just smiled back at them, not understanding a single word and said, "Si, soy inglés."

My window didn't have any glass in it, just iron gratings. Outside, at the end of the street, a high mountain cloaked in thick jungle rose up into the dark clouds. I sat down on the bed and had one of those "oh my God what have I got myself into now" moments. Here I was, on the other side of the world with a whole year stretching out in front of me like a sentence of solitude. I'd never felt truly alone before. But there I was, truly alone, solísimo, by myself on a strange new continent. There were no relationships, family, or friends to seek solace in. Everybody I knew was at least a 14-hour flight away or an expensive phone call on a very faulty line away.

A very loud thunderclap exploded like a bomb overhead. It drummed my chest with such a sudden force that I was nearly blown over. Some mangos thudded onto the roof from a large tree that was starting to waver and shake like a mambo dancer. Then the boom rumbled up the valley, and then turned around and came right back down again. It was the loudest, longest thunderclap I had ever heard. Time for the daily 4 o'clock storm.

Gigantic raindrops started thrashing down onto the city, chasing parrots back under cover into the trees and sending more mangos whomping onto cars below. Warm spray splashed in through the window like an open shower curtain that I couldn't shut. A pool of water collected on the floor. I moved my bags. Another explosion boomed its way through the sky sending a crash and a rumble reverberating along the steep slopes of the mountain. My teeth rattled. Then came a cataclysmic clap of thunder smashing its way through the air, literally blowing the wind out of my chest. Jesus H Christ! I yelled, clutching the bed in horror. I felt like my room was about to be gunned down by a gangster God doing target practice.

Steadily the dark sweaty night started pressing down, and the rain turned into a steady deluge, rinsing away the dirt of the city on a steady spray cycle until, suddenly, someone somewhere flicked a switch and the storm stopped. But we were not left in silence. In Venezuela you don't get silence. Out of nowhere a loud, piercing, electronic, synthesizer-like bleep started up. It was nearby. Then another beep came from a bit further away. Within a few seconds the whole neighbourhood started beeping. Where was the noise coming from?

I looked at my window-sill, and there, in a puddle of water was a small, bright-green frog. It looked straight back at me. It's body suddenly expanded and contracted and let out a loud ear-piercing beep. I moved a finger to touch it, but it jumped off. The moment I walked away it came back. It continued beeping, along with a whole frog chorus, all night long.

The mountainside lit up with white lights that twinkled like a Christmas tree making the ranchitos look beautiful and enticing. But the life that hid within the narrow alleys was brutal and ugly, and, as I would learn, poverty turns good people like you and me into thieves.

That first night in Venezuela I could hear police sirens circulating from time to time. Sometimes I could hear people yelling on the street. Sometimes I could hear a gunshot echoing up the valley, but it wasn't this that kept me awake. It was the flipping frogs that squeaked for hours on end, with nothing to shut them out, sometimes making it into the room and closer to the bed, and finally shutting up and turning in to rest just when it was time for me to get up and go to work.

Days arrive quickly in the tropics. One minute it is dark and humid, then, suddenly the sun is up, and it's bright, hot and steamy again before you have even brushed your teeth.

I soon found my feet at the small school where I taught. I had lovely colleagues that showed me the ropes, and eager students who were keen to soak up every last bit of English I could share with them. I enjoyed many invitations to chat over a Toddy Frio, that delicious, iced, malted chocolate drink, or a guanabana juice and hot ham roll, talking about the difference between life in Caracas and London.

The advice flooded in. "Take a taxi to the bank when paying in, just in case." As it turned out, machine-guns greet you at bank doorways anyway to protect you from robbery. "If you drive at night-time, never let your arm hang out of the window at the traffic lights," one teacher told me. "Your watch will be snatched off at gun-point. You may even lose a hand…" I gasped in horror.

"Never walk through the slum-town. It's not safe. You will be mugged." I wish I had listened to that one. "You look too smart, too much like a gringo. Wear scruffy clothes. Don't stand out." "Always lock every lock on your door and do not trust anyone." The Caraqueños were an anxious lot but I quickly learnt the rules. Within a few weeks I got around in the local yanqui Spanish. I learned to say "Qué chévere - How cool." Or "Epa chamo deja la vaina quieres - Hey man, will you just back off!"

Life was edgy here, but, for a twenty-year-old, it was exciting. I quickly learned to haggle down the prices of a taxi, and check my change. My moderate Venezuelan salary meant I couldn't afford to be ripped off.

I quickly moved into a flat with a colleague and two Venezuelan guys. We needed six door keys to get inside. Once in, Enrique would be at the table caressing the next door neighbour's hands in a telenovela tale of true love, reciting poems, knowing looks, tears, and amor amor Amor! Edmundo, or "jungle bunny" was from somewhere between the Orinoco and the Amazon, and in this city bursting with long-haired, long-legged, tall, green-eyed and full-busted sensual, sexy girls, would be trying to handle an irresistible catwalk of gorgeous Caracas girls on-heat, all looking for a man like him.
At midnight Edmundo and Enrique would whisk me off on outings to "fuentes de soda" or cafes to eye up the local talent over a batido of blended juice from the endless supply of pawpaws, soursops, guanabanas, chirimoyas, guavas, mamones, nisperos, custard apples, papaya, red, white or yellow bananas or jack fruit. Their polite yet unceasing attempts to pick up the gorgeous slinky Caraqueñas took courting to a new level.

At dawn one morning, two of Edmundo's guests woke me up and asked me to let them out. "Si. Como no," I said politely while I was fumbling for the keys. I opened the door and saw them out. When we woke for breakfast a few hours later, many valuables from the flat had been stolen. I remembered seeing one of them carrying a large bad with her, but I never even considered that it would be full of our stuff, besides, I was fast asleep at the time.

But when the power cuts that came along our dancing parties turned into impromptu truth kiss or dare games around candles, and when the water failed and made the bathroom very unpleasant for days at a time, we just went to the pool every day, when a bank transfer took ages to arrive we literally lived off peanuts and papaya. We were young and resilient and the laughter and camaraderie carried us through.

From our flat on the 12th floor in Los Dos Caminos we looked down along the valley of the city and a view straight up to the Avila Mountain, cloaked in jungle. I would go to the nearby park and follow a magnificent line of chaguaramos palm trees to the reptile house, and force my face up to the glass staring straight into the eyes of a giant anaconda to try to overcome my fear of snakes. It's head was as fat as mine. I must confess it seemed to help somewhat.

At many school parties I was grabbed and danced with over and over again until my hips turned to liquid and my shoulders shimmied and legs lilted to salsa and merengue, leaving me just feeling happy, no matter how miserable or lonely I was. To date I still don't know anything that is more instantly effective at lifting the blues. Gliding and moulding together, effortlessly connecting to a dance-partner, you find yourself understanding them more after a two minute spin across the floor than a lifetime of chat. All the movement in the pelvis seems to open up the lower half of your body like a big smile that sends a warmth upwards that you never knew was there, rising and filling the heart with pure joy. It is the greatest tonic on earth. It fills you up until you pop with joy. ¡Qué alegría, qué felicidad, qué chévere. Más nada!

In Caracas the music flows in like a magic potion onto crowded busses, busy offices and markets making everyone move their hips and smile without even thinking. At the first excuse, dances would erupt in classrooms, street corners or in boardrooms, with merengue and salsa bringing grannies hip to hip with hot young men, and little princesses being whisked off by gentlemen. Any hardship just fell away as Venezuelans showed just how good they were at dancing. This was a national treasure that everyone shared. So when "Ojalá que llueva café en el campo," Juan Luis Guerra's tender voice filled the air, wishing it was raining coffee in the square, life was so happy, so carefree, so full of energy.

Merengue's sexy, driving bass-drum beat: Ra Cucuta, Cucuta, Cucu Rata Ta Cuta, and salsa's rhythmic trumpets seemed to blast through any worries and put you directly in touch with something that is just fundamentally happy and connecting. Try to be miserable during a salsa class. It's impossible. If you're a bit down, just merengue. In Venezuela everyone knows this. This dancing music was and still is the most liberating language I have ever learnt.

Crammed onto a small "Por Puesto" bus, clinging on for dear life, as we zoomed past grand houses and boulevards, sky-scrapers and ranchitos, we were all kept in time by a small tinny speaker blaring out happy music next to a picture of the Virgin Mary and Simon Bolivar over the driver's head. No matter how serious the moment was, music in Venezuela made everyone's hips wriggle slightly and mouth to turn into a slight smile. Somehow, a sense of love and fun had to burst through and open like tropical flowers. It was the elixir of life.

"Volveré, Volveré, porque te quiero, hasta tu puerto volveréeee," the classic song of the times by Wilfrido Vargas played on every street corner, on every bus and in every club. "I'll come back, I'll come back, because I love you, back to your port I'll come back.
In the first few weeks of my year in Venezuela I felt my senses waking up and bursting out in a way that never happened in England. The view of the shanty-town rising up the mountain at the end of the streets was a start reminder of the poverty and hardship that forced people into difficult lives. This edge meant that on my meagre Venezuelan salary I had to fight too so that I could get by without paying the tourist price. As the months passed I found myself turning into a bit of a Caracas ninja snapping at taxi drivers before they could even try to rip me off, walking along in a "don't mess with me kind of way" so that any beggars or pickpockets knew to stay clear. I started bracing myself against a sense of danger that was always lurking just around the corner.

Without realising it, I was starting to run on adrenaline, and instead of resting comfortably in my body, my focus went up into my head and I felt very switched on. As my attention moved up and out the chatter got faster and more intense too.

Before, when I went to a café, I would have a juice, slurp it down, love its deliciousness and stay with the texture as it went down. I would look at the people around me out of interest. Who was interesting? Who was sexy? I would wonder what was going through their minds. There was a basic sense of trust in the world, and things felt safe, like a child in a happy home who can just hang out without needing to tend to his. He can just play knowing that the roof overhead is not likely to come crashing down. He doesn't have to think about anyone else. He can just lose himself in play, or drinking the juice.

But after a few months in Caracas I found my new normal was to rush ahead, prepare for challenge. Being "OK" on my way to the café meant rehearsing the lines, "Now look mate. I'm on a Venezuelan salary too. Give me the proper price." Checking my change, I would then sit down and look around, sussing out the people around me. Are they ok? Do I need to keep an eye on my bags? My focus would be out monitoring everyone like a radar. I would barely notice the juice as it slipped down because I was tracking the environment, wondering if I was safe.

I had gone from an "in and down" person feeling happy inside my body, to an up and out person, rammed into overdrive, focusing out there, senses switched into a state of red-alert, checking on everyone and everything all the time, getting ready for difficulty. I had lost my sense of safety.

Instead of just walking along the road with my feet on the ground, smelling the coffee, feeling the sunlight on my face, looking at the brightly coloured patterns, enjoying the faces, the interactions, amazed at a fruit shop with things to eat that I had never dreamt of, I cut myself out of this reality, took one step inside and barricaded myself behind a wall of being careful and wary.

The wonderful ease of Europe that I had taken for granted, where I could sit at a café in a timeless square by the cathedral, in a burping, post-lunch haze, full of ice-cream and coffee, as people had done for decades, all this had gone. How many times did I used to stare off into space, feeling at ease, enjoying watching the people coming and going, thinking about what to chose from the menu, shaded by the trees, listening to that happy sound of bon-viveurs enjoying their lunches. Maybe I would feel a bit tipsy, I might think about work, or who I would like to meet up with, move the body gently to digest better and release any discomfort, drifting off like a dozing cat only coming back to myself if the waiter asked me if I needed anything.

In Caracas you had to be sharp.

One Saturday afternoon, I was walking back from a lunch party near my flat. It was about 430pm. Because it was the dry season the sun was still burning down through a limpid blue sky. I was not drunk but definitely enjoying some kind of inner fiesta having drunk a fair bit of Cacique rum and fruit juice. It was barely a ten-minute walk back along the main road of Los Dos Caminos to my flat.

The pavement was full of afternoon shoppers dipping in and out of small businesses. I walked past the paper shop, and then the bookshop, and then a fruit shop stacked to the ceiling with long papaya with their slightly rancid pong. Then on my left I could see down through a gap in the buildings to some shacks and noticed the foul stench of the cloacas or open sewers. I stopped for a minute and looked down at the brown river. How can people live down there? There was a narrow walk-way that followed steps down between ramshackle shacks made out of bricks and corrugated iron. I could see more alleys branching off into the gloom.

Someone tapped me on my shoulder. I turned around and a small guy was looking at me angrily. "¡Dame tu plata, catirito!" he said. At first I just looked at him, and wondered why he was angry. He prodded me impatiently in my chest. "¡Dame tu plata!" he yelled. Then an automatic reaction kicked in as I made sense of the situation. I'm not giving you my money. What a bloody cheek. Without thinking, I just pushed him away like an irritating fly and shouted, "¡No! ¡Vete al carajo!"

With that, two more guys stepped up onto the pavement. They were tall and skinny and their faces were bony and dark. All three of them were staring at me like hyenas. My heart started thumping hard in my chest. My mouth went dry. Holy Shit. One of them has a broken bottle in his hand.

"You give me all your money now, you stupid gringo, or we will kill you!" They pushed me off the pavement and several steps down the path.

I came to my senses and fumbled quickly for my wallet. I had insurance, for God's sake. Just give it to them. Don't be an idiot. Just do whatever they ask.

I handed over the wallet. The short man grabbed it and put it is his pocket. He signalled for me to give him more. I was confused. I pulled out my empty pockets and said, "No tengo nada más."

The guy with the broken bottle lifted it up over my head and tugged at my shirt.

"Mi camisa?" I asked, incredulously. I started taking my shirt off.

"Si, ¡pendejo!" he said in a broken voice. He then tugged at my jeans.

"¡Ai no! ¡Dios mio!" I yelled out. He shoved his face into my face and pushed a sharp tip of glass against the skin of my chest. I gasped in horror. His breath stank. His eyes were empty and dark. Oh my God, is this really happening?

"Ok ok ok!" I said.

He pointed to my shoes, so I took them off too. Beneath my feet the step felt tacky with all the grime.

Before I knew it I was standing in my underpants. For a moment we all looked at each other. I felt like my life was in their hands. I stared back at them hopelessly. Now what? There's nothing more to give. I started to feel sick. What are they going to do?

At that moment a group of people walked past. I turned round and, in desperation I took a risk and yelled out at the top of my voice, "¡Socorro!" They stopped and looked down. A man moved towards the steps. "¡Socorro!" I yelled again.

I turned back round to find the last of the three muggers disappearing out of sight below. A way down the alley, a woman peered out of a small doorway, looked at me, tutted, shook her head and then went back inside.

"You ok?" the man up on street level said.

"Uh yes. I live near here. I live in the next block. I just want to get home."

"Are you hurt?"

"No. I'm ok."

"You shouldn't walk through the ranchitos. It's really dangerous."

"I know, I know."

I walked back up to the pavement.

"Can you make it home alright?"

"Yes, I'll be fine."

"Are you sure?" he said looking into my eyes.

I could see my block of flats up ahead. "I live just there," I said and pointed down the road.

I thanked him and started walking back along the busy pavement in just my underpants. People stared at me but I didn't even notice. I was still down those steps running the scene back over my mind. I was furious. I felt like I had been violated. Those bastards! How dare they!

I got to the main gate of my block of flats and the guard greeted me.

"What happened?"

"I was mugged," I said flatly and walked straight towards the lift.

For the next few days the frightening faces, the smell of the brown river of sewage, the man's breath that smelled like the bottom of a stagnant pond, the grimy sticky feeling of my toes on that foul pathway, kept on flooding back in. Every time I thought about it my stomach lurched with fear.

I would try to calm myself down with thoughts such as, "Oh well, I'll get the money back on the insurance..." But the feelings took a while to subside.

But the real cost became clear over the following few weeks. I felt violated and dirty, like something of those men stayed with me. I felt like I had been contaminated with a sense of their disgust for life, their hatred and the hell of their poverty. A piece of their world had joined my life and I had learned to mistrust the people around me much more.

For the rest of my year in South America, a large part of me walked around on the lookout, making sure that I would not be mugged again. Those men had not only stolen my money, but far more importantly, they had robbed me of my sense of safety.

Worst of all the ringing in my ears became loud like a policeman's whistle being blown in the same room as me. This whistle followed me around wherever I went. It whistled in the staffroom while I was preparing my English classes. It was there at mealtimes and whistled into my ears while I was trying to enjoy my food. At the time I was making great progress with learning Spanish but the tinnitus got in the way of that too as I found it hard to pay attention to what people were saying.

Worst of all was night-time. When I was tired and was trying to sleep, the whistle blew right inside my head. It took ages to get to sleep. The noise made me feel like I was trapped.

"Oh my God. Is this ever going to go?" That horrendous question started to weigh down on me like a tombstone. In response, my stomach would lurch and I would feel a sense of dread gripping me like an iron fist inside.

I started to feel afraid of my own head. I couldn't switch this damn thing off. I felt like I had been taken prisoner and I was locked inside with a scary cellmate. A pressure started building up in my head, and from time to time, this turned into a headache.

The noise did abate a bit after a few weeks, but it didn't drop down to where it was before I was mugged. It stayed around a moderately loud hiss, like a kettle going off in the same room. I just put up with it and didn't do anything about it. I didn't know I could.

This kettle-like hiss came with me on a trip to Colombia to visit Paula, a classmate from university, who lived in the beautiful city of Pamplona, up in the tierra templada or temperate zone of the Andes. After the boiling heat of Cúcuta, trying to find which collective taxi to take amongst a hoard of harassing sellers and beggars, I found myself relaxing as I watched the vegetation change as we wended our way up past banana trees into minty eucalyptus forests. For the first time in months I could feel cool fresh air pouring in through the window.

Every time we went past a dangerous bend, with a sudden view falling away down to the valley floor thousands of feet below, several crucifixes stood in loving memory of people who had obviously not been paying attention, and had driven over the edge. Out of respect, just at the most dangerous part of the road where the crosses were, the driver took one hand off the wheel to cross his chest, and the other hand reached up to touch a picture of Jesus shining next to his rear-view mirror. In the back we all held our breath.

Suddenly a policeman was standing up ahead, pointing a machine gun at the car, signalling the driver to stop. The driver braked abruptly. The officious man with a big black moustache peered inside, took one look at me, and then called me out onto the road.

"Where's your bag?" he demanded.

"Here." I pointed.

He opened it and with the briefest of glances he said, "You're carrying drugs, aren't you?"

"What? No I'm not." I was so taken aback I just stared straight back at him, gobsmacked.

His eyes widened in the middle of his pudgy face, and he moved uncomfortably close.

"You've got cocaine on you. You're a gringo wanting to take cocaine back to your country, aren't you?"

"Uh no!?" I was just lost for words. I turned round to look at the man who was sitting next to me in the taxi who promptly looked down at his newspaper.

"Look I don't understand. I do not have any drugs on me," I answered

The policeman stretched out his hand, which was pudgy too, and said in an officious tone, "Dollars!"

I heard a "Pssssstt," and turned around.

"Just give him a 50 dollar bill if you've got one," the man inside the taxi said, under his breath.

I reached inside my wallet, took out a note and then placed it resentfully into the crooked git's hand. As I turned round to get back into the car I was afraid he would ask for more. But he didn't. As I slammed the door shut, the driver then set off quickly on our way again and said in a loud voice: "What an asshole!" he said.

"Bloody hypocrite!" a woman muttered on the other side of the taxi.

"Welcome to Colombia!" the guy next to me said, raising his eyebrows apologetically.

The woman on the other side of the taxi leaned over and, squeezing my arm, said, "Listen darling, you don't go paying any attention to gente de polla! You're going to have a lovely time in this beautiful city of Pamplona. Lovely people... Just forget about him!"

As we set off, I tried to forget about it like everybody else in the taxi was doing, and enjoy the spectacular scenery that was looking more like Scotland with every turn in the road. But I felt shaken by how blatantly I had been robbed in broad daylight.

I was relieved to get to Pamplona with its green hills and cloudy skies. There was a slight chill in the air, which smelt of wood-smoke, barbecued corn on the cob, and freshly fried crisps. Everyone was dressed in Ruanas, thick local ponchos to keep warm. It was great to see Paula, a familiar face. We had plenty of exchanging notes to do with our new found South American lives.

That night, while trying to learn how to dance Vallenato and La Cumbia with some of the warmest and friendliest people on the planet, I could feel my tinnitus drilling into my awareness a bit. But the music was loud enough to drown it out and the good company more than enough to distract the attention away. Their Spanish was crystal clear and so easy to understand. By the time I went to bed I was too exhausted to even react to the noise in my head. I had a great, long week-end cooling off in the high country of Colombia.

When I look back the tinnitus was quite bad at this time. As a coping strategy I didn't tell anyone about it. I was partly in denial about it and also pretended that it would go away. If I had told people about it, this would have made the whole thing more real. They would start talking about it and, consequently, it would perhaps cement itself in more.

It was just a noise, and it would go away one day. It was just a noise, and it would go away one day. I just kept on with this mantra, trying to soothe myself. It was just a noise, and it would go away one day. I don't know where this positive belief came from, but it was strong and like a message from the future sending me some guidance.

The rest of my year in Venezuela went by without too much upheaval. I loved sleeping in hammocks on sugar-white sandy beaches that glowed green at night when you brushed your teeth in the salt-water, or splashed around. The jungle was vast and awe-inspiring, especially having been jolted around for two days on a bus with two high walls of dark trees on either side. When the road suddenly started going up the side of a table-top mountain or "tepuy" the most incredible view of nothing but rainforest came into view, from horizon to horizon. I will never forget the moment when a man clapped. The bus stopped. And several hours after the last sign of human inhabitation, literally in the middle of nowhere, with no track to be seen, this man grabbed the couple of chickens that had been flapping about in the roof rack overhead, climbed down onto the red dusty road and walked off into the leaves. Where did he go? How could he survive in such a place?

The mosquito bites would leave red circles of pain that would hurt for two weeks. The jejenes, or ferocious, tropical sand-fleas, would attack in seconds and leave you dotted with pinprick sores for most of the night. If you were stupid enough to get up for a wee at dawn and bare your crown jewels to the world beyond the mosquito net, the pain would be excruciating.

We often went to Choroni, a tiny village at the end of a perfect Caribbean beach lined with coconut palms at the foot of a tropical mountain range. To get there you had to drive through rainforest over the coastal mountains rushing with rivers and washpools. We found a waterfall where you could climb behind the wall of water and then dive headfirst into the deafening roar, to be tumbled down and shoved around in a booming washing machine of movement and then very quickly be spewed out onto the surface again in a cool froth about ten metres further down river. It was divine and made you want to yell out like Tarzan.

And then there were los Tambores…

When the evening started to cool off a bit, ten or more drummers would meet at the end of the beach and start beating out an incredibly thrusting rhythmic beat that caused even the most frigid and repressed souls to start twitching and swaying, and wiggle their hips.

Soon quite a crowd would gather around, and in the middle of a circle of onlookers, a man and a woman would start dancing together, showing how much they appreciated each other. Under the hot Caribbean night there was only one rule here: just one man, and one woman at a time. So trunks with lumps and bikinis with their bumps would bound around in the hot sweaty air and briefly touch, sending up a cheer from the crowd.
"Dale, dale, dale," the men would cry. "Give it to her, give it to her."
"Que mamasonga!" "What a gorgeous mamma!"

This encouragement would get him crouching down even lower with one hand behind his bum, the other just above his bulge and then he would thrust ever more courageously, letting himself get even bigger.

The women watching would howl with delight, some would even scream with wide staring eyes, mesmerised by this rare and unfettered meeting of male and female. Then the women would shout back,

"¡No se para! ¡Cuca! ¡Dáselo!" "It's not getting hard. Pussy. Let him have it!"

If you liked the way the woman was twerking her bottom and jiggling her breasts inside the circle, then you could jump in. It was up to you to have a mock fight with the man, show him your worth and then shove him out.

Once inside you could feel the circle of passionate drumming and arousal filling you with a strong energy like an elixir of life, lifting you up and then sending you thrusting and writhing in a body full of intense joy, freedom and aliveness.

Then, once inside, if a woman fancied you, she would then jump in and push the woman who was dancing with you out of the way, and then come on to you as much as her body could get away with, seducing you with each pull in of her body, thrusting her shoulders forwards and backwards and luring you into her hot thighs; you would push forward with your hips and bottom thrusting daring a tiny bit more with each movement, touching where it matters, not being ashamed to let yourself show slightly, pushing into the thunderous applause of the drums and being egged on by the crowd. And then, you were out, and he was in...

We all drank Guarapita, an illegal passion fruit liqueur that was bought wrapped in newspaper through a secret window. This helped free up the inhibitions and fuel los Tambores into a frenzy until the energy became so strong it sent people running off with a partner to the nearest quiet place, a backstreet alley, where they could and mingle and burst together like tropical seed pods, rocking in hammocks and sending explosions all along the beach. When los Tambores were playing soon all the hammock hooks of guest houses would start swaying.

Yes, of course the loud drums made the tinnitus worse but I didn't care. I had far more interesting pursuits to enjoy in the trees. There is definitely an art to loving inside a hammock, and there is an art to sleeping in a hammock. It is all about angle.

In Choroní the way people walk in the morning is so very different to the night before. It was slower and definitely looked worked out, even sore. It always made me chuckle. There were so many collusive smiles over a morning "guayoyo" or coffee. Here the restraints of city living were loosened and the natural lore of living took over and held sway. Experiencing Los Tambores changes you fundamentally.

At Chichirivichi, a mini-Venezuelan Maldives, I had a terrifying night on a yacht where I awoke almost upside down in a storm. When I stuck my head above the deck, Jorge and his dad were yelling as they fought against the horizontal blast of rain, and a howling gale with white lashing waves all round, trying to stop the boat from being dragged off its anchor. We managed to stay put, but a neighbour's anchor didn't hold. Their boat was ripped from its moorings on the reef and sucked out into the monstrous night. It was totally terrifying. I sat down and held on for dear life.

The following morning the sea was eerily calm like a gently undulating mirror. As we sat eating swordfish arepas for breakfast in the silent sun, lapping over the most brilliant turquoise water I have ever seen, everyone was so chilled it made the storm seem like some strange psychotic episode. Having been scared to trembling point during the night, my tinnitus was up again. One of my worst fears is being lost at sea at night, and I wondered for a good hour whether we were going to be sucked out to see by the storm too. My head was buzzing like a family of cicadas were sitting on my shoulders.
But the idyllic turquoise light was too irresistible a pull and so I dived in dozens of times with my face mask and twisted and turned like a dolphin in and around yellow, red and blue fish. Soon after climbing back on board the sea darkened with some manta rays, who flew under gracefully.

I went water-skiing around the cays of Morrocoy, flying over sugar white sand that suddenly goes dark as the reef edge drops into the deep blue. I nearly went flying into a huge black spider monkey hanging upside down off a mangrove bush. Once when I came off the skis in the warm black water of the lagoon, I found my skin being nipped by hundreds of baby turtles. It took a couple of minutes for the boat to pick me up again and all the nipping and biting was incredibly ticklish.

The Venezuelan coast is paradise, and all the excitement it brought was enough to send the noise inside my head to a loud frothing surf which kept up for a couple of days. But then, with the undertow, it would gradually recede back to the more usual high-pitched hiss.

Sometimes too much excitement, exhaustion, or fear, sent a tidal wave of raised tinnitus surging through my life for a week at a time, but the energy and relatively uncluttered mind that a twenty year old has, meant I was able to bounce back quickly. Besides, Venezuela was like a dream come true for me and served as the perfect masker and distractor for the ringing, because, on most days, the beauty and interest of this country won hands down. Up and out was far too interesting for me to just sit around and hang around inside my own experience.

On the flight back to England I cried for hours. As the plane took off and pulled away from the coastal mountain range, I stared without averting my gaze from the jungle mountains dropping steeply down into the white beaches, getting smaller and smaller until they vanished from view. "Volveré, volveré, porque te quiero, hasta tu puerto volveréeee."

We flew over the coral atolls of Los Roques where I had been dropped off on a sandbank in the middle of the sea with a friend, a parasol and a hamper of rum, arepas and limes for the day. I remembered how the sea turned green underneath a dark storm cloud, and how the fish swarmed and slipped around our legs like living fish soup.

I must have been crying loudly next to the window on the plan because the woman sitting next to me kept on giving me looks of concern. Maybe she thought I had been bereaved. In many ways I had been. I didn't want to leave Venezuela. During that wonderful year out, all my upright, letter-box Britishness was shaken free by this wonderful, colourful Venezuela that I fell in love with, a land that turned the living up loud and intoxicated me with her fast and colourful dream. I wanted to give up my degree and stay. I wanted to set up a new life in Caracas. However, with a heavy heart I decided to return home and continue on with St Andrews. I was to mourn this decision for months to come.

Chapter 5 The Sound of Anticlimax

Autumn Cottage, West Sussex 1987

Wind Blows

Wind blows
leaves remain
wind rests
leaves fall

Autumn strangeness
shows me
myself

James Low
Sparks

"Hello darling. Lovely to see you." My mother greeted me at the large, brown gate to Autumn Cottage.
"How did it go?" she asked, giving me a big hug and a kiss.
"I've had the most amazing time. It's been the best year of my life."

I looked at her face. The camera stopped rolling, and my mother was wheeled off, her make-up redone, clothes replaced and then a slightly more wrinkled and shrunken version of her was wheeled back in. Back by the gate, filming started again. It was a year later. My mother's younger face updated itself with an older one, like a time-lapse film of a withering flower. But this was not a plant that was withering and starting to fold in on itself before my eyes. It was my mother. I didn't want her to wither or fold in on herself.

A rush of reality raced through me like a giant sieve passing through the earth, snapping a potato from its roots, wrenching it out of its safe, homely soil. The life I knew and loved was being replaced by something else.

Standing by the sturdy, brown gate, taking in my mother's older face, I realised that Autumn Cottage was built on shaky ground, and that one day I would have to leave, never to come back. As sure as birds eat worms, one day, my mother and her cosy, oat-cake cottage life would be pulled away in a flash.

Angus the black Scotty dog was barking and jumping excitedly under the inner gate. I walked over and pushed it open. He hurled his puffing, grunting nuzzle and scampering paws against my ankles and started buffeting, yelping and snorting frantically. It was sheer joy to be greeted by his tail-whacking, sniff-puffing, nose-nudging happiness. I reached down and picked him up. I squeezed his familiar, chunky little body and inhaled the sweet chocolaty Scotty smell of his neck that I had kissed so often over the years.

His legs carried on racing with delight even though they were no longer in touch with the ground. I loved this about him. Then I placed his furry black undercarriage back onto the paving stones, and as his feet re-engaged with the ground, he shot off in a circular dance around me as I walked into the garden, barking out to the whole neighbourhood that this was a moment of great celebration and joy.

It was time for tea. I sat down with granny, grandpa, mum, the tinkling waterfall by the pond and one of grandpa's freshly baked cakes. Angus sat underneath my chair and, every so often, beat his tail against my leg, reminding me that he was still pleased to see me.

"South America is such an amazing place," I ventured. "A couple of weeks ago I went on a walk into the jungle with a Paracoto Indian who showed me how to spear a small animal with a serbacana, or blow pipe. The table top mountains there are staggeringly beautiful."

Granny raised an eye-brow and slurped on her tea.

"I travelled up to the snow-line in Ecuador and was so high up I had to suck on some 'panela,' which is a piece of sugar-cane rock, to stop getting dizzy from the altitude."

Grandpa reached over for a Rich Tea biscuit and dunked it into his cup of Yorkshire Tea.

"I went on a walk into the largest cave network in South America. It was really scary when we turned the lights off and looked into total pitch-black darkness. When we switched our torches on again we saw a scalopendra centipede which is so poisonous it can leave you screaming for days."

Grandpa gasped and gave a quiet shake of his head.

"Don't they smell lovely," Granny said to mum. She looked at the roses just behind her. My mother raised a finger in that let's-wait-and-see gesture, lifted her nostrils, took a sniff and then nodded back at her proudly. Granny knew what was important.

"One night I slept with a fisherman, well not with him, but in his hut, next to a beautiful lake high up in the Peruvian Andes. He didn't even speak Spanish. I woke up with 'sorroche,' which is altitude sickness, and I had to chew on disgusting tasting coca leaves and crunch into chalk to release its medicine to feel better."

"The deep-red ones are the best," mum added. Granny looked back at her and raised a finger with that you're-absolutely-right gesture.
"The altitude sickness was so bad I had to go back down to sea-level as fast as

possible. I got a lift in the back of a truck full of labourers, a scared dog and three loose piglets. Each time we went over a bump, it felt like my brain had come loose and was bruising itself inside my skull."

"Oh, by heck!" Grandpa gasped. He finished his tea, got up and wandered off to do some gardening. Angus got up with a bark of approval and ran off to help him.

"Golly! That sounds horrible darling," my mother acknowledged.

"Well it sounds a little bit like an ego trip to me," Granny muttered under her breath, as she struggled to her feet, picked up the tea-tray and hauled her hunched and sore-hipped frame back up the garden to the kitchen.

"Oh Mum, Venezuela is one of the most beautiful countries in the world. I love it so much."

"That's nice dear. Anyway, it's lovely to have you back. Now 'Eastenders' is on in a moment, so we must get ready." With that she got up and walked back up to the cottage and to the remote TV control.

My audience was over. I found myself sitting with the pond and a trickle of water that was running over stone slabs down into the green algae-filled water. Some fish were moving about gently. Then they stopped moving. The water trickled a bit more. Then a dark red fish with black speckles on its back just wavered a dorsal fin slightly. Then they stopped moving again for a moment.

My head was hissing. Tsssssssssss. The noise was calm and steady, like a background hiss of a sound system. It was strangely comforting, like an old friend even.

My mother's garden was long and beautiful with fruit trees and neatly kept flower-beds cutting into the lawn like a long, deep theatre set. The large tamarisk was laden with pink flowers and hung down like a thick curtain. The large ceanothus formed a vibrant blue tunnel that led down to the yellow shed-door at the bottom of the garden, where I used to have parties. Beyond the raspberry and blackcurrant plants, and tall netting to keep the deer out, a large field dropped down to the woods. Birds twittered in trees that were beginning to slouch under the weight of apples, pears and plums.

I sat there bursting with enthusiasm for South America, alone, on a fold up, collapsible garden chair. It was the same chair that Granny had fallen through a couple of summers ago.

Looking back to life as a twenty-one-year-old I was still attached to friends and family, which meant any change in direction or any rift hurt like a plaster being ripped off a wound far too soon. A fifty-year-old, however, has tougher skin, and is used to losing friends into the thick of life, and love affairs that once glowed as brightly as suns, but now lie like faded photos at the back of the bottom drawer.

At twenty-one, death seemed far off, and only occasionally did a person pop off to the next world. Back then it was like a cataclysmic bang. But from where I am sitting now, life is rapidly heating up like a pan of popcorn that is starting to pop faster and faster until soon a whole generation will be exploding out of this dimension into the next.

But thankfully most things in life move on gently, like sweeping away autumn leaves. Friendships end and we realise that we have gone beyond the point where it is too awkward to get back in touch. And then there are lovely, poignant, almost delicious endings when we savour the last blackberry before the garden shuts down for winter. We know there is a long wait till next summer when the garden will once again swell with fruit, and yet this wait feels manageable, because the cycle will return.

But there won't be another mother or father next harvest. There is no circle of life when it comes to harvesting parents. When they finally go they will be gone. When the roof-like protection of mum and dad has been taken off, we will be left exposed to the vastness of life under the stars with nothing more than memories to cling on to, and an increasing amount of gone-ness.

Do memories get more precious with age or just more painful? Remember the time when we were laughing deliriously in the swing-chair, quivering with wet-eyes? Well, it's gone, and it feels like a real wrench of the heart pulling it back out from that forgotten place. Remember the raunchy sausage dipping into salsa picnic amongst the poppies? Remember running at top speed across the dunes with pleasure pointing skyward? No. Stop it. Just stop now, shut down or you will cry. The moment has gone. Shut it down. It is best forgotten. Otherwise we will cry as we try to capture it once again in our hearts and just find really it has got sucked into emptiness along with everything else. All we are left with is the present moment and actually a lot of emptiness that is here if we really notice.

Tssssssss. The noise broke me out of a reverie. "Bloody tinnitus!" I got up from the garden chair and too, wandered up the garden to the cottage and plugged myself into TV and biscuits and cups of tea for a couple of days. Then, a few weeks later, I tried to squeeze back into third year at St Andrews. But it felt a small and uninteresting place after the heat and excitement of Venezuela.

In fact, as I tiptoed into the new term, the days seemed to slow down and move like a slug along the grey, stone walls of the ruined cathedral and its damp mossy pathways. Empty holes in the castle walls stared blindly out towards the cold, grey-green North Sea. The daylight weakened and a terrible, steely-blue gloom pushed earlier and earlier into the day, pressing against steamed up windows of students trying to stay awake in the last, tired lecture of the day. Soon, a sense of low-grade depression sank in like a sea-fog, draining all the colour out of University life.

I found myself sharing a flat with two girls, floating around like an untethered buoy awash in a sea of girl-talk, art-history and musings on things that would probably never happen. Life became so flat that the pile of books at one end of my desk rose up like an irresistible doorway out of the gloom. There was nothing better to do than get lost inside the covers. By the time finals started to loom over the horizon and threaten me with having to write eighteen essays in one week, I had finally succumbed and had turned into a book-reading student.

I was surprised to find myself laughing out loud to the hilarious ingenuity of Don Quijote, and was so gripped by the labyrinthine world of Hugo's sewers of Paris that I read Les Misérables in just one week, and went for days without talking to anyone. I was taken in by Baudelaire's evil flowers and I found myself longing for times past, yearning for some kind of Pays de Cocagne, full of "luxe, calme and volupté."

My desk was built into a bay-window which looked over the Castle Sands to the sea. This view kept me sane. Often I would look up from a play or literary criticism floating in ideas, sometimes not knowing where I was or what month of the year it was. But then the rippling, choppy waves reverberating backwards and forwards across the chilly sea provided a constant homing ground to come back to and rediscover myself sitting there again, as a student in St Andrews.

There is something so morbid about books. They put us directly in touch with the minds of the authors who have often long since gone. For a short period of time, these ideas that had been lost in the sea of time, flick on again, like a lighthouse at sea, and for a few glorious months crash through us students like tidal waves, sending a froth of essays, tutorials and excitement out into the world, before pulling back with that heavy, shingle-sucking roar, into the ocean of forgetting.

Then it would be over. Nobody there to care about those feelings and insights anymore. Back into the emptiness that is always there. We can read and fill our minds with shared experiences, but what happens if we just dare to stop for a moment. Do we dare meet the emptiness that is there too? Just unplug everything, sit alone with no input and wait. When the body settles and the thoughts eventually slow down the emptiness comes in like an ocean of stillness, waiting to soak right through the middle of you and show you just how small you are.

Outside my window, I noticed that the swimming-pool built into the rocks had emerged again from underneath the waves. For a moment I stare at the heart-stoppingly cold water offering its icy plunge to your naked skin like some sadistic joke. How can they swim in that… Then I would look back down at the words on my desk and get re-absorbed into worlds that took me far away from where I was sitting. When I looked up again there was no sign of the pool. It had gone back under. It was out there somewhere, lost beneath the waves.

I pick up my coat. I run downstairs and across the street to the steps that drop down to the beach. The wind slaps my face awake with its salty freshness and stink of sea-weed. Soon my feet are crunching down onto the shingle and, overhead, the castle ruins are screaming with seagulls. They are flying like thugs round the black towers looming up into the twilight. The surface of the sea is agitated. Every so often, a large rogue wave comes marching in with thundering self-importance, only to be tripped up by a leg of rock sloping out from the castle tower, and reduced to froth on the other side.

The waves are dramatic but it is the tide that scares me. It's often the quiet forces in life, the ones that you cannot see or hear that are far more powerful in the long run. You can't really notice them without first becoming very still, and only then, in the quietest moments, is something revealed. You can't see the tide move with normal everyday consciousness. To catch it you have to settle down, perhaps wrapped in a warm blanket, as you focus your gaze onto a place where perhaps the sea touches a rock. If you focus on the waves you'll miss it.

To meet the tide at its own speed you need to let go of the normal rush of the thinking mind. You slow your breath right down and focus single-mindedly on that one place, letting the waves come and go, come and go. As you become more focused the mind becomes stronger and clearer and the twitter falls away. With one view and slow, calm breathing you wait until the visual world starts flickering through like an old-fashioned projector. Slowly, very slowly, with sustained attention, the water laps back and forth, back and forth, again and again, hundreds and hundreds of times, until you start to see clearly that the whole horizon of water is marching towards you.

With a slow mind, waves can accelerate until they almost vanish from sight, so that you can focus on the slower movement underneath. It takes time and heightened awareness for the deeper patterns to reveal themselves to you. From a small beach you can start to sense that there really is a giant celestial object two hundred and thirty thousand miles away pulling the whole horizon of water along with it. Everything really is connected to everything else.

I didn't know about the Long Tide then. I didn't know that it was possible to sit calmly and slow down enough to feel a great space open up and have an immediate experience of a body connected to everything around, a locus of awareness hanging there in space, quietly reverberating in all directions, like a vast, interactive, yet completely silent hologram. Little did I know that it would be the body that would reveal this to me years later.

The night-time sea looked terrifying from the Castle Sands. Rough, dark water was punching, slapping and pushing and pulling out into deeper water, moving further and further away from safety out into the icy, black space. The shock of the sea, with its cliff-shattering strength, and planet covering immensity would always stop my tiny head from overheating. The sea had an ability to clear my head in minutes. It was this cold, floating world outside my bay-window that helped push the reset button and was responsible for getting me through finals.

Two other things helped me get my degree: running into the front room with my flatmate Melanie and hopping up and down, laughing hysterically like five-year-olds, and, throwing South American parties with Paula where we got everybody dancing salsa and merengue in a desperate attempt to rekindle the fire of Colombia and Venezuela on cold, dark evenings in Fife.

My tinnitus had moved in for good. A noise like a pressure-cooker whistling right next to me followed me into lecture halls, libraries and into bed. Even through it wasn't loud, the noise felt like an unwanted stalker, and yet I was just able to ignore it then. So that is what I did. I just kept my head down and ploughed on through to the end of finals, and to the end of St Andrews and didn't talk about it to anyone.

Chapter 6 The Sound of the East

Obama-shi, Fukui-ken, Japan 1989

The crow has flown away:
Swaying in the evening sun,
A leafless tree

Natsume Soseki

I got my degree and set out on a ridiculous plan to go to Japan, learn Japanese and then come back and work in the City as a Commodity Trader. With French, Spanish and Japanese under my belt, and a grass-roots knowledge of life in South America I would become the ideal coffee or cocoa trader. Needless to say it didn't work out like that.

I got a job teaching English in a Fishing High School in Wakasa, a beautiful un-bombed region of central Japan, over the mountains from Kyoto. A highly indented coastline faced northwards across the sea to Vladivostok, and steep mountains, cloaked in bamboo and cedar forest, opened up an exquisite world of temples, hidden coves and some of the most beguiling and surprising people I have ever met.

I arrived in Obama-shi in the late summer and immediately explored its narrow lanes of wooden houses with ornate roofs and the smell of drains and drying fish.

Strange looking faces poked out through door hangings like characters in a Bunraku puppet show and gasped at my strange gaijin face. At first I would smile back and say a polite "Kon nichi wa."

I jumped on my moped and putted along the humid valleys discovering beautiful rivers, temples and monasteries at every turn. Then I would turn uphill and chug slowly higher and higher to an occasional Shinto shrine, up in the cool, forested sky. At times the view would plummet off to bright green coves and tiny islets far below.

As I spluttered round each bend on my two-stroke engine, monkeys would scatter, and once in a while, to my utter horror, my wheels would suddenly go "bam bam" as they ran over a snake that was defiantly stretched out across the tarmac in the afternoon sun. I never looked back.

I decided to visit Kaminegori, a village high up in the mountains where autumn had already burned the trees into dramatic brushstrokes of red, orange and gold. The cottage roofs were made of thatch and were steep enough to shrug off the first heavy snows of winter. These thatched cottages huddled closely together near the flanks of the mountain.

I got off my bike and walked towards a brace of elderly ladies bent double in conical pointed hats. Some were hanging out long, pendulous horse-radishes on wooden fencing along the lane. Others were piling up fat, russet-red persimmons into baskets. Their bodies were bent double and looked as if they had given up all hope of ever seeing the world from an upright position. Indeed I think the first lady to catch sight of me had done so upside down, through the comfort of her legs.

In Japanese towns the sight of a gaijin or foreigner can still be somewhat of a surprise for the locals. However, in more remote mountain areas, a sighting of a hairy, western man is a rare experience and a frequent cause for great concern, as I learned only too quickly.

The first cry of alarm "Aréééé!" started slowly and deliberately, a little bit like a cockerel at dawn, rising in both pitch and loudness. A couple of hats twitched and then unbent themselves enough to look up. Then a more obviously shocked sounding "Ehhhhhh!" rose out more urgently. I looked over at a whole row of wide staring eyes. Their mouths were now wide open and crying out, "Aaaaaahhh!"

I couldn't believe it. I felt like I was a gorilla or an axe-murderer on the loose. They all darted off started shouting "Gaijin! Gaijin!" and shuffled off as fast as their hunch-backs would allow, out of sight. Within seconds the mountain village was plunged into silence.

My mouth fell open in disbelief. What a welcome! I walked around the cottages somewhat defiantly, hoping to find someone to talk to but all I met were faces darting away from windows. "Kon nichi wa. Watashi wa Igirisu-jin desu!" Hello! I'm from England!" I yelled, but nothing. I gave up after a few more minutes and thought I had better scarper before causing any more upset. So I put my gorilla legs over the saddle and sped hairily off back down to my new hometown, Obama.

The next day, I had to go and meet my supervisor. The other three Westerners, who lived in the same town had already met theirs. They turned out to be young, trendy men who would help break them into the Japanese way of life and make sure they survived. In Japan they say, "The nail that sticks out gets hammered back in," and we unruly, independent-thinking gaijin would need our supervisors' help to make sure we fitted in appropriately. Now it was my turn to meet my "buddy" for the year.

I was dropped off at my supervisor's house near the beach. The garden was exceptionally neat and tidy with white gravel that had been raked into a swirl and a straight line. Around the edge stood a couple of wise, gnarly trees that had been shrunk down to toy-sized, ikebana trees. Behind a proportionally perfect plum tree with curves in all the right places, stood a porch with chains dropping down in exact symmetry from eaves to ground. Drops dripped off the last link of the chain into small drains at exactly the same time as each other.
I pushed the door-bell.

Immediately, as if the bell cable was connected directly to my supervisor, light flooded into the corridor, and through smoked glass I could make out a small figure shuffling up to the door. It slid open. On the other side, down on the floor below, kneeled an elderly woman dressed in an intricately embroidered kimono. She stared straight at me. She was holding her lips tightly together in a small dot and her eyebrows stretched high up on her forehead like two question marks.

"Nakayama-sensei?" I asked awkwardly?

She pressed her hands together and closed her eyes as if she was just about to start praying. Then she bowed very slowly until her head touched the floor and slid her hands out in front of her head onto the immaculately clean, polished wooden surface like she was worshipping a Buddha. Then she continued to stay down there in that position. I didn't know what to do. So I looked at the embroidered figures, rivers and mountains on the cloth in the middle of her back.

A moment later she started to rise slowly back up again with her hands back in praying position in front of her chest, and her mouth still in a dot and her eyebrows still looking amazed at the top of her forehead. She was holding her breath in.

Once upright she then opened her eyes and stared directly at me. I found myself staring back at her with equally raised eyebrows. But my mouth had fallen open. I too was holding my breath. We stayed in this position for what seemed like an awkward amount of time. We stared far too deeply at each other too, which made me blush profusely. Why do bodies do their best to embarrass us even more?

"Welcome Jureun-sensei to Wakasa!" she burst out, releasing the breath suddenly. Then, very slowly and instructively, she added, "Jureun-sensei wa, Wakasa ni, yokoso!" Then she stopped and waited.

"Domo arigato gozaimashita - thank you," I said.
Suddenly she smiled so deeply that her eyes nearly shut again. Then she let out a loud and totally unfettered laugh that clattered about her midriff as if she had just told joke of the century. I gave a polite and somewhat bewildered laugh back. Then she settled down.

"I am very happy you are here," she said. She then continued to kneel there looking straight at me, allowing her words to sink in. Her smile looked like she was pleased with me. I stood there and felt taken off-guard. I closed my mouth again. I couldn't really pretend to look anywhere else. So I just received her welcome in that open-chested, slightly awkward silence. I wasn't used to meeting someone through their eyes before. I blushed again.

The rush of red to my cheeks made me feel really uncomfortable so I laughed to cover it up. She noticed with a smile.

"Prease take off your shoes." She pointed down to my feet with the palm of her hand stretched out flat like an artist's mannequin doll. She then translated this carefully and slowly into Japanese as if she were introducing me to something special and worth treasuring. There was a kindness and warmth in her words, like a mother helping a toddler to walk.

"Prease put on your srippers." She pointed proudly across to a pair of blue slippers. They had poodle-like tufts of fluff over the top strap. She bowed to them affectionately as she would to a dear friend, and smiled. I put them on.

"Prease step up – Hai, dozo o agari kudasai," she said, still on her knees, pointing to the door-way. I stepped up.

"Prease come in," she said with a bow. As I stepped inside she bowed so low that her forehead touched the floor. I towered over her like woolly mammoth.

Still partly bowing, she managed to locate the door and carefully slid it quietly shut. She then edged her way on he knees, a movement I had never really seen before Japan, along the polished wooden corridor to a paper screen and then kneeled towards me. "Prease, Jurean-sensei, will you take tea?"
"Er, yes please. That would be lovely. Yes. Thank you." I said, feeling clumsy next to her finesse and formality. She slid back a white paper screen and pointed into the room.

In the middle of tatami mats were two flat cushions. Next to one of the cushions was a fairly deep hole, which contained an ornate cauldron of water. I could hear the sound of boiling water bubbling gently away under the heavy iron lid.

"Prease sit down." She pointed to a cushion. I slid off the poodle-slippers and placed them neatly together in the corridor. Then I stepped across the threshold onto the cool, firm, even matting beneath my feet and then sat down cross-legged in the middle of the room on a cushion. Then she slid the screen slowly back to a silent stop, returning the room to a perfect white square. For a moment she paused to acknowledge that this had been done.

Sunlight poured in through an outer window sending a horizontal blaze of light across the wooden squares, dissecting each one into half-light, half-dark triangles. Then the elderly woman turned towards me and then, to my surprise, came over, right in front of me and knelt down. She settled into position and then looked up again and took up eye contact. Her eyes must have been a metre away from mine.

"I am Naka Yama," she said proudly. "I am very preased to meet you.
"'Naka' means 'middle.' 'Yama' means 'mountain.' So 'Nakayama' means 'Middle Mountain.' Call me prease, Mrs Middle Mountain."

She smiled deeply and then rested her gaze on the floor. The room returned to silence except for the bubbling water noise coming out of the black pot. She stayed in that position. We both sat for a moment just long enough for the sense of space and stillness to start pushing in again.

On the wall behind her was an old parchment with a beautiful kanji character painted in black ink. The symbol swept in a great arc, then twisted downwards until it spattered off into tiny strands and a thousand specks. She sat there and waited in silence. What should I do now? I felt slightly uncomfortable and so I ventured, "Hajimemashite!"

"Aré!" she said, and looked elated, almost shocked. She took a deep bow then replied, confirmingly, "Ha ji me ma shite!" Then she did something that I would grow very used to over the next year. A deep frown appeared on her forehead looking like she was in pain. She tipped her head forward and went "Mmmmmnnnnn," like a growling cat. Then suddenly she said, "Bery nice pronunciation!" and with that, she laughed again, letting her entire upper body shake freely.

"Oh thank-you," I answered.

"My preasure," she answered, like a Collins Phrase book, regaining her composure. The room fell silent again.

"Jureun-sensei?" she asked, "Are you ready to take tea?" Her sudden seriousness took me aback and suggested there what was about to happen was important and needed my full attention.

"Yes I am," I answered, feeling suddenly a bit nervous.

She stopped and said something in Japanese solemnly like she was talking to spirit, and closed her eyes. We both sat quietly for a moment and then she took a couple of deep breaths.

While I was sitting there I felt a slightly odd thing happen. In the silence it felt like something was gathering in the room, as if an atmosphere was forming gently around me and was starting to gently hold me. As I sat there I distinctly sensed that Nakayama-sensei was focussing on me in a special way, creating a force field of some kind. My body felt like it started to float gently inside this force field.

Nakayama-sensei looked like she was deep in meditation. Whatever she was doing was so calming that, even though I had never felt anything like it before, I just accepted this as if it were just something ordinary and everyday.
My body started relaxing and I felt light, and yet, rooted to the ground at the same time. Without any effort I found myself just staying focused on her calmly waiting to see what would happen next. We were both very aware of each other and yet at ease too, something I don't think I had ever experienced before.

Nakayama-sensei put her hand into the wide belt or "Obi" that went around her waist and pulled out a red cloth. She stretched her arms out straight and folded it slowly with careful, precise movements. I watched in fascination. Then suddenly, she snapped it tight, sending a loud crack into all four corners of the room. I jumped out of my skin. It gave me such a jolt that I laughed out in surprise. The crack went straight through me and seemed to wake me up more than ever. And yet I still felt very relaxed. The room fell silent. I could hear the bubbling water clearly against the silence of the room.

Mrs Nakayama looked relaxed, and yet focused, and I found myself being relaxed and focused as well, as if this state of mind were a transferable thing. Mesmerised, I watched as she held the cloth out vertically and then carefully folded it and placed it into one hand. She picked up a small lacquerware pot and wiped it carefully around the top and sides before placing it onto a tray. She then lined up two earthenware tea bowls on another tray in front of the boiling water, lifted the lid, and let out a small cloud of steam like an escaping genie. Then she took a long bamboo ladle and tipped boiling water into each bowl before returning it to the top of the cauldron, then rotated it round so that it was in alignment with the tatami mats. She swirled the bowls round and round before tipping out the waste-water into a receptacle out of sight. She then dried them with the red cloth.

Next, she took a long thin bamboo spatula, took the lid off the lacquerware pot, took out three scoops of bright green powder and placed them carefully inside the bowls. Each time she tipped the powder into the bowl, she tapped it three times, with a "tack tack tack" against the silence. Then she ladled some water onto the powder and whisked it into froth until it was just the right consistency and temperature. Finally, she moved carefully like a yoga teacher so that she lay face down on the floor right in front of me. To my surprise she lifted my bowl of tea lifted above her head. I found myself sitting there in a deep state of stillness.
It took me a moment or two to realise that this elderly woman was lying completely prostrate with her nose pressed to the ground, on the floor before me. The bowl of tea was steaming as she was straining slightly to lift it off the ground towards my lap.

I reached down, lifted it out of her hands, and said, "Arigato gozaimashita."

She then pushed her body back up into a bowing posture like a caterpillar and neatly placed herself back opposite me with her bowl in the palm of her hand. She looked at me and raised her eyebrows as if she wanted me to copy her, and then studied the bowl carefully, turning it round gently in her hand.

I examined the dark-blue glaze on my bowl. It was full of tiny flecks that reflected the light like a starry night sky. As I rotated it in my hand I saw how it had a slight wobble in its form with a shorter rim on one side compared to the other. And yet it felt balanced, strong and light, and was perfect in its imperfection. Cupping the form in my hands I imagined how the master potter formed the final shape on the wheel in a long, slow and final out-breath.

I slurped up the pungent, bitter froth. It didn't matter that I didn't like the taste particularly. I just remember that, as we both wiped our mouths with the napkins and looked at each other, it felt incredibly peaceful. I realised that the twitter in my head had switched off.

As the tea-ceremony came to a close there was a sense of just sitting there, looking through my eyes and seeing what was there in front of me. I wasn't listening to the thoughts in my head because there weren't any, other than what was going on in front of me. It was like an internal theatre with its own play inside my head had switched off, and the stage had gone clear. The internal twitter stopped and, as a result, there was just a gentle tracking of the sound that was there in the room. The bubbling of the water had died down. I could hear a very gentle almost imperceptible hiss. The room was quiet and my ears had really dropped down. I could still just about hear the noise but I felt still and calm too.
The noise in my head had all but gone. I could just hear the sound of two people breathing. My tinnitus turned right down and almost fizzled away. What on earth was going on? Did she have some strange magical power over me? As we both sat there I felt really well and incredibly grateful. A layer of discomfort that I didn't know was there had melted away and I felt at ease inside. How did she do it? My tinnitus had gone. I couldn't stop smiling at her. My eyes were watering up.

I went back to my flat next to the rice fields, and, for an hour or two, noticed how quiet everything was. It was delightful and made me laugh out aloud. I got acquainted with my flat and learnt how to slide my paper-screen open. When I checked, there was not a peep from my ears. I worked out how to operate my sit-in-up-to-the-neck bath with its boil as you bathe switch. Even after plucking up the courage to switch on the self-boil bath switch once inside, and feel the eddies of kettle-like heat swirling up around my bottom and turning my face purple, my head was still quiet and clear. Still no noise. It took me a while to get the knack of the gutter-like toilet with its violent horizontal flush that blasted everything to smithereens in a very exposing kind of way. Even though it sounded like a roaring jet-engine and made me jolt every time I pulled the lever, my ears stayed silent. For a short while I kept checking to see that the stillness was still there, and it was.

My year in Japan couldn't have been more Japanese. From my base school on the beach I could literally see red sunsets behind volcano-shaped mountains, and cedar trees hanging off the rocks leading down to the sea. I windsurfed across jelly-fish infested water to inaccessible beaches across the bay. When I met a local potter and threw a pot on his wheel, much to his amazement, I appeared in the local press: "Foreigner makes a Japanese pot!"

Mr. No-Seh, the local karate champion, welcomed me into his clan of he-men with a foot-slap to my face. It made me jump out of my skin and the ten other guys fall about laughing. The room was barely large enough to contain all the yelling and punching. But it felt great to push into the rock hard abdomens and vigorous precision of this strong group of men and to be welcomed whole-heartedly by them. I found there was a fair amount of anger and this was the perfect place to get it out.

At the beginning of each karate class we would sit, chant and take a moment to enter into the spirit of karate. Then at the end we would all bow to each other, and look into each other's eyes and feel a sense of respect. Then finally, we would burst out of the room, covered in sweat and buzzing with young man energy. As we roamed through the town people would bow to us knowingly and girls would point and giggle and sometimes follow us for a while.

The barman in each whisky bar would hand us the special karate group bottle and slowly the conversation would get more and more rowdy, and connections with women in the bar would sometimes heat up. But the attention always came back to us men. There was an unspoken rule not to stray into the women around us.

From time to time one of them would stroke my arm jealously and say, "Takusan heya. Nnnnn sgoi na..." which means "Lots of hair. Mmm that's really great, isn't it." They would insist in me taking off my shirt and then they would tug the hair on my chest and then the women in the bar would clap and cheer. From an alcoholic point of view, I was often the last one standing and helped some of the drop to the ground drunk guys get home. It was fun and I loved the strong, loyal camaraderie they gave me and really appreciated the effort they made with my bad Japanese.

I learnt how to dry out my sweat-drenched futon in the sun on the most hideous sauna-like days where steam seemed to come in through the window. I had to pick the occasional snake out of the wheel-arch of my car on the road that ran along the river to school, which made me cringe. But apart from that, life in Japan was great, except for work.

I was an English teacher, but at my base school nobody wanted to learn English. The kids seemed a bit rejected and there was a general air of not caring or mattering. I soon discovered that my job was more a token gesture of putting kids in touch with the outside world rather than teaching English.

The Japanese government had decided to import us gaijin en masse from all over the English-speaking world and drop us like alien tubs of yoghurt into the dairy-free classrooms all the way from Hokkaido to the Okinawa islands in the south.
Walking intoa room of 30 faces all with black hair, and military-cum-sailor-styled uniform staring at you was daunting at first. When I found students fast asleep at the back of the classroom I tried to wake up them up. I thought they were being rude, until Nakayama-sensei took me aside and told me that it was cruel to try and wake Hitoshi-san up. He had been out all night fishing and needed to sleep.

At the week-ends I would see my students dressed up in a baseball uniforms marching along the side of a road like soldiers off to war.

"What are you doing?" I would ask winding down my car window.
"Why aren't you having fun on the beach?"

"We want to be the namba wan team in school," would come the reply.

"Oh really?" I said back to them, just not getting it. "Ganbatte Kudasai – please do your best," I would add a bit sarcastically.

"Sank you sensei!" they would all reply in unison as they returned to robot marching towards the baseball pitch.

One morning the staff-meeting was disrupted by an explosion in the block next door. A father was so ashamed he had lost his job, he decided to blow himself and his family up in a massive breakfast explosion.

Another day, a mother hit the headlines when she couldn't face the shame of her child's stutter, so she strapped her to her back and jumped off the cliff to their deaths.

One morning I stormed out of the staff-room in disgust at the way children were put on desktops and punished by terrifying gangs of male teachers yelling at them like machine guns.

After a Christmas holiday travelling across frozen China, I was ordered to shave my three-week-old beard off or face leaving the school. Begrudgingly I obeyed.
The only way I could get through to my students was to blast them awake with exciting videos of Madonna. This seemed to get through to some of them at least, but I slowly realised my job was simply not to give up on them and keep trying.

In winter so much snow fell out of the sky that ghostly white fingers grew out of the tops of rocks in the still green water of the sea, and bamboo forests bent down to snapping point over the narrow roads creating an exquisitely beautiful cathedral roof of white lattice overhead. Even after a meter of overnight snow, the students, of course, would still ride up to their midriffs in their uniforms, often without overcoats and manage to get to class on time with blue fingers and chattering teeth. They reassured me that the bikes gripped well in deep snow.

The rivers of Wakasa are unusually pure and their waters are believed to contain special properties. One night, I crunched along a frozen path behind a long line of monks in white habits and pointed hats like the Ku Klux Klan, lighting up the snow-filled forests with burning torches. They filled the winter silence with the deafening sound of conch shells that echoed off the mountain slopes all around. Some of the people accompanying us were carrying the old-style Japanese flag, the Hinomaru with its red-sunbeams.

In a moment of solemn silence, the monks poured water taken from a sacred well into the small stream, and sent it off with small rafts of floating candles and a blessing. We watched in silence as the small trail of flickering lights bobbed up and down before disappearing off through the trees into the dark winter night. It would take ten days before the water would be received at Nara in the next prefecture. Once the small rafts appeared the monks would then take water from the stream and use it to bless their own temples. This ritual called "Omizu Okuri," the sending of the waters, revealed a deep reverence for the local spirit of the land.

My tinnitus came back gently without me noticing at first, and switched on and off for a while, and seemed to have a mind of its own. But I was totally fascinated by this extraordinary country and found life far too interesting to focus on a quiet noise inside my head for too long.
I fell in love with the beautiful temples and monasteries of Wakasa. I often went to meditate at Myotsu-ji temple, which lay along a road deep in the forest. I would cross over a bright-red, hump-back bridge over a stream, climb up the steep stone steps and come to the curved roof gateway where the ordinary, everyday world was left behind.

Paintings of wrathful deities welcomed you with terrifying eyes, exploding skulls, splurging brains and demonic fire flying out in all directions, waking you from the everyday slumber. Nearby a bamboo pipe conducted a trickle of water into a clear pool of carp. Every so often the pipe would fill up and then tip over, sending a regular "tock" echoing off the boughs of the surrounding forest.

Stepping up into the large, wooden meditation hall, you could still sense the vast, silent swirl of incense and stillness hanging in the air from the last sitting. It was the kind of stillness that quietly permeates you like water onto a tea-bag. The longer you steep in it, the more you are opened out into the bigger space.

The few monks I saw there were quiet and unassuming, and yet they were continuing a practice of Vajrayana Buddhism that had been filling this space in an unbroken line since the 14th century. They had steeped in stillness for years and no longer inked the water.

In summer the hall was wide open, extending its wide platform of tatami as an open invitation to the forest of trees waiting all around. At the centre stood two enormous pillars, like the legs of a giant Buddha stretching up and supporting the huge, heavy, curve of the wide sloping, wooden roof. There was a tremendous sense of connectedness to the forest around, especially when a downpour of rain crashed down out of the hot sweaty sky sending a rush of air smelling of cedar, pine and bamboo across the hall. The old trees stood guard in every direction like a wise sangha, or congregation.

Up more steep steps and out of breath, you reach the final three-roof pagoda at the top, standing like a giant Van-der-Graaf generator. It seems to give off a powerful field of energy that passes through your crown and goes out through the soles of your feet into the ground. And yet this beautiful wooden tower is hidden by tall pine trees all around and just stands there like a colossal secret, only for those who wish to discover it.

I was very privileged to meet the monks, nuns, and master of inji, a Zen Buddhist monastery in Obama. I started learning about meditation here, surrounded by shaven heads dressed in black, sitting bolt upright on a raised tatami platform staring straight ahead at a paper screen.

Just sitting in their presence, I felt slovenly and all over the place, and struggled to stay put with the endless theatre of chattering that used to dominate my head. They, by contrast, felt like twenty verticle midlines that sat with quiet, centred strength. It was intimidating, but I really appreciated it. I loved the gentle, wooden architecture and beautiful gardens, and the space and stillness that helped me settle and start to see through the thinking, thinking, thinking.

Sometimes walking, sometimes sitting, I learned to find a simple focus. For the first time I found that I could just follow the breath, or feel the feet touching the ground and not get lost in the endless twitter. Breathing, I saw the thoughts that took me away from breathing. Walking, I saw the thoughts that took me away from walking. Eating, I saw the thoughts that took me away from eating.

For twenty-three years I had been taken over by a weird addiction to thinking. I had been lost in an endless stream of twitter appearing out of nowhere, and then disappearing back into nowhere. Could I really just step back and not jump onto the trains of thought as they came into the station? Could I just stay on the platform, breathe and feel my feet on the ground, and not get carried away by it all?

It seemed so simple, and yet such a radical change.

Every so often a monk would whack a shrill wooden block with a hammer, sending a shock wave through the meditation hall. This made me jump out of my skin sometimes, and once, gave me such a start, that I broke wind, and spent the next ten minutes trying not to laugh.

Often I would be looking at the paper screen, watching the squares change shape, wondering how I was going to get through the next two hours of sitting. I would feel tremendous aches and pains stabbing across my back or find that my tongue was in fact jammed up against the roof of my mouth. Then "Bang!" I would be jolted out of my reverie and find myself sitting bolt upright again, next to the monks, wide awake and aware. This would be enough to interrupt the "programme of Me" that was running, and just find something sitting there. Slowly, slowly a little bit more of the ego would be leached out of me into the clear, empty water like a tea-bag, and I would step a tiny bit closer to the monks who exuded an emptiness of self. They had long since given up getting lost in the personal and were steeping in a deep sense of equanimity.

By the wooden block was a phrase written in English that haunted me. It was both touching and brutal in its simplicity:

"Each of us must clarify the great matter of life and death. Time passes swiftly. Do not be negligent." Every time I looked at this sign it was like a wooden stick crashing down next to me, which woke me out of my daily stupor.

A translator, who once had gone to visit the monastery and ended up living there for many years, asked if I would like to meet the master and very kindly offered to interpret for me. I eagerly said yes, even though the whole idea made me nervous. The interpreter monk led me through a whole series of preparations involving chants, lying face down on the floor, ringing bells and meditating for periods of time closer into the centre of the monastery. Eventually we waited before a large screen on cushions. My heart was thumping, and I could sense the presence of the master on the other side of the screen. The energy caused a very gentle rocking sensation to float down my spine. After a period of time sitting, the interpreter got up, whispered through the screen, and then pulled it back. I found myself looking directly into the master's eyes. The contact was powerful, yet peaceful and he exuded a very palpable, clear presence. I felt an extraordinary emptying sensation gently pass right through me as if my clutter was being cleared out, and being replaced by a strong, empty, space.

I had never experienced anything like this before and instinctively knew that it was a great honour and privilege to be sitting in front of such embodied wisdom. Here was a man who was a living form of Buddhist teaching and he was sharing this directly with me, transmitting this awareness to me, heart to heart, eyes to eyes, being to being. It was deeply humbling. The teaching was meeting a fresh mind, and I sensed that my own chaos and lack of clarity was somehow falling in line and being attuned to stronger forces of coherence.

"Your question please, Julian Sensei," asked the interpreting monk solemnly. Kneeling there with his bald head and black cloak, he stared straight at me with wide-open expectant eyes.
"Eerr gosh, well, please could you tell the Rosshin that I am terrified of death and dying. Please ask him what is a good way to overcome this deep fear I have…"
He looked at me, smiled, closed his eyes, and then bowed.
Then he turned to the master and relayed the question to him with his head bowed forward out of reverence. They spoke to each other briefly and then bowed to each other. Then the interpreter turned back to me.
"The Rosshin says you should look into your life and find the answers there. Become aware of the mind and how the body connects with the mind. Developing this awareness will help you."

I listened to the words and tried to commit them to memory, but I was in awe of these two men. This experience touched me deeply. It opened my eyes to something extraordinary and new, that I had never even contemplated before. Something moved in me for the first time opening up a pathway of enquiry that I am very grateful for, thirty years on, as I write this. It means far more now than I was able to grasp at the time. I started visiting the monastery for regular sittings and this provided a backdrop of calm for extraordinary goings on in everyday life in Japan.

I was very caught up in trying to make sense of a very different kind of land, and trying find my feet as a teacher. The four of us gaijin in my town helped keep each other stay sane by our regular meet ups at the Dear My Friend Have a Nice Music Café. It was opposite "Fresh Fruts," the local frut shop. In the loo there were slippers, on top of which was written the rather appealing slogan, "Let us Merrily Gather Moustache Men." On the wall was a picture of two cats peeing into a pot with the words, "It's refreshing, it's so refreshing." Why not?

We had regular rants and marvelled at the extraordinary experiences that rural Japan afforded us every day. A typical conversation would be filled with either laughter or shock horror:

"I was shopping yesterday at the supermarket and a woman looked at me, gasped, and then grabbed her son and ran out, shouting "Gaijin! Abunai! Abunai! – Foreigner! Danger! Danger!"

"Well I was looking for something to eat at the supermarket and I picked up a cold pack of dark looking things next to the lettuces in the cold counter and it moved and nearly bit my finger off."

"Look at my lovely new T-shirt. It says: 'Let's go out into the summer night to sniff the breezes, oh my love.'" Why not?

"Have you seen the latest learning English technique? There's a group of girls with their fists clenched into their armpits, raising and lowering their arms in time to a disco beat, singing a chorus of, "I've got a bad case of diarrhoea." (You can still see this today on You Tube. It's a classic.)

"Well can you believe this? A woman came up to me yesterday, and said "Welcome to Japan Mr Teacher," and gave me a present. Inside this bag are 75 pairs of lacquer-ware chopsticks. That must be about £300 worth."

"Well what about this then: we had to catch fish and then cook them for this TV documentary series. We thought it would be fun and they gave us £500 each. It turned out to be a piss-yourself-laughing-to-foreigners-behaving-strangely programme. The studio audience were crying with laughter when Mark started cutting off the fish head."

"Well I went to yet another school party and had to do the same old karaoke number and sing my heart out to the whole bloody staff-room. No surprises there. But this time the headmaster asked me to take off my shirt. When I stared at Mrs. Nakayama in that "What the hell should I do now" kind of way, she raised her eyebrows and looked the other way. Before I knew it I had male teachers feeling my hairy chest and hairy arms, and they were panting and grunting. What is it about bloody hair in this country!? It felt like a scene from a zoo. This keeps on happening to me."

Encounters with the truly bizarre were a daily occurrence. At train stations we got used to whole platforms of people staring at us in fascination. We learnt that if we turned round too quickly we could stare back at them and catch them all out before they had a chance to turn away. All the women would then cover their mouths with their hands in shame and start giggling in impossible high, shrill voices. Life in rural Japan was interesting but always a bit disturbing. And yet we had a great time laughing our way through it.

But then came the toothache. It started suddenly one night. I had been watching TV on the floor of course, with my head pressed against the wall. I heard a clap of thunder and the wall started moving quite radically behind my head for about two seconds. But nothing fell over. I walked outside, and a neighbour was shouting "jisshin, jisshin!" It was an earthquake. We waited for about ten minutes and then he reassured me that there wouldn't be another one for a while. So I went to bed.

I woke up in the morning with a stabbing pain in my lower left jaw. It felt like someone had stuck a carving knife down into the bone. I winced with tears in my eyes all the way to work.

"Mmmmmmmm," came that familiar growl and deeply furrowed brow as Nakayama-sensei rattled her brain as to who to send me to.

"Jurean-sensei, I think you cannot work today. You must go to the dentist.

"Aarrgh" I replied with my hand over my jaw.
"Mmmmmmm." She growled again, thought about a couple of dentists in her head, and then, rather alarmingly shook her head to herself. "No no no. Not him."

Then she went over to Hayami-sensei and asked him for a recommendation. They both shook their heads in equal disapproval after considering a couple more suggestions to each other. Then Mrs.Nakayama came back a bit cagily with a rather apologetic look on her face.

"Prease go to Mr. Nosaki. He is quite a good dentist," she said, and then dropped her face forward, trying not to look too worried. She handed me an address and then gave me a local map with a big red X marking the spot.

I bowed to the staff room and said, "I'm sorry I will be rude and leave before you," as you do, and then sloped off. I walked uregently round the tiny streets asking several times for directions before a small lady with a white mouth-cover recognised the name and pointed with her open palm up to a pair of stairs opposite. She bowed gracefully and waddled away.

I walked in and a small woman shrieked out, "Irrashaimase - welcome." She looked at me and was taken aback. "Oh you are a foreigner. Where are you from?"

"I'm English," I said barely managing to form the words through the pain. "I have tooth ache. Please help."

"Aré! You speak excellent Japanese. You're really fluent."

"Aarrghh," I nodded, not caring at all.

I sat down and put my face into my hands. The knife-like pain was searing into my jaw bone. I had tears streaming out of my eyes.

Ten jaw-throbbing minutes later a door squeaked loudly open as it wobbled and rattled open on its unoiled casters, and a rather portly man presented himself and bowed. On top of his furrowed forehead were two giant eye-brows which bristled straight up like porcupines.
He fired out some machine-gun Japanese at me, which I didn't understand, and ushered me into a tiny room full of metal contraptions and a huge ashtray. I clambered onto a rackety chair making lots of dangling things rattle above.

He lit up a cigarette, stuck it into the corner of his mouth, and prised my mouth open. As he looked inside, he exhaled a whole load of smoke into my throat and up my nose. I coughed. He muttered to me in Japanese but it might have been Korean for all I cared, because I had not a clue what he was going on about. I started to feel a bit floaty.

He put the cigarette down. With a very nicoteeny tasting finger he then shoved a piece of plastic uncomfortably down into the gums behind a tooth, grabbed my finger and signalled for me to hold it. He then picked up the fag again and took another deep drag in. As he placed it back onto the ashtray, he had to flick the ash off the end of his finger because it had become temporarily glued on with my saliva, which was acting as a mild glue.

He then wheeled round a rather worn out looking x-ray gun and bumped it up against the painful part of my jaw-bone.

"Arrgh!" I yelled out.

He flicked a switch. He didn't get up as other dentists would do and vacate the room. Instead, while the short imperceptible buzz filled the room and all of our bones lit up in a sudden Chernobyl-like flash, Mr. Yellow Fingers started picking at a smoky bogie sticking out of the end of his nostril like a dried up piece of sea-weed.

He then took one of those long, I've-given-up-on-life kind of sighs, and then, with the same finger, took the piece of plastic out of my mouth.

While I was left to savour the organic taste left in my mouth, he took another couple of puffs on that hideous cigarette and then stubbed it out. He looked at the small x-ray photo, grunted a couple of times and then showed me the small white blur as he gave the unintelligible diagnosis in a machine-gun Japanese.
 "I'm sorry I don't understand," I said to him in sore-mouthed Japanese. "Do you know the word in English?"

"Please wait," he said as he slid the squeaky door open again. He had a quick chat with the receptionist and then came back and said, "Lootoo canaroo tooreet tumento."

"Bloody hell!" I said out loud. My heart sank. Not root canal treatment. I'd had it done a year before and it was awful.

In Japan, you learn to recognise the "katakana" pronunciation of English words really quickly. Anything Western, such as a table or an elevator or root canal treatment is turned into Japanese by transcribing it into Katakana, the alphabet designed specifically for foreign, mainly English words. This miraculously makes it understandable to the Japanese. So if you say "Good morning" to your students, they won't understand. But if you say "Goodu morningu," they will get it. This teaching approach is not recommended.

"Is that ok? It will take about an hour," the dentist asked, rather kindly.
"Ah yes. Please do it. I need it. It hurts."

He took a deep breath and reached over to get another cigarette.

"Excuse me!" I snapped.
"What?" he said in surprise.
"Please don't smoke. I don't like it. It is not clean." I coughed angrily.
"Daijobu daijobu, Ok," he muttered, and cleared his throat noisily and swallowed the contents.

He pulled out a syringe and stuck it under the jaw-bone, sending a searing pain that made my left eye tear up immediately. He pushed it too far as I'm sure I felt a spray of liquid come out the other side and wet my neck.

I wanted to grab his hand and push him off and run at top speed out of that terrible place. But he quickly pulled out and then re-aimed the needle and filled my jangling jaw nerves with anaesthetic. This time round it felt right and after a couple of minutes, to my great relief, the pain subsided.

The drill sounded wobbly the moment he started on the floor pedal. It wasn't the nice neat hiss of a precision instrument, but instead had a rather jumpy tone that sounded like a faulty train set. He moved the grinder into my mouth and then went down onto the tooth head with some force. It started graunching and grinding and caused my whole head to vibrate strongly. He was a bit rough, but it felt like he was going in the right direction.

He drilled down into each root and then blasted them with air that brought up a hideous smell of burning. Then he stuck long pins in and started twiddling them around, scrunching and scratching deep down into the bottom of the nerves.

I sat there with my mouth held painfully open. If I closed my jaw I would bite onto the pins stuck into the roots of my teeth. Suddenly a deep sense of hopelessness came over me. I felt trapped in a nightmare in strange country on the other side of the planet where I was either a monster or a VIP and I just wanted to go home. A wave of panic passed over me. I started crying quietly. I don't think he noticed. But tears started streaming down the side of my face. It was still painful through the anaesthetic. "I don't know if I can stand this much more," I thought, as my mind started to spiral.

Then, to my utter horror, I stopped crying, and noticed a small, bright red patch of blood on the white cloth of his coat, near his shoulder. That wasn't there when we started. Oh God no. I'm going to be sick.

I grabbed his hands and pushed them out of my mouth. He tried to keep them there but I forced them off. I reached in and pulled out the pins, grabbed a wad of tissues and shoved them between my teeth and ran down the steps to my car. I climbed inside and started crying. I didn't care about the faces that peered in. I got home a while later and climbed into my futon. My body was shivering, but I managed to fall asleep. In my dream I went straight back to the dentist chair and watched Mr. Yellow Finger picking his nose and then turning towards me with the drill. The high-pitched squeal started up and I woke up, bathed in sweat. The drill was deafening.

As I came round, I realised that the sound of the drill was still going on inside my head. The pain in my jaw was unbearable. The noise literally sounded like the drill and I had never had tinnitus like this before. The noise was loud, in both ears, and was pushing into my awareness making it very hard to concentrate on anything. I went for a pee but it followed me and bored its way into everything I did. I was trapped inside my head with this monster.

The wound inside my head had stopped bleeding, but I knew I had to go back to the dentist. There was a big gaping cavern inside my mouth, with very sensitive and exposed nerve endings, ready to jump in pain at the slightest sip or nibble.

I didn't go to school the next day. In fact the pain kept surging all week-end and made me cry, it made me squeeze my temples with my hands, it laid me low, it made me curse and swear, it made me beat my hand against the wall in despair. In two days I had turned into a heap of sparking nerves. I called Mrs. Nakayama.

She picked me up in her car on Monday morning and took me to another dentist. "I think he is better than the other one," she added, with a furrowed brow, which I didn't find reassuring in the slightest.

At the new dentist I watched Nakayama-sensei explain to the dental assistant what had happened and felt relieved that they knew. As she left she looked at me with an expression of deep concern and said, "Good ruck." I waited for just a short time this time before being called into the dental surgery. As I walked in I was amazed to find a large room with several reclining dental chairs and four people lying down. Next to each chair sat a female dental assistant who was waiting patiently. I was ushered to a chair, and lay down.

Mr Matsuda, a rather strapping dentist, appeared with a big chest and a proud smile. He strutted around handsomely and twiddled inside one mouth and then drilled into another. I heard some spluttering and a cough. Then he moved onto a new mouth and scraped and banged and chatted. Then after few more suckings and slurpings he moved onto the next. As he arrived at each chair, the relevant dental assistant puffed up and smiled with pride or maybe desire. She seemed honoured that it was her turn to be working with the big man, with the big drill.

Then he came round to me. He looked at the notes and shook his head. He filled the hole with antibiotics inside and covered it up with a temporary surface. Then he handed me a packet of painkillers and said,
"See you again in one week. Is that OK?"

"Yes," I replied. I didn't care. I just wanted the pain to go away.

I had to take another day off work and went home. The noise in my head had risen to such a screeching pitch that I honestly don't think I could have heard what any of the students would have said, had they decided to speak any English. It felt and sounded like I had a pneumatic drill hammering into the side of my jaw. I couldn't focus. I couldn't work. I flitted about my flat like a bird in a cage. I wanted to get away. I wanted to fly out across the sodden rice fields, and croaking frogs, over the mountains back home.

I tried to sleep. I crawled inside my futon, which was normally a place of refuge, but the screeching followed me there and hissed away at me ferociously. I turned over and tried to get more comfortable but the noise wouldn't leave me alone and yelled back at me on the pillow.

I got up again. I tried to watch a film. I couldn't focus. The screeching was like a million Japanese cicadas, not Mediterranean ones. These bastards were incredibly shrill and were screeching right inside my head. I couldn't get away from them. I took painkillers and the pain got a bit better. But the sound didn't. It felt like the noise was coming from inside both ears. I may as well have had two cicadas down both ear canals that were screeching away, it was that loud. But it sounded like there were cicadas screeching away in the room too, and outside. They were everywhere.

Millions of them. The sound was coming from all directions, both inside and around. I climbed into my upright boiler bath. I filled it up to chest height and switched it on. The heat started building around my feet and swirling upwards in hot eddies around my legs. I remembered Mark saying how every year some people fall asleep and never wake up. Their families found them cooked, sometimes boiling in their juices. I sat there getting hotter and hotter until my face glowed bright pink like a lobster, and then flicked the heater off. There was no way I wanted that to happen.

I pulled the plug out, needing to submerge my face in order to do so, and let the heavy, stress-ridden water slowly drain down, taking all the electricity and nervousness away with it, dropping down, returning me to my normal weight like an astronaut coming back into the earth's gravity, getting heavier, sinking down until I lay like a bag of boiled potatoes at the bottom of the tub. I felt like my own plug had been pulled out. Flat. Non-responsive. Exhausted. Heavy like a sack of lead.

It was night time. It took me all my effort to climb out and walk across the room, still steaming like boiled cauliflower. I dropped in between the cool sheets of the duvet and futon and passed out in a dark, dreamless and heavy sleep.

Twelve hours later I woke up. The cicadas had flown back to the trees. The sound was still loud but they weren't screeching down my earholes any more. But they were out there in the trees. There was some space.

I went back to school. My attention over the next couple of days gradually shifted away from my ears and re-engaged more and more with the students. I settled back into the usual rude questions like "How biggu isu itu?" pointing to my crotch, or two kids with huge spiky haircuts throwing things at each other. One girl started imitating my accent causing much hilarity, but thankfully, it didn't bother me. I was just very glad that screeching was backing off.

Over the next couple of weeks the sound settled back to a more manageable level, but it was a new normal. The level was definitely higher than it was before the dental episode. I was now living on a higher plateau of sound.

Chapter 7 The Sound of Getting Lost

The City of London, 1990

Stop, what's that sound
It's the death rattle of this rusty old town
Stop, listen again
It's the sound of laughter all along the Thames

Hey, what's my line
Do I have to stay here 'til the end of time
I'm, good looking and bright
I want to see life after ten at night

Joe Jackson
Down to London

When the plane pulled up, up and away from Japan I felt a tremendous sense of relief. In fact I even lifted my feet off the floor of the plane to leave as fast as possible. I was sad to leave Mrs Nakayama, my fellow Gaijin friends, the Buddhist Temples and the exquisite ancient culture behind. But, as for the crass, pressurised, modern lifestyle, that was best left as far away as possible on the other side of the planet. I loved and hated Japan intensely.

It took me two months to get home, gliding across Asia, sweating my way through Hong Kong, which, after deepest rural Japan, felt more familiar, like the West End of

London. In Malaysia I gorged myself on rambutans, and "came a crapper" on a boat that broke down one night in the middle of a storm on the way to Tioman island. Fortunately the thunder and wind was loud enough to conceal my evacuations off the back of the boat.

In Singapore the street food was delicious and the eponymous cocktail classy. In Indonesia I fought off monkeys who tried to steal my camera, windsurfed around idyllic Riau islands, and meditated amongst the Buddha-shaped pillars of Borobudur. Then I came back down to earth and landed with a hefty thump onto the desks of a commodity trading firm in the City of London.

I was to become a trader by asking questions and watching these sleek businessmen and women do their work. I was plonked next to a cocoa trader and had to bug him for two squirmingly uncomfortable weeks at a time. "Gosh, so you got a first in music from Cambridge. That's amazing. How did you get from something like that to here?" Stony silence. "Do you mean your trades alone affect the entire Venezuelan economy? Wow. I lived there for a year. It's an amazing country. Have you met many Venezuelans?" "Er no!? Look, sorry, I must make a phone call. Please excuse me."

In the long periods of silence where I pretended I was turning into trader material I ended up looking across the Thames to Hays Galleria. Could I really fit in amongst these high-powered people who think nothing of popping off to Bahia for a week-end, or borrowing a ski chalet in Crans Montana to impress a new partner? It looked good on the surface but none of them seemed to be enjoying what they were doing very much.

The clincher came when I was positioned between two Forex traders straddling phones, screens and hundreds of numbers flying past their faces. A prim and proper woman walked past. On my left, sun-tanned Matt with manicured hands, expensive cufflinks and classy cologne reached down to a drawer, and pulled out a small box. On the front there was a button. He pushed it. A recorded message flew out of the speaker filling the space with "Bitch, Fucking Cow, Slut, What a Whore…" Laughter erupted in the immediate vicinity, but there was not enough time to look up from frantic conversations and scribbling out figures.

Ten minutes later, David on the other side of me picked up the phone. "Konnichi wa Nishimura-San. How are you today? Good, good. Glad to hear you are 'genki.' Anyway last week we were reading about Jackie who had been raped, tied up and left in a cupboard. Today's chapter is called, 'Jackie's Smell.'" He laughed. I could hear laughter coming back down the phone. He started reading an S&M porn rag down the line to someone who must have been an important client on the other side of the world.

For weeks now I had been fantasizing about leaving this job. Nose-browning was not something I was prepared to do. It wasn't me. Here I was, back in my home country where I wasn't a gaijin at all and yet I still felt as foreign and lost as ever. Sometimes the phone rang and I answered "moshi moshi," by mistake. It took me ages to stop bowing.

I found myself staring at my coat on the other side of the room. I pictured myself grabbing my bags and coat, and running. It felt so irresistible. Was I overreacting? Could I really do it? Could I really get up and go, take off, run away, out of this wrong turn I had taken. If I did, there would be no turning back. This would be acknowledging a big mistake and would cause a major life crunch.

My pulse quickened. David next to me was chuckling loudly with a tortured grimace across his face. I didn't have any choice. I couldn't stand it any longer. How much did I really want to become a cocoa trader anyway? Did I honestly think I would ever make sense of all those numbers and make the right choices? I would probably end up losing a fortune for the trading company.

Sun-tanned Matt started guffawing next to me, sending another blast of cologne across the desk. Everywhere I looked faces were babbling away in various languages with strained smiles. Many had slightly bulging veins at the temples and hands that rapped and tapped and flipped pens nervously. These debonair people were bright, well-mannered, and charming, but at the end of the day, it all boiled down to clinching the deal and pocketing the money. Did I really love money-making enough to put myself through all this hassle? The dream of buying a lovely house in the country and exotic holidays started to flicker like a failing cine-camera that started to reveal large gaps of empty space in between the frames. In my heart of hearts I knew that I was walking down the wrong road. My life in cocoa was about to go up in smoke.

One last look at the plucky movers and shakers around me and I felt my legs standing up, almost against my will. My heart started pounding. I found myself running across the room. People often ran across that office. If anyone had bothered to look up beyond their urgent conversations, they may have thought I was late for a meeting or needed the loo. But they were wrong. I was running for my life, running to get it back. I grabbed my coat and bag, and plummeted down the stairs like a bearish market.

"Bye." I smiled at the security guards. "I'm not coming back!" I yelled. They looked at me in surprise and waved goodbye. I ran along the street and up onto London Bridge, which stretched open and bare like a great runway out of the glamorous City and into, well, Southwark. I accelerated across the river, leaving the towers of power behind me, sprinting away from my dream of becoming the Man from Del Monte, and ran headfirst into unemployment.

My small, bare-bulbed, minimalist flat in Borough, seemed very unhomely and horribly quiet in the middle of the day. I sat down in the chair. The rest of the world was at work, and there I was, not at work, or to be more accurate, out of work, alone and sitting in silence. It was so silent it was shocking. I sat there staring at the unlit gas-fire and was hit by a wall of screaming tinnitus. It was really loud. It sounded like a thousand brokers yelling all around me.

But my body was still buzzing with the thrill of escape. I had done it. There was no going back. Good-bye wealth and luxury. Hello money problems and uncertainty. My head was vibrating like the surface of a speaker.

I looked into the eyes of the green moneyed demon who had been clutching my hands with his bristly fingers for a while now. His seductive and sulphurous pull towards wealth, glamour, and high status felt revolting. I looked into his yellow goat slit eyes and said, "You are not what I want. What you offer doesn't interest me." I reached out and grabbed his little goaty beard and shook his face from side to side and said, "There must be more to life than this. I need something more meaningful.

Sorry mate." And with that, the demon closed his eyes, put the jewels back into his pockets and clomped off back over the bridge to the City.

I sat in front of the bare white walls of the flat and, for the first time in my life, noticed a great expanse of nothing stretching ahead of me. There were no plans. Just a big, open empty space. Mind you, at twenty-three, being unsure and lost is definitely better than doing the wrong thing and then becoming trapped doing the wrong thing for the rest of your adult life.

I moved into a flat overlooking the woods of Tooting Bec Common and languished in a swill of unemployment and doldrums for months. Slowly the fires of ambition cooled down and I learned to accept that reading the paper and going for walks was good enough for now. The ringing in my ears had turned into a constant kettle whistle that showed no signs of letting up at all. It was loud but just about bearable.

I tried to find jobs to squeeze myself into, but they were designed for other people, not me. There was a bad recession and so I felt even more obliged to push harder to fit into one. I filled out a long questionnaire to determine which job I was best suited to: introverted, sensitive, risk-averse... After hours of thinking and deliberating and then waiting a couple of weeks, the result came back: MONK. Great. Lots of prospects there, then. So, reluctantly, after ten months I eventually gave in, and went back to teaching English as a foreign language. I had never been to Eastern Europe before and a friend of mine offered to get me an interview in Hungary.

I got the job and loved it. For two years, in between classes, I soaked in the heavenly thermal baths of Budapest, with their Turkish domes that let in shards of coloured light down through the steam. I knew which waters were best for clearing a hangover, which ones eased aches or pains and which ones filled you with energy.

In summer I would often be first to dive into the vast, swimming pool of mineral water on Margaret Island in the middle of the Danube. It is filled fresh every day so you can literally drink as you swim. Hungarians really know how to do water. Whether its mineral, soda or healing water, it's all on tap.

I made lots of friends in Budapest and in winter we had the time of our lives skiing in Austria. Often we were last to leave the mountaintop bar, soon after the red winter sun dropped behind the freezing dark-blue mountains. Glowing with Glühwein, we would then ski back down through the dark forest slopes sending bright sparks off the edges of our skis.

When we drove back, the Austrian villages looked neat and orderly under an even blanket of snow. However we were always happy to cross the border back into Hungary, where, on the side of the road, Huns would still be in passionate debate about life, smoking, cooling off from the Dance House, and reeking of Palinka.

I gorged on opera and the rich meaty, creamy, paprika cuisine, and drank my way through too much Tokaji and Villany wine. I danced salsa with Cuban scientists and university lecturers releasing their frustration through their hips in a club down a forgotten, back alley-way.

Living in Hungary meant engaging with a people who are sincere and hearty like their goulash, and have a strange, lilting intonation that makes them sound slightly depressed, even brooding, but never flippant. I loved floating past the large-bellied, men with strong, serious features playing chess in the hot steaming water with snow falling on our heads.

Budapest looked just as I imagined communism would look with roads spluttering with Trabants and their eye-stinging smoke, people in heavy trench-coats and furry hats, racing home to their enormous hot stoves covered in beautiful tiles. Behind Chainy Bridge and ice-slabbed Danube, the castle district lit up like a frosty Christmas card, the Paris of the East.

But unlike Paris where you can feel horribly isolated and left out, in Budapest you slot in with Hungarian values. If you don't give up your seat for an elderly woman on a tram, then you are thrown off and sneered at collectively! And yes that tiny piece of cloth is really all you wear over your bits when you climb out of the hot thermal waters, so you may as well take it off. Who cares what goes on under the water, or in the parks behind the bushes as long as you do not draw any attention to it. We are all adults in Budapest.

My large flat in the middle of Pest was still covered in bullet-holes from the student uprising in 1956. Every time we had a party I was afraid the front façade would come crashing down into King Paul Street below. From the roof there was a fantastic view across to the Buda hills where we would sit and laugh, and down more of Polgar Zoltan's wine.

For two years the noise in my head poddled along quite happily and had become part of the furniture, a rather boring and forgettable background that followed me everywhere I went. I guess I had habituated...

One morning, towards the end of a long, freezing grey winter, the paprika looked a bit dry and shrivelled on the side of the market, and the slabs of ice floating along the bitterly cold Danube had lost their appeal. And then that fateful, dangerous, life-changing list appeared on the noticeboard at work. "Next term there are vacancies for British Council teachers in Argentina, Botswana, Italy, Mexico, the Philippines, Pakistan and Romania."

Before I knew it, I was on a plane to an interview. The frozen white flatlands of Hungary gave way to the warm plains of the Po valley and I landed in sunny Bologna bursting with indulgent, warm apricot blossoms. The tiny medieval streets around the Piazza Maggiore were stuffed full of Parmesan cheeses that were 'stravecchio' or extra-old, which gave them that crispy, crystalline crunch. Mouth-watering hams hung down at nose-level like fragrant thighs, and tortellini lay so freshly made on the trays they were still slightly loosening themselves, and all this sensual heaven was presented by handsome and immaculately-dressed Bolognesi men and women.

I took the job and settled into life in Italy like a fine tomato sauce soaking onto an al dente strozzapreti pasta. The first year was great fun. I shared a Bohemian flat with a Sicilian brother and sister in the central square of the city. I could already speak Spanish and so the frequent dinner parties, full of laughter and outrageous behaviour were the perfect place for Italian to take root.

Sometimes Renato would take off his clothes and stand on the table, reciting his favourite Mina songs. Sometimes Erminia would talk toplessly from the bath through the open door, across the dining-room table to anyone who was in the house, no matter who they were. Lovers of both sexes would come and go. Sometimes there would be tears. Often there would be singing and drunkenness. But they knew the words to the songs and cared about what the words meant, because they both had big, generous hearts. It was only when the shutters brought the cavernous old house into pitch darkness to keep out the hot sun, that the drama would finally go quiet for a few hours.

My tinnitus sounded fairly allegretto in Italy and for the most part was quite 'pianino' or level. There were far too many gorgeous people and places to explore, and endless wines and delicious restaurants to snuffle my way through to bother too much with tinnitus. There were lots of irresistible phrases to learn like "mi fa impazzire," he drives me crazy, which you have to say with your hands in prayer position and move them up and down fairly violently. I used to see how much I could get away with exaggerating my hand gestures to a ridiculous degree, completely screaming out in an over the top, melodramatic, almost shrieking intonation. But the more outrageously I did it, the more the Italians stopped noticing I was foreign. Renato and Erminia taught me how to speak and be Italian, and my reaction to everything became 'sconvoltu tu luttu,' which is their own neologism that means as 'completely flabbergasted.'

With all this excitement my tinnitus felt thoroughly disgruntled and had to take second pew for a while. In fact it dropped down to 'pianissimo' for a while until November, when that wretched and terrible winter fog that forms over the Po valley started pressing down in between the narrow medieval streets, and mixed with the dismal two-stroke-engines to create that thick, poisonous, choking fog. 'La nebbia" would last five smotheringly-long months, casting a sickly yellowish haze over the snowy medieval streets. On day two, 'la nebbia' sent me wheezing with bronchitis to il Medico.

"You must eat more spaghetti with olive oil," the doctor cried out in a great crescendo with wide starring eyes, and waving pinched fingers and thumbs together as if he was revealing a secret of the universe right there before my eyes.

"Davvero?" I answered in surprise. "I have a cough and you think spaghetti will help?"

A few months later I went back to il Medico with strange fainting spells and indigestion.

"You must eat more spaghetti with olive oil," he begged me, gesturing dramatically with praying hands.

"Veramente?" I replied, slightly amazed.

Sfortunatamente, or unfortunately, lo smog took root inside my sinusses and bronchi and made me cough for months on end, which gave tinnitus something to grab, then climb onto like an unwanted rat, and then take more centre stage in my head with an unrelenting 'sforzando,' until I was shouting "Porca Miseria!" at the sky and beating my fists against my bedroom walls.

So I went back to il Medico. He listened as I explained in my fairly fluent Italian by then, that my life was being filled with this irritating alarm. "Mi fa impazzire! I yelled. Its driving me crazy. Then for greater effect I started screaming: "Mi fa impazzzzire!" with my hands shaking and pointing up to the heavens above. He put his pen down and looked impressed. For five minutes I ranted and gesticulated in hysterical, full-blown Italian, garnering all his respect. He thought for a minute, letting the room drop into silence, and then and finally declared:

"You must eat more spaghetti with olive oil."

"Ma stai scherzando!?" Are you joking, I asked him. "Ma stai scherzando!?" I started shrieking for more Italian effect. I didn't go back. But I did take his advice.

I ate tons of spaghetti and chose the raunchiest of olive oils. In fact, at least once a month I treated myself to some freshly hand-rolled tortellini that lured me in through the elegant glass window of Zanarini, on the edge of the Piazza Maggiore. They (the pasta pieces) looked so delicious that I had to make sure my mouth was closed so I didn't spray against the glass as I peered in through the window. (In English, when we talk about pasta, we disrespectfully use the pronoun 'it,' for example: It is delicious. This is far too dismissive for an Italian. Because each individual piece of pasta is worth its own weight in gold, and may be judged on its own individual merit, pasta in Italy is much more respectfully referred to with the use of the pronoun "they," for example, "they are really delicious.")

The olive-oil came from Maurizio's holiday home just further along the Appenines in Romagna, where the climate is warmer and the oil nuttier. Maurizio was my new flatmate and fellow "buongustaio" or gourmet. His olive oil left a long persistent tang at the back of my throat. So I say "grazie" to him for showing me the finer foods and wines of his land, and "grazie" to il Medico for his fine advice. The pasta did me lots of good.

In Bologna there was the Piazza delle Erbe where you could run along whole aisles of rocket grass or 'ruccola' tasting your way through to the best, slightly tangy, fiery, nutty grass of the day. Italians taught me how to unbuckle my Britishness and let my emotions pour out. I eventually managed to get genuinely worked up about whose tomatoes were the best. Snap went the tomato stalk. "Smell this!" said a women defiantly thrusting her finest, fat and juicy pomodoro up against my nostrils. I would inhale deeply, with my eyes shut, sniffing up all that peppery, hot summery, sappy green perfume. With wet lips I would savour and snuffle as much as much as I could get away with without becoming inappropriate, and then release, loudly, suddenly, unashamedly, "Prioprio sconvolgente!" absolutely mindblowing, my voice flying out across the tomato stall like an opera singer.
"Oddio! Questo è una vera maraviglia!" I would say with hands held close to my heart and eye-brows raised. Oh God, this is a marvel. You had to sniff it to believe it. Italy had been working its magic on me for months now, and my alerted nostrils could recognise quality when they met it.

Maurizio was was a dentist. He used a whole Parmesan cheese that he had been given by one of his patients to step up to the top of the fridge to reach the extra good bottle of Passito dessert wine and Cantuccini to round off the end of the meal.

He and I joined the local wine-tasting society and enjoyed arguing about which wine went best with the 'mortadella' and loved being shown how the rather searingly tannic, dry, dark-red fizz of Lambrusco, when paired up with a fat greasy lump of Cotechino sausage turned into the most delightful marriage in the north of Italy.

We raced off to the Cinque Terre to try the quirky Sciaquettra white. We spent an entire week-end drinking and sampling our way around Montalcino, and, because I was writing for a wine magazine, we were invited into the most exquisite medieval

Fattorie overlooking the Tuscan countryside. There in front of crackling fireplaces in huge glasses were treated to some of the best Brunello di Montalcino on offer. Even the name sounds appealing, like a full-bodied, brunette, and for me, these wines are some of the best in the world. I quickly learned that wine-makers are some of the loveliest people around and that they like nothing more than someone who can really appreciate their wine. That was a job Maurizio and I could both do.

At home a huge map of Italy appeared on the wall, but not with Naples or Rome marked on it, but Amarone di Valpolicella, Coda di Volpe and Morellino de Scansano. We learned the names of all three-hundred and thirty four wine denominations in every region of Italy.

Maurizio took me to his favourite restaurants where we ate sixteen-course meals, and had pasta pressed through a colander right into the steaming broth in the plate in front of you, bringing a whole new meaning to the idea of fresh pasta. Thank you Signor Medico. I will carry on eating spaghetti and olive oil and it definitely does make me feel better, even now. But, unfortunately, as much as my palate wanted to stay in Italy, my heart had a different journey to make all of its own.

I met Ili on holiday on a wild open beach in Cadiz province, SW Spain, where the Atlantic is warm, pale blue and full of light, hence the name: Costa de la Luz. Ili and I hit it off immediately. Before I knew it I was whisked off my feet and taken to Jerez, arriving at night with the smell of orange blossom filling the air and a gypsy strumming a guitar, singing a 'bulería' in the square outside the window with its lilting rhythm that just got you tapping and clapping. The moon shone through the palm trees and the young students clapped with amazing rhythm that ricocheted around the white courtyard. Ili knew the words, and sang and danced around the flat, moving like an expert and poured a glass of Palo Cortado. We crunched into some roasted almonds. It was hot. I fell in love.

We both jumped on planes and started a long-distance relationship between Andalucia and Northern Italy, which fanned the embers of our love for each other even more. After a year of trips backwards and forwards I eventually decided to throw caution to the wind, and packed my life into my car, and set off on the long drive to Southern Spain. I was sad to leave the great red city of Bologna, with its magical porticos behind. I was sad to leave the safety of the British Council with its stable career path. As I drove out of the city gates, past Il Cassero, my favourite club, I played Mina's "Parole Parole" at top volume in tribute to Renato who helped convert my Spanish into Italian over the first year.

It was mid-summer. There was nobody about. Stretching ahead was a wide open motorway snaking its line over the hills in the shimmering heat. Normally I would have stopped for a break, but I was happy, and in love and couldn't stop driving. I soon crossed the Pyrenees into the dazzling sky of Spain, and just kept driving, past Barcelona, past Castellon. I kept listening to a song called "Before Today" by Everything but The Girl: "I don't want your smiles. I don't want to feel like we're apart a thousand miles. I want your love and I want it now." I kept going, speeding past Valencia, and Alicante, barely stopping the whole way down, deeper and deeper into the brilliant bouncing white light of Southern Spain, all in one day. I kept playing "Long to be Lifted by your Love," by K D Lang. I was happy. There was no reason to stop. I wanted to be with Ili.

I pulled up to a halt in front of my father's front door in Agua Amarga a day early. It was twilight and the white walls of his house were still radiating out heat like a giant toaster. I pushed the door-bell. A moment later he appeared.

"Oh it's you. What are you doing here?" He looked really surprised.
"I just kept on keeping on."
"Come on in, out of the heat. You must be knackered?"
"No, I'm ok actually." I said with a smile. "I'm really well." We hugged.
"I can see that! Want a Highland Park and soda?"
"Sounds great."

We sat down on Dad's large balcony under the hot starry sky that looked south to the sea with a small pinnacle of white houses lighting up like fireflies in the middle.

"I just couldn't wait another day in Bologna. I have to be with Ili."
"I understand. When you're in love you're in love," Dad said, taking a long, knowing

sigh. "Yes, yes, yes, I know that feeling well," he added, clinking his Scotch against mine. We both smiled, took a large glug and then, at exactly the same time, placed the cold, heavy glasses rattling with ice-cubes onto the table. We were both starring straight ahead at the stars.

"Yeah, good luck to you," he said pensively. "Good luck to you," he repeated, breathing out another large sigh. We sat in silence, letting the Scotch soak its way deep into our veins.
"Sometimes I think about following my heart too…"
He stopped and I looked at him and held my breath.
"But then I look at this place and realise that I have found what I love. It's peaceful here. Sometimes it's so quiet you can hear the sun set."
"Yes. It's an amazing place… I love it here… "
We both took another cold slug of our drinks.
"It can be so overwhelming, can't it?"
"What do you mean?" he asked.
"Following your heart. When your heart is set on something, not doing it is torture. And yet when you do follow your heart, it can been overwhelming."
"Yup," Dad replied.
"When the heart opens up, it's so overwhelming. I can't listen to certain pieces of music because I feel like I'm going to start crying and never stop."
"Tell me about it!" Dad agreed, with a chuckle. "I've got plenty of pieces of music that I can't listen to either."
We both picked up our whiskies and took another large glug.
Suddenly, and much to my surprise, I felt a rush of tears come up.
"I'm giving up my whole career to follow my heart." Tears streamed down my cheeks.
"Yup," he said. "You said it," he added with a sigh. "But then, you have to go. If you don't go you will never forgive yourself for not trying."

I stared straight ahead at the masses of stars flooding the blackening sky. Dad noticed my tears but kept staring straight ahead. He had tears in his eyes too.
"Yeah. Feelings. Synchronicities. Same Wavelengths," he added.

We sat in silence and understood each other. It was one of those rare moments that only lasted just a few minutes on the clock but actually took place outside of time. There seemed to be no separation between us and our feelings and the sense of connection belonged to the eternal moment like the stars in the sky.

"Look, there she goes." He pointed up overhead to the ten o'clock satellite moving across the sky.

"Oh yes. I see it." We both watched a tiny pinprick of bright light moving through the purple afterglow into the dark blue then black night sky.

"Every time I see a night-time satellite it makes me think of you," I ventured.

"Oh really?" he answered, and chuckled in a chuffed kind of way.

"Top up?"

"Yes please."

We moved onto the Abelour.

"Yes. What's it all about?" Dad pondered. "What do you think happens when we die? Is it inky blackness once you have exited stage left?"

"No. I think, when the body falls away something carries on. I think it is going to be a bit scary finding yourself without a body. Just imagine what it's like coming round and just finding yourself in infinite space with nothing to hold onto or slow you down except your mind, your fears, your beliefs!"

"Nah... Don't buy it. It's inky blackness as far as I am concerned."

"Ok Mr Atheist. But I guess we will find out one day...."

We both took another slug.

For the next hour we had one of those memorable chats when we talked about life, love and what mattered. An unfiltered honesty poured out of both of us like treasure, and for a couple of hours I really liked him, and for maybe an hour or so I sensed he liked me. Maybe that was enough. Because after this meeting the vault quietly closed, never to open again.

The following day I set off through the endless poly-tunnels of Almeria, over the mountains of Granada, and down into the miles of the blazing olive groves that were baking in the sun of western Andalucia. Five hours later, like a dried out sponge, I pulled into the narrow white streets of Jerez and found the impossibly narrow lane where I had to fold in the wing-mirrors to squeeze through to get to my garage.

I found Ili laughing with friends under a purple jacaranda tree. On the table was a glass of ice-cold Manzanilla Sherry and roasted almonds waiting for me. I slotted straight into a life of laughter, and lively talking that was loud even by Spanish standards. Ili's friends welcomed me with open arms into the "pandilla" or group. Their only rule was to share stories in the most colourful way possible and make each other laugh.

Ili's friends got me a job teaching English in a grand Sherry House that felt more like a cathedral than a winery. It was indeed a place of worship, especially when we got to taste the most revered wines from the "sacrestía." During the furnace of high summer, when temperatures soared up to 45C, it was always an intense pleasure to step into the cool, musty world of casks and that familiar smell of the "flor" or yeasty growth on the surface of the wine, and taste the cool, dry Finos and Palo Cortados.

The very first week-end after moving to Jerez we were invited to stay at the Casa del Coto Doñana, a large hunting lodge at the centre of a spectacular marshland and bird sanctuary owned by members of the well-known Sherry family. We drove across the chalky white vineyards to the Guadalquivir river and then, after a ferry crossing, entered a wild, unspoilt wilderness.

Minutes after arriving at the a great white walls of the Lodge, we were welcomed by Jose, the estate manager, and were given an obligatory glass of ice-cold Alfonso, that irresistible and delicious tangy, walnutty Oloroso Seco that I would get to know too well. Then Ili and I were ushered off to the tackle room where we were booted up, and greeted by two large white horses with blue grey eyes. The moment I felt my legs sit into the saddle I could feel my horse's strength. He was impatient to get out and bolt across the open space.

Unlike British saddles, the Spanish saddle had a huge spur sticking up at the front, which I grabbed onto as the horse lurched forward and trotted off down the dusty track. My legs couldn't grip much at all, and I just bounced up and down precariously, quickly learning not to lean too far forward for fear of inflicting a lot of pain.

We trotted past a huge expanse of water teeming with hundreds of birds that stretched out under the blazing sky as far as the eye could see. The horses knew the terrain well and gave us a really good view of the swamplands and dried out scrub stretching out all around. Yellow gorse bush scratched up against my jeans and Ili's horse in front sent smells of rosemary and lavender up into the air. All around patches of asparagus were growing everywhere like clumps of grass.

Then the sandy path opened out onto a clear stretch of parched land and the horses accelerated into a canter, starting to snort as they flew through the hot air. My bottom left the saddle with each rise and fall and, had I not gripped onto the spur at the front, I would have come flying off. Behind us clouds of dust flew up into the air. Suddenly Ili shouted "Jabalí. Jabalí!" Up ahead two large wild boar dashed across the track in front of us with a long line of spotted piglets trotting along behind. We followed them for quite a while before they suddenly veered off and disappeared into the undergrowth. The horses seemed completely unperturbed by them and vice versa. We cantered off again sending whole clouds of birds soaring into the air and kept on going until we were all out of breath.

We approached a large pine grove where the horses slowed down to a trot, and I could feel the sweat coming through my trouser legs. The pine needles gave off a pungent, sweet sappy smell and provided welcome shade from the sun. We ambled slowly through the trees for about ten minutes and then came up against wall of white sand. As we approached, the horses picked up a bit of speed and then climbed up on sinking hooves sending us swaying strongly from side to side. I had to grip really hard onto the saddle to stop myself from sliding off the steep sloping back of the horses. Then, when we reached the top, the horses suddenly levelled out again revealing a huge, open vista of crashing Atlantic waves. A vigorous cool breeze brought a great sense of relief from the terrific heat. From the highest dunes on top of the horses we could see right back across the sea of green pine trees and lakes to the church of El Rocío floating like a vision on the shimmering horizon. This was the sacred destination of the great Andalucian pilgrimage that brings hundreds of devotees singing and dancing flamenco every year through the Coto.

We found a sheltered part of the dunes tied up the horses and made love in the hot sun and cool air. Then we trotted back towards the house to find Jose under a large pine tree, who had prepared a seafood paella over a fire on a huge round dish. We all gathered round and ate a delicious lunch and drank dizzying amounts of ice-cold Alfonso, my favourite, and Tio Pepe. Then we took a long siesta on rugs in a semi-drunken haze beneath the trees. Around 8 o'clock, when the sun was definitely starting to cool down a bit, Liliana and Guillermo took us on a tour in a jeep and pointed out nightjars, warblers, hoopoes, eagles, bustards and other birds I have never heard of, in perfect English.

The Casa del Coto, was a great hunting lodge with thick white walls to keep out the heat of summer. In the courtyard stood a magnificent, fragrant yellow mimosa tree, and outside the large white gates stood a pajarero, a large tree that had been stripped bare by hundreds of nesting birds. Once inside you were greeted by a wall of antlers looking onto the dining-room table where we ate and drank late into the night, marvelling at Jose's tales of wild boar hunts, endless droughts, and strange snakes and toads. The conversation flew from one funny story to the next, and very occasionally launched into song. It was such a great privilege to take the small ferry each time across the Guadalquivir river to the wild Coto. I felt like this was Spain at its best, and we had the warmest, wittiest and most generous company.

In Jerez, when the poniente wind blew in from the Atlantic, the whole town relaxed and took a breath of fresh air, as the thermometers plummeted to a comfy 25C degrees under a brilliant blue sky. We ventured out and marvelled at the sound the women made in the fish market, returning back home with bags bursting with tuna and the juiciest green peppers and tomatoes. I loved watching the handsome men in grey riding suits and flat hats of the Spanish Riding School jumping and dancing with immaculate white horses.

When we went to a Peña and heard the flamenco cante jondo I found it jarring and harsh at first. But then, one evening, I found my heart becoming bewitched by its duende or spirit and found myself stamping my feet in thunderous applause with tears in my eyes.

When the levante wind blew in from the east, the sky turned a feverish yellow for weeks on end, and the temperature soared to 45C. The wind rattled and shook at everyone's nerves, sending dust and leaves whistling through the window grills and around every street corner. Schools and shops closed early and everyone took refuge in front of air conditioners and had the longest siestas possible.

During the "feria" everyone dressed up in suits and flowing skirts, and spent hours laughing, dancing Sevillanas, and knocking back Sherry. Some would swipe the head off the bottle with a clean sweep of a knife and then pour a glug onto the floor to thank the ground for this bounty.

By far the most haunting time was Semana Santa when the town's churches opened their doors and the Virgin Marys were carried out on top of ornate floats through the narrow streets. Down below the heavy, gold frame weighed down onto twenty grunting men with bright red, sweating faces. As they staggered along this movement gave the wide-eyed and staring Mary above an eerie gait, with intricate glasses with their candles shaking and rattling around her. A long line of penitents wearing white cloaks with sinister pointed hats, trailed along behind, like a scene out of a nightmare.

The perfume of orange blossom hung thick in the air like cologne, and the streets filled with the smell of frankincense. Behind the float carrying the Virgin Mary and a long line of penitents, the Jerezanos followed, dressed in their Sunday best, walking in time with the slow, melancholic march of the trumpets and drums. The notes were high, but perfect, from weeks of practice, and the large drums resounded out in perfect time, echoing solemnly across the town. Then suddenly, the foreman banged his staff twice against the ground. The float dropped onto its own sturdy legs and the men heaved a sigh of relief beneath. The whole road fell silent. For a moment everybody stood still in the swirling incense and looked down, as if in prayer.

After a pause, as the people waited expectantly, a shutter overhead would open, and a beautifully dressed gypsy with golden earrings and necklaces, in the finest flowing brocade, would breathe in, deeply, and then let out the most mournful lament of an improvised poem or saeta, sent out flying like darts through the air, a song with such heart that many were moved to tears. The voice wailed, gasped and even yelled at times, with tight fists and closed eyes looking skywards, breaking into moments of silence, and the releasing in heartfelt pain through the ears and minds of the people standing spell-bound in the narrow streets. The heart sang with such compassion that people nodded their heads as if she were speaking individually to each soul, waking them up, and making them feel the depths of human suffering. Then her head would drop, and the crowd would clap furiously at the end wiping the tears from their eyes with silk handkerchiefs. Semana Santa opened the Jerez nights up into a sacred space allowing the collective wound of being human to be touched for a while. For a while the suffering of an entire community lifted and then gently dispersed somehow.

For a while Ili and I were blissfully happy. On summer evenings we would go to the sea and cool off in the breeze and look out for the green flash when the sun pops just below the horizon. We perfected the recipe for our gazpacho and found the best cafes for seafood tapas. In winter, when the rains lashed against the iron gratings at the window we would keep warm by pulling the table-cloth over our bodies and huddling in the warmth of the under-table heater enveloping us in the warm table-leg, wood-smelling air.

Jerez is a lovely old town, full of history, pride and colour. I felt very at home there. But all the Sherry and good-living was causing something to change inside me, and slowly but imperceptibly a feeling of tiredness and heaviness moved into my body and by the end of the first year I felt like I had a heavy weight dragging me down to the ground.

My wrists and ankles started tingling, and my head felt foggy like it couldn't think clearly. The worst thing was that my ears felt like they were clogging up. It was like someone had opened up the sides of my head and had filled them up with cottage cheese. This muffled feeling blocked my hearing and made me feel distinctly deaf. I felt hemmed in. Cut off. Isolated. The ringing was getting louder too and sounded more like a white noise hissing in the same room as me. At times the pitch started getting in the way of hearing what people were saying. At the time I thought my Spanish needed improving, but actually I was going deaf.

One day over lunch I found out that Ili had to change work. Having set up a mini-language school, which gave me quite a good income, within a few weeks, we would have to move to Algeciras for easy access to a new job at the hospital in La Linea. So we rented a flat in Getares, a small village on a lovely beach. From our balcony, eating barbecued sardines and green peppers, we could see straight across the bay to the Rock of Gibraltar.

In this small town I quickly started to build up some local students. I enjoyed being able to go for a swim before breakfast every day with the beach just a few stairways down from the door. My favourite place to unwind was a short drive up the mountain to the wind turbines where I would sit with them whistling overhead while I looked out across the straights of Gibraltar to Africa across the water. This place was full of energy, where Atlantic meets Mediterranean, where Christianity meets Islam, where ships line up and pass through one of the busiest waterways in the world. Sometimes the cars in Morocco glinted brightly enough to send a flash of light across the water. It was a place of great freedom and contrast. I loved it up there.

But Ili was clearly struggling. Living away from home was like being a fish out of water. We tried to make things work for several months. I even worked as a translator in a giant steel mill converting Kentucky drawl into Andulucian slurry Spanish. But I soon realised that the mounting anxiety meant that we would soon be moving back to Jerez where nerves could settle and recover. All too soon we found ourselves driving back across the windy road to Jerez.

The prospect of creating a new source of income all over again for the third time in just over a year felt like hard work. I realised that I was feeling a bit worn down. My tinnitus was constantly pressurising my head and would not leave me alone for a minute. My hearing continued to feel muffled so that I felt like I was under water. Slowly it dawned on me that maybe I was not going to be happy living long-term in someone else's life.

We loved each other, but there were strong feelings of strain creeping in, and, I knew that in my heart of hearts I had to return home and build a new life for myself. So a few weeks after moving back to Jerez, it became obvious that the dream was over. Ili needed space. So did I. So one sad day, and with a very heavy heart, I wrenched my life away from dear Jerez, with its laughter and brilliant light. I was heartbroken. We both were.

Driving north along the Ruta de la Plata, past Merida and Salamanca, I had to pull over onto the side of the road from time to time and cry for a while. Slowly the light started to loose its brilliance and fade to a more subtle shade. I took the ferry from Bilbao to England, and after two days at sea we approached England lying under a low blanket of cloud. I drove back onto a country I had been running away from for years and noticed how the sky looks smaller in England and the hedgerows and woods much closer in.

Chapter 8 The Sound of Falling

Autumn Cottage, West Sussex, 1997

Sometimes I have wanted
to throw you off
like a heavy coat.

Sometimes I have said
you would not let me
breathe or move.

But now that I am free
to choose light clothes
or none at all

I feel the cold
and all the time I think
how warm it used to be.

Vicki Feaver
Coat

I arrived back at my mother's house with no job, no relationship and no future. She came to greet me at the garden gate. She gave me a strained smile and a hug, which felt heavy and anxious. Granny had died leaving the cottage in a state of chaos and imbalance. It was great to see Grandpa, but he was grieving painfully behind his brave Halifax face and stoicism.

The small cottage was starting to descend into the fading gloom of autumn. The large garden was starting to shut down, and the living space rapidly shrunk back to indoors only. I couldn't stop thinking about Ili, love in the sun, and the life I had left behind. I cried myself to sleep for months. We both did. Slowly the tears diluted the memories, and, feelings of love started being replaced with letting go and forgetting.

My head hurt with the ringing. I had a choir-boy singing a very loud and high "Ahhhhhh" right between my ears. It was a bit disturbing and carried on day and night and sometimes kept me awake. Sometimes this voice turned from being a clear pitch to more like a scream. This scream was strident and drilled through bath time and TV programmes, and hijacked my awareness. Sometimes, underneath this scream, I had an accompanying low and dull hum, forming strange chords that followed me to the kitchen. The noise followed me to the shops and down into the woods. It was really irritating, but did my best to ignore it.

I got a job working for a wine-travel company, taking people to the best restaurants and wineries all over Europe. It was run by a lovely couple who worked hard to provide the best service possible. As a tour manager I had a never-ending list of hotel, restaurant, and winery bookings to make, ferry and plane tickets to buy, and itineraries to write. I got to hear the British Airways jingle for hours every day waiting to speak to someone.

The best part of the job was flying somewhere new and tasting my way around the best restaurants and wineries, and rooting out the most comfortable places to stay. "I might be bringing large groups of wine-connoisseurs to eat here on a regular basis. Would it be possible to try some of your cuisine? What would you recommend tonight?"

Almost immediately the Maître D' would run over, sit me down and ask, "Can I interest you in a glass of Roger Brun, Grand Cru Reserve to welcome you?"

"That sounds perfect. I love a good Pinot Noir from Ay," I would reply smugly, jotting down the name on a little intimidating pad of paper.

"Ahh Bon!" he would reply, raising his eye-brows and his game.

"Now tonight I can offer you a selection of our favourite dishes. Perhaps you would like to have a glass of Jurançon with your Risotto de Coquilles de St Jacques? They marry so well."

"Sounds just lovely," I would reply.

"You must try the 1996 Chablis Grand Cru, Les Preuses, by Fèvre with the Andouillettes à la Moutarde Façon Francine,"

"Sounds mouth-watering," I would add.

Off he would go to the kitchen and give the signal to the chef. He would then make a special effort to throw together a masterpiece. Soon the first wave of scintillating flavours would grace my palette with their wet, velvety textures, slopping about in my mouth with truly breath-taking wines, coming together in an ecstatic marriage of pleasure. After a long day travelling and snuffling around hotels and wineries like a truffle hunting pig, I would then scratch out some notes, trying to capture something of the magic before it disappeared off back again to the place that all flavours and experiences return to.

Then the Maître D' would reappear with raised eye-brows:

"Monsieur, I don't think you will be disappointed with the Maigret de Canard aux Groseilles with a Morey St Denis, Clos de Tart, perhaps?"

"Gosh, what fabulous idea," I would say with slightly flushing cheeks and a rather pleasing feeling of melting inside.

"To follow that, can I interest you in a surprisingly good Loupiac to go with the Brillat Savarin and Bleu de Bresse?"

"You can indeed," I said with a subtle smile, maintaining a professional air of restraint, and off he went.

And so it continued, on and on, until I was stuffed to the nines with gizzard salads and lavender ice-cream and raspberry coulis, and a good glug of the finest Calvados before waddling off with a burp to bed.

As much as it was great to learn how to distinguish Billecart Salmon from a Krug, or learn what makes a Brunello di Montalcino just so incredibly persistent and delicious, the downside was when people did not get what they had ordered.

I remembered arriving at a château in Burgundy and a woman starting to scream at the top of her voice. "Julian! Julian! Where are you? Get down here right away!" I walked down and found a woman in the middle of the courtyard hyperventilating. "Where is my chandelier? Where the fuck is my chandelier? I did not get on a plane and fly all the way to Europe to have this kind of shitty service. I ordered a room with a chandelier. Just what the fuck are you going to do about it? I'm not moving until you sort this out right now!!!" and with that she stamped her foot down.
"I'm most dreadfully sorry. Leave it with me," I said, showing a certain amount of concern, and then ran around the back where I found the hôtelière who was standing with her mouth open. "Ah mon Dieu. Elle est americaine, n'est pas? Quel rage! Ah mon Dieu, ces gens sont tellement exigents." Some clients were demanding indeed, but fortunately, I managed to sweet-talk a more amenable client out of his room into a non-chandeliered room.
"Thanks so much for helping me out here." I said.
"I don't give a bloody toss whether I have a chandelier or not! What a carry on, honestly! She can do with the chandelier just what she pleases. Let's hope it calms her down!"

Another time a wine VIP of Ay was proudly driving us up a very steep vineyard slope. In the back sat another very demanding lady and a rather snooty British connoisseur.
"Sortez, s'il vous plait Messieurs Dames," the VIP said, suddenly stopping the car.
"Please get out of the car. I think he wants to show you some special vines," I told them. We got out, but the two ladies stayed in the back.
"Les voici. Mes vieilles vignes," he said with a big sigh. "Dans ce terroir idéal qui donne vers le sud, le cépage Pinot Noir prend son essor."
"Here are his favourite old vines. This terroir with its ideal position facing south..." I stopped interpreting. To my horror I saw the car starting to roll slowly backwards. There was a sheer drop about five metres below us. In his enthusiasm he had forgotten to apply the hand-break.

"Quick! Help stop the car!" I yelled, diving inside and tugging as hard as I could at the hand-break. Three guys had to run behind the car and bravely stand in its way to stop it from plunging over the edge. At the same time the VIP jumped in and drove the back wheels into a spin sending chalky stones and mud flying high into the air, nearly blinding the rear defence guard.

"Oh my God." The ladies started screaming. "Oh my God, there's a cliff right there. Ahhhh!" The car dug into the slope and suddenly found some traction and with a violent start, lurched off upwards to the top of the hill. Both passengers in the back screamed out at the top of their voices.

Sheepishly the VIP and I got out of the car. I reached back to the trembling arms of the ladies and helped them climb out in a stunned silence. We stared at each other, speechless.

"Time for a drink!" I announced medicinally, and quickly reached down into a bag and pulled out some rather special Bouzy Rouge that we had picked up from yesterday's tasting. Before they had time to utter any words of dismay I funnelled more fizz down their necks, the perfect antidote for shock.

I knew that if I just as so much mentioned the word "Sorry," the barrage of outrage would lose me my job. Thankfully we were saved by lunch-time.

As is the case in France, from the Pas de Calais all the way down to Perpignan, everybody, from lorry drivers to prams-pushing mummies, and from the highest fonctionnaires in the land to the most wretched of tourists, lunch takes over everything. In France midday is like a giant reset button. Everyone bee-lines for the table.

The two horrified women's faces started to soften with the pink fizz. A short while later all the members of the wine tour were sitting around a table. I started dashing about making sure the service was extra snappy before the Domaine Laroche, Clos Grand Cru, Chablis started working its magic with the Salade Campagnarde aux Gésiers de Volaille.

Being a wine tour manager makes your skin toughen quickly. When a man on a Rioja and Navarra Tour came up to the front of the coach and said, "If you don't stop this bus in a minute or so, I am going to piss myself. Please stop as soon as you can."

"When's the next garage or toilet stop?" I asked the driver.

"Ten minutes or so. I can't really stop here, look!" Outside we were driving across a bleak, open landscape. There were no bushes to hide behind and there would be thirty prying eyes looking out to see what on earth was going on.

I secretly handed the man a cup and pointed with my eyes and raised eyebrows to the steps leading down to the door.

"I can't believe he is about to do what I think he is," came a disgusted, aloof voice from above.

Quickly summing up the situation and working out the path of least furore, I turned round calmly to the man, took back the cup, and said: "You're going to have to wait, sorry."

The man looked up at me desperately. "Please stop, please stop."

Outside there were still no bushes or trees anywhere to be seen.

So I turned round I looked back up at the girl with a slightly forceful "don't you dare tell anyone about this" look on my face and signalled for her to turn the other way. She tutted in disgust. I handed the cup to the man. He stopped holding his breath and his face went from red to normal. I quickly handed another cup to the man. He took a deep sigh and filled that one up too. Then I handed a third cup to the man. He didn't need that one, and handed it back to me with a smile. He then walked back to his seat past all the gourmet passengers. The girl flared her nostrils back at me accusingly. So I looked sternly back at her with a tight finger across my lips.

We managed to pull over at a service station ten minutes later where I managed to sneak down and pour the pale yellow liquid with tints of golden straw down a drain, without any of the high-class connoisseurs noticing. The driver just looked at me and laughed, "I don't care, hombre, as long as you don't spill that piss all over my coach."

The job was demanding and exhausting. I bought a small flat in a nearby town and worked hard to make it work. But no matter how much I tried, there was always one who was still dissatisfied. Unfortunately, I found myself starting to fantasise about picking up bowls of gazpacho and tipping it over the snobhead or imagined using a large quenelle de brochet to silence a really annoying mouth that would

149

not stop whinging and whining. As much as Champagne breakfasts and lavish lunches sound great, by the time I hit bed, I was utterly exhausted and felt like my liver was going to explode.

I grew more and more tired and my body became heavier and heavier. I had regular periods of thrush on my tongue and my digestion became bloated, and I started to sleep badly. But worst of all my head started ringing loudly like a siren, and I started making mistakes with bookings, and couldn't hear what the winemakers were saying when I was interpreting in the wineries. I felt like I had two Camembert cheeses strapped over each ears.

One day I went to my answerphone to find my boss shrieking at me in a message. "Where are you? Why aren't you answering the phone? We've got a whole group of people waiting outside a hotel in Reims, which you didn't book properly. Pat is absolutely beside herself. Please call me immediately!"

"How did I miss that call," I wondered.
I got ready and grabbed my things, but as I walked past the answer phone there was yet another message. "Julian, Why aren't you answering? I am really not happy about this at all. Where the hell are you?!"

What was wrong with the phone? Why wasn't it ringing properly? I stood there and listened to a shrill ringing inside my head. It sounded a little bit like the phone ring. "Wait a minute. Is that the phone ringing now or is that my head?" I answered the phone. "Hello? Have you got any of my messages?" "Sorry, can you speak up? I can hardly hear you." I realised that the sound in my head was so loud I couldn't hear the phone ring. It was starting to deafen me literally.

My boss called me into her office. "I'm sorry Julian, we cannot allow this to carry on any more. You are making too many mistakes. I'm afraid we are going to have to let you go."

I couldn't believe it. The shock went straight through me like a bolt of lightening. How was I going to pay my mortgage? What was I going to do now? The others in the frantic office looked away as I gathered my wine maps, walking books and a bottle of jet-black, 150-year-old Lustau Sherry Vinegar, and headed off for home. When I got back my head was screaming. It was so bad that I couldn't sit still. So I walked around the small lake in front of my flat. I paced backwards and forwards and just didn't know what to do with myself. Instead of sleeping I spent hours sitting by the window starring out at the moon hovering over the water. My head felt like it was on fire. It was screaming. Tsssssshhhhhhh! Screaming. Tsssssssshhhhhhh! I'd had six hours of the worst, most relentless screaming. Screaming. Screaming. Tsssssshhhhh! I tried squeezing my head. If I moved my jaw or craned my head to the side the sound got even louder. I started feeling really scared. How was I going to get out of this? "I can't stand this. I can't stand this. This is going to drive me mad." I tossed and turned in bed. I put the radio on, but it was no way near loud enough to even compete with the sound in my head.

Before dawn I fell asleep and dreamed I was in a black car. There were huge mountains all around heavy with fresh snow. The snow came thundering down in an avalanche, which crushed down over the car sending me into darkness, and silence, all except for the ringing in my ears. I sat trapped inside this metal container unable to get out. The air was hot and my tinnitus had pressed itself into my dream. Was I dreaming? I woke up. Tsssssssshhhhhh! The noise was there like a giant insect. It was drilling itself into the centre of my head and I couldn't stand it. The noise was deafening. I couldn't stand it. I just couldn't stand it.

I tried the radio on again. I listened to someone talking. I fell asleep again and heard many voices talking to me all night long, in many different languages. I dreamt of angry clients and impossibly difficult words to translate. I was standing in front of a row of expectant faces and I couldn't get the words out.

The next day when I came round from an appalling night I was shaking slightly. I went to the letting office and put my flat on the market. I packed up a couple of suitcases and that afternoon I drove back to my mother's house. My life in wine was over.

Grandpa was breathing oxygen from a cylinder when I arrived. Mum had put on more weight. She looked really strained. I gave her a hug and told them both what had happened.

"How about a nice cup of tea?" she said in that comforting way.

"Oh deary, deary me," said Grandpa. "Just look at us all," and he started laughing and coughing, sending steam into his small plastic mouth breather. The conversation didn't last long and we all looked at each other hopelessly, realising that we couldn't find any positive resources or distraction. So on went the TV and for weeks we all struggled with three separate, different kinds of hell.

My tinnitus erupted onto a whole new level. I developed a roaring jet-engine which set the thunderous bass-line. Then a horrible electric sound formed a mid-section of noise that twinged and changed tone constantly like an out of tune electrical radio station, and then in the treble section I had the same screaming Tsssssssshhhhh like a million insects buzzing, which seemed to hurt my ears.

I was in pain. When a knife dropped onto a sink I jumped, and winced in pain. I had to leave the room when theme tunes chimed up on the TV. Dramas with ambulances, and everyday jingles turned into electric shock therapy that whistled down my ears and seemed to pinch something inside. It was like the TV room had turned into a torture chamber that was connected directly to the insides of my brain with electric wires.

This torturous pain of sound, continued relentlessly until I started to feel like I was going to fall apart. At night I had to leave the radio on loudly to help me stop being taken over by what sounded like a rushing tornado. When I fell into an exhausted sleep, tornados would appear in dreams and race down the road towards me. When I woke up, the sound would still be right there, bearing down on top of me. I found myself bathed in sweat and literally gritting my teeth. I remember punching the wall in the middle of the night in frustration to try and take the focus off the sound. The resulting pain in my knuckles provided me with at least some tangible distraction that gave me something else to focus on.

"How can I carry on like this? I can't. I can't live like this anymore. If this noise doesn't shut up I don't know if I am going to be able to stand it. What can I do to get away from a life-time of noise torture?" These thoughts started to pray on my mind. I felt like there was no way out. I felt like there was no future. If I am honest, I did want to die. I was never suicidal as in planning anything, but I definitely didn't think I could carry on with this torture. The drilling, roaring sounds were hounding me and felt like they were shaking me to the core. I could feel my body vibrating. The sound was turning my whole nervous system into a shaking, trembling wreck.

And then I would stare across at Grandpa's grief-stricken face and terrified eyes. I loved him dearly and yet there was nothing I could do. I just watched in between TV programmes how he was suffering without his dear wife. Dougal the West Highland Terrier stood on his knees smiling and panting proudly. He was the only thing that gave Grandpa something to live for. There was a sense that he was going to die soon. When I looked at him in that state, it made me realise that, even though I was going through hell, anything was better than facing the end of one's life bereft of the one we love.

One particularly bad night I felt like I was floating out of my body to try and get away from the "Tsssssssshhhhh!" I felt like I was literally climbing the walls of the bedroom. When I realised what was happening I lay there in bed and felt the whole room starting to spin. I gripped onto the sides of the bed and could not stop the room from turning round and round. It was like the tornado had touched down on the small cottage. I felt sea-sick and had to get up. I went downstairs and made some tea. I was a bit shaken from this and so I resolved to go and see the doctor. I managed to get an appointment later on that day.

"Hello Julian, please come this way," said the village doctor. "How, can I help you?"
"Well I am at the end of my tether. I've got tinnitus. It's really deafening and I don't know how I am going to be able carry on with this."
"How long have you had it?"
"About twenty years, but it has got so bad this last year."
"Really? Gosh that is a long time. Sounds awful. Look, there's not going to be anything much that I can do for you I'm afraid, so I am going to refer you to an audiologist and to the ENT department. They will test your hearing and may be able to help. How are you sleeping?"
"Terribly. I wake up constantly with this wretched noise. It gives me nightmares. I've got this roar at the moment with intermittent ticking. It sounds like a hot engine cooling down. Every time I yawn it is deafening."

"Well, I'm going to write you out a prescription for Temazepam which may help take the edge off things and help you get to sleep. I hope you feel better soon."

I got the pills, took them and on the following day I had the strange feeling that I was sitting in an elevator in the living room and it dropped down into a heavy and listless gloom. I felt locked in with the roaring and ticking sound, but now on top of this I was now sitting in a layer of drugged listlessness to boot. The pills didn't help me sleep, so I decided that feeling more awake and terrible was better than feeling listless and terrible.

I started to wait eagerly for the ENT appointment. Maybe he will be able to help me. The noise was relentless and gave me no moments of respite. The weeks stretching ahead to the audiology and ENT appointments moved by at a snail's pace. I developed a screeching sound that was just like chalk on a blackboard. It made me wince in pain and sent shudders down my spine. At times I broke into a sweat because the sound was so excruciating. I had become a restless trapped tiger and I had to keep getting up and going for walks. I felt a burning sensation at the base of my spine and could not sit still at all.

Night-time was a perpetual nightmare with an ocean of silence in all directions causing my tinnitus to stick out even more violently. Sometimes I would get up and go for walks around the village at three in the morning. Somehow feeling the fresh air, or rain on my face and my legs walking helped me feel like I was getting away from things. I walked up to the church at the top of the hill and found my grandmother's grave. It was still relatively new and had lovely flowers on it. She was buried deep down to allow space for Grandpa to go on top. It all seemed so brutal and awful.

But the "Tssssssshhhhh," dominated. There it was blasting its hellish din over the top over all other experiences. The squeaking chalk on blackboards in the middle of my head brought wincing pain that at times made me feel like I was going to pass out. There were more bloody jet-engines roaring. I was sick and tired of dreaming about the fence at the end of Gatwick airport's runway. There are protesters shouting about something and I am standing there transfixed by the noisy plane booming overhead. Except that when I wake up the noise is still there, booming overhead. I can't stand this. I can't stand this. I can't bloody well stand this anymore. I smash my fist against the wall again.

At times I felt like I had electricity all over my body. I found just talking really noisy and uncomfortable. If I put plugs in my ear it made the sound louder. Mum and Grandpa looked at me hopelessly. So to stop burdening them, I got up and went down to the woods to try and let go of my distress alone.

The noise became part of my whole body and space around. It was like my head had become a giant loud speaker. The final straw came when I was sitting by the window and someone rang the bell by the door. It jingled with such a force I jumped out of my skin and started shaking. Then to my horror, the noise kept going. I could hear the jingle reverberating through my head like the auditory function of my brain had broken and now the torture was opening up a new can of worms. I was hearing bells. It kept on playing like a broken tape-recorder. I winced at the imaginary sounds too. The door bell tinkled and jingled for days. So did the TV theme tunes. All the noise was swirling round and round inside my head so loudly that it was hard to distinguish between imagined sound and real sound.

Finally the audiology appointment arrived like the slow train from Calcutta.

"Good morning. Just a few tests then. I see you have bad tinnitus. Sorry to hear about that. Please put these on your head and when you hear a sound I want you to push this button."
I listen out for sounds and hear a fairly quiet hiss, and then a low buzz, and then a middle C, then a tiny very high squeak. I keep pushing the button. I push it again. I hear another lower buzz. I push it again. I hear a medium whoosh.
"OK you can stop now. We've finished."
"Oh have we? Sorry."
"Don't worry, that often happens with tinnitus people."
"Is that it? What shall I do about the ringing in my ears?" I asked desperately.
"Try to get some rest and relax, and you will get your results when you see the ENT." I left completely at a loss.

The next few weeks passed very slowly. One night was forced out of my bed and onto the village lanes at 4am by a brass band. I woke up with the sound of a brass band having a very bad rehearsal. A sound of trumpets, trombones and particularly a tuba blasted in my head and was producing a loud cacophony. It kept on playing over and over again in my head and became part of the prevailing tinnitus noise. I thought I was going to go mad. I know some people hear voices, I was hearing brass bands. But then the ENT appointment finally arrived. Thank God.

"Mr Cowan Hill, your ENT is ready to see you down the corridor on the left.
"Good morning. Let's take a look inside your ears. Mmmmmm," he said as he thrust a cold metal tube down my ear canal.
"Nope, nothing there. And the other one? Nope, nothing there either. That's all fine."
Then he put his hands over his mouth and started making a funny, muffled noise.
"What? Sorry what did you say?"
"Oo carn earmi mecor oo are eff."
"What? Sorry I didn't hear you."
"I thought so, he said rather jovially. You're deaf and you are lip reading."
He then put his hand over his mouth and then made this strange muffled sound again.
"Oo carn earmi mecor oo are eff."
Then he took his hand away and said with really exaggerated lip movements, like he was talking to a complete idiot:
"YOU CAN'T HEAR ME BECAUSE YOU ARE DEAF. Now you can hear what I am saying can't you, because you are reading my lips." He smiled.
I jumped inside my skin and felt shaken. "This can't be right," I thought.

He put his hand back over his mouth and spoke with such exaggerated face movements that I could cheek and forehead-read him. "You can't lip read me right now can you because you are deaf."
"OK, OK I get it," I burst out irritatedly. "Gosh – are you saying I am deaf?"
"Afraid so. Your tests have come back and you are moderately deaf in your left ear and severely deaf in your right ear. I'm afraid you need hearing aids. Also there is a slight anomaly in your semi-circular canals which may affect your sense of balance, but I don't think that is anything to worry about."
"What? Really?"

"Yup. You'll get a referral come through in the post in a couple of weeks and they will sort you out with hearing aids. They should be really helpful. Ok?"

"Umm wait a minute, what about my tinnitus?"

"What do you mean?" he replied blankly.

"What can we do about my tinnitus?"

"Oh nothing. Um, I'm afraid you are just going to have to learn to live with it. There is nothing that we can do to help that. Sorry... Anyway I hope the hearing aids help. Now good luck."

"Is there really nothing I can do? This noise is driving me insane."

"Sorry. I'm afraid you will just have to get used to it. Anyway, thank you Mr Cowan Hill. I wish you all the best." He looked with an apologetic smile towards the door.

With that I got up and walked back to the car. I opened the door and slumped down into the seat. I felt like I had been hit by a sledgehammer. "I'm deaf. Moderately to severely deaf in fact. I need hearing aids. And I can't do any fucking thing about this sodding noise in my head. I can't cope with this. I can't carry on with this torture." I didn't cry. I kind of just slumped forward and rested my head on the steering wheel. I felt utterly, utterly bombed. "The rest of my life like this? No way. Oh no, God, please no." I sat in stunned silence for a good half an hour trying to compute the consequences of this message of doom. Inside something just shut down and disappeared.

I needed to go for a walk before I was with it enough to drive. So I followed a path along a small river across the fields into some woods, and then threw up over some rotten logs. I was gutted. I drove home and told mum and grandpa the bad news.

"Oh crikey. Whatever next," he said, steaming up his oxygen breather.

"I'm not going to be much good company I'm afraid."

I went up to my room and slumped onto my bed. I felt myself closing down again. My body felt like it was dropping through the bottom of the bed. I felt like I was falling down through the covers, through the floor into a pit of numbness. I was floating and falling at the same time and felt trapped in a dismal dream world. My mind went dark and I plunged headfirst into an ocean of hopelessness.

"I'm 36 and I don't have a life. I don't have anything any more. Just hell to look forward to. No future. Nothing. Failure." Thoughts started filling me with terror. My stomach smarted and lurched with every realisation, and filled with electric butterflies. "I'm living with my mother and I am 36." I flash back to the ENT conversation over and over again. "There is nothing I can do. What kind of a life is this? Sorry Grandpa for being such a dead loss. I can't carry on like this."

Something in me goes into slow motion. Days turn into a bit of a blur. The noise is there, but I am not. I'm elsewhere, in a dark cloud of heavy, terrifying thoughts of nothingness. I'm falling into a void, nothing there to stop me, with no end to this suffering. A feeling of dread grabs the pit of my stomach and grips tightly in, squeezing hard with no sign of letting up. I feel sick. I'm not going to be able to deal with this. "I mustn't kill myself. It would be too awful for mum and Grandpa. It's wrong to commit suicide. I will go to hell if I do. Why do I think that? Why is it wrong to commit suicide? Maybe it is a way out? Who says its wrong, anyway? Killing myself will turn this hell off, it will shut this screaming torture off inside my head."

"What if I pretend to get a job overseas and just get lost somewhere and do it quietly, gently, carefully, make it look like an accident? I could go to Canada and walk North and get lost in the woods. Nobody would find me except the bears. Maybe I could fly South instead..." I imagined flying to a bleak desert land and catching a bus into the mountains and then walking out into the middle of a desert with no food or water. That would be a natural way of doing it." I remember a friend telling he was once so heart-broken when his girlfriend dumped him that he flew to Canada with a bike and rode off into the winter intending to freeze to death. But when he unpacked the bike in the snow, the brutality of the winter woke him up and brought him to his senses. So he rode south and stayed close to the sea until Spring arrived and melted his heart and his dreams of suicide.

"I am afraid you are just going to have to learn to live with it!" resounded in my head like a death knell. Each time this passed through my mind, I felt terrorised. I had no idea that a sentence coming out of one person's mouth could cast such a devastating spell of death on someone else.

"There is nothing we can do to help. Tsssssshhhhhhhhhhhhh!" Every time this thought passed through my nervous system, it seemed to make my ears ring even louder.

"I am afraid you are just going to have to learn to live with it!"

"There is nothing we can do to help. Tsssssshhhhhhhhhhhh!"

"I am afraid you are just going to have to learn to live with it!"

"There is nothing we can do to help. Tsssssshhhhhhhhhhhh!"

This idea was taking root inside my mind like a killer octopus and was burrowing lots of harmful tentacles deep inside my brain and down my spine. It took less than five seconds to say, but this message was drilling itself deep inside my being like some demented and twisted torturer. Because I believed the ENT, his message turned into one of the most destructive and deadly mantras I have ever heard.

I'm sure the ENT had no intention to harm me. But he showed a deep lack of understanding about how this condition works. It is true that the medical model at that time had no way of helping tinnitus, but delivering a message like this to someone in my state was utterly damaging. Because I believed him, his message pushed me to the edge of a cliff where I sat staring off into the abyss of suicide and darkness. Off the edge this darkness roared back at me like a thundering, endless black hole waiting to suck me into eternal damnation. I believed what he said because there were no other messages out there. It took just five seconds of his life, five seconds of words to destroy my future. His words kept firing into my mind like a machine-gun moving me closer and closer to that terrifying noise on the other side of the cliff. "Shall I jump? Will that bring this hell to an end?"

The only things holding me back were my mother and grandfather whose hearts acted like thin strings keeping me attached some small vestige of meaning and purpose. In front of me the giant screaming void was waiting, opening its mouth wider, encouraging, and enticing me into its oblivion. My head was buzzing with the sound of a million of screaming voices yelling out, in terror, from the void.

Chapter 9 The Sound of Hell

Autumn Cottage, West Sussex, 1999

I do not find release
From humming, strumming, banging, clanging,
Slapping, clapping, hissing, sizzling, howling, growling,
Orchestrated sounds.
There are no bounds, no limits set
To my regret
For this destructive torture.

No one understands my pain.
My only wish is to stay sane.
I learned to hide what bothers me,
Therefore, not a one can see
The devastating state I am in;
The horrible calamity
That frightfully engulfs me,
Keeps petrified me in my chair
In agony, and deep despair,
Not knowing what's in store for me,
Praying: "Please God, let this be
The last of these unbearable attacks.

Neil Bauman
The Sound of Hell

The following day I woke to police sirens going off in my head. They were loud, wavering sirens that sounded like they had faulty wiring. The sirens were crackling and sizzling. The sirens came on without any warning or predictable pattern. The sirens were so loud they made my head hurt. When I moved the sirens changed pitch and a sudden rush of electricity exploded through me like internal fireworks of pain. The sirens left me smarting in terror.

I sat on my bed and squeezed my head into my hands. The tighter I pushed the louder the sirens screamed back. If I jutted my jaw out the noise went up a tone and the sirens got louder. If I strained my neck to the left the sirens became even more distorted. If I moved it to the right the sirens went down a bit. I felt like I was trapped inside a robot nightmare, inside an alien body of pain that was waiting to attack any movement that was out of line with an electric shock.

I became terrified of walking too quickly for fear of triggering a shriller, more unbearable siren, which would send me into wincing pain. I moved about my room like shell-shocked soldier whose nervous system was like a circuit-board that could burn itself out at any time.

I edged downstairs and shuffled up to the table where I joined mum and grandpa for porridge and tea. "You're really suffering today aren't you darling," Mum sighed, rubbing my back sympathetically.
"Awful, just awful."
Then Mum and Grandpa turned to each other, and then we all looked at each other and said, "Ooooh dear oh dear oh deary me!" and burst out laughing.

Grandpa dropped a spoon against the side of his cup. The clink sounded like two wooden blocks were being snapped together either side of my head, and sent a knife of pain searing through my upper body. I braced my hands against my ears to try and shield myself from the noise. He then started stirring the spoon against the earthenware mug causing a grating sound, which felt like it was sending irritating vibrations grinding into my teeth and down my spine.

"It's really bad. It's actually diabolical today. I think the news the ENT gave me has knocked me for six. I can't believe I'm deaf and this is what it's going to be like for the rest of my life…." I stared off into space.

"Its not going to be like this forever darling," mum chimed in. "You'll be alright. You wait and see. You're just going through a really tough patch, but it'll back off." I loved Mum for saying that. It didn't matter if it wasn't true, but I was willing to believe it.

"Do you really think so?"

"Yes I do," she said, clearing her throat and putting on a reassuring face. I pretended to believe her and smiled. But behind this smile I quickly slipped back into a sense of despair.

I ended up walking around in a haze of agony and torture, braving seconds of screeching, whole minutes of loud alarm bells ringing, and hours of tormenting, deafening screaming, hounding me for days, for weeks, leaving me feeling utterly exposed to the tyranny of the deafening din. I tried to watch TV but my focus had been utterly taken over. I tried to listen to the words and follow the story-line, but my mind had been kidnapped by this wretched henchman who had taken me prisoner in my own body. He was there and drilling like a pneumatic drill into my awareness the whole time.

I watched the opening credits to a grim accident and emergency programme. Over the course of a minute the theme tune hammered its way inside my brain and then started repeating itself over and over again with the sound of the life-support system, the electronic pulse and infuriating jingle that hounded my mind all night long, as if a sadist was rewinding the show back to the beginning to annoy me, replaying that jingle over and over again. So instead of hearing the quiet of the bedroom I was held ransom inside my head by the sound of the relentless, harrowing music, and electric monitor, raised heartbeat, of the ear-worm that I couldn't switch off.

One afternoon a particularly piercing and painful sound started drilling into my skull. I simply could not bear sitting with it any longer. So I got up, put on my coat and sloped off down to the bottom of the garden. It was a grey, drizzly summer day. I walked over the field down to the woods, wincing in pain.

This noise that I had been living with for twenty years had become absolutely and utterly unbearable. It was a living torture. I walked with half-crazed eyes up to a tree and started bashing my head against the hard bark in despair. It really hurt. I saw stars. Bang. Bang. I felt my forehead whack against the tough surface. The pain and the shock of the impacts were strangely distracting. They were strong enough to be an escape in some way from the tinnitus and the terrifying thoughts that were flooding into my mind.

My head throbbed. I yelled out in frustration. "I can't bear it!" I yelled out. "I can't stand this fucking sound anymore!" I hit my fists against the bough of the tree. I kept hitting them hard against the strong, hard, surface. The harder I hit my clenched fists, the more they hurt and the more I felt the hardness of the tree. The shock of the impacts was distracting and helped me float out into a different perspective. I found myself looking down at an exhausted man who was lost and out of control and suffering intensely, bashing his head against a tree in the middle of a wood in the middle of a drizzly summer afternoon. "Oh God, my life has come to this," I remember thinking. I was shocked. "Look at me... What on earth am I doing?" I slumped down onto the muddy soil and started to cry in a very gut wrenching way. Nobody heard.

One morning, in the middle of scraping butter onto crunchy toast, Grandpa, who was trying to ignore his failing health and slow suffocation, and mum, pouring a cup of tea, who was trying not to notice that her father was on the way out and her son was going through hell, one morning, somewhere in between the porridge and the marmalade, and Dougal, the West Highland Terrier, wagging his tail under the table, waiting for the next bit of toast, Grandpa mustered up some resources and ventured:
"Listen lad, why don't you go for a swim? Take car and go to Cranleigh and have a good float in pool. I bet that'll make you feel a bit better. It'll take your mind off it at least. Why don't you?"

The thought of just mooching around at home all day driving everyone round the bend did seem pretty grim. I was locked inside a dark stream of thoughts, but, for some reason, this idea popped in like shard of light. I was so taken aback with the suggestion that it actually got through and lit up something inside my head.

"Do you know what? I think you're right. I'll give it a go. This is driving me mad."

"I can see that," Grandpa added. "That's why you should go."

I helped clear up and settle Grandpa back into his chair with the oxygen cylinder and Dougal on his knees. I grabbed the keys and set off. Even though the noise was deafening, and sounded like highly pressurised air pump rushing forcefully out of a valve, the driving forced me to pay attention to the road, and took my mind off the sound a tiny bit. I meandered slowly along the country lanes and found my way to the car park in front of the sports centre. Having to interact with people, undress, shower and get changed also took my mind off the tinnitus a tiny bit.

I walked up to the edge of the pool. The sun was streaming in through the windows and down to the bottom of the water, sending ripples of light that looked like shimmering sapphires and diamonds sparkling out in all directions. My ears were blasting out three loud sounds at the time: there was loud, high-pitched, piercing squeak, then there was a loud pfffffft sounding like a strong release of hissing air out of a tyre pump, and a hideous, wavering siren that was going "wah oo wah oo wah oo wah," right through the middle of my brain like a child imitating a fire-engine. My body was trembling slightly from head to foot. The noise was so loud I could barely notice the shrill sound of the kids playing in the pool.

I dived in. Suddenly I was plunged into that suddenly muffled, deep sonorous underwater whoosh that reverberated like a submarine sonar. In that moment it was like I went into slow motion, and felt millions of bubbles pouring over my skin, echoing up to the surface. In a split second my whole body came alive with the contact of the cool refreshing water. A wave of pleasure juddered through my body.

As I had done many times before, I found myself starting to swim along the bottom of the deep end until I came to the part where the pool rises up suddenly. I gently pushed my chest against the incline and then let my body take off and just float up slowly to the surface. It felt really peaceful under the water. It was so much quieter down there.

As I surfaced, I listened to all the trickling and sploshing water, dripping and splashing around my head. For a moment I enjoyed feeling my body being supported all around by the water, then I pulled myself out with one movement onto my feet and felt the water come crashing down to the ground, feeling the trickles running around my forehead, tickling down my cheeks and through my beard. I held my legs and buttocks firmly together, positioning my feet into the lumpy patterned tiles along the edge of the pool that stop you slipping, feeling strong and athletic for a moment. Then I dived back down into the sparkling sapphires of silence at the bottom of the pool, into the deep muffle where everything is still and peaceful. I slowly allowed the body to float up again in that tingling, tickling rush of bubbles, feeling the weightlessness and support of the water that was so intensely comforting after what felt like weeks of pain and hell. My body juddered with pleasure and started to relax and settle a bit.

This was the pool I had learnt in. We used to go swimming there when we used to be a relatively happy family. I remembered pushing Bargie into the deep end from school years ago, and seeing if I could beat Gigglees or Hodgie down to the bottom. We had such fun. As I started gliding through the smooth, cool water, positive associations started flooding in like nectar to a thirsty mind.

Maybe it was a survival instinct that kicked in, but the swimming definitely de-prioritised tinnitus and sent it flying down a few notches in my experience.
I did a few lengths gently and then enjoyed feeling the tough hot blast of the shower pummelling my back and squirting around my eyes and nose and mouth. It sounded good and felt strong and clear and real. I rubbed the dry, rough surface of the towel into my legs and bum and across my back, which revitalised my body and made it tingle and feel almost comfortable. Walking back to the car I was able to smell the fresh air, breathe it in and feel it against my face. There was something really calming about these simple, strong body sensations that managed to take my mind off the tinnitus a bit. In some ways Cranleigh Swimming pool helped save my life, flipping me from suicidal thoughts to finding something worth living for.

The noise in my head walked me back to the car, of course, but I felt a bit better with it, and this was a massive step forward. I felt a tiny little bit soothed. If water is a powerful enough sedative to help ease mothers through childbirth, then maybe it is good enough to help me find some comfort with tinnitus.

For the next couple of weeks I went swimming every morning, and slowly but surely started to feel my fitness return and my body strengthen. I started doing the shopping, which helped Mum and Grandpa. Although this may seem a small thing in itself, this simple action gave my life a bit more meaning. Although I slumped back into the pits of despair every afternoon with the unbearable noise, daily exercise meant my sleep definitely started to improve and my body started to de-stress itself.

Night times started to provide me with hours of sleep providing the "balm of hurt minds" that I started to have a proper break away from the onslaught of tinnitus. Better nights, in turn, stopped me feeling so hemmed in. Swimming was the first thing that helped me feel a bit better, and that sense of slight improvement gave me some space in which I could start breathing just a bit more.

I came home one day to find a friend of my mother's talking over tea. Sue approached me and said, "You know, I have been talking to your mum and she has been telling me all about your tinnitus. Have you considered having Craniosacral Therapy? I think it could help."

"Cranio what did you say?"
"It's brilliant. It's a gentle hands-on way of working with the body. I've had it done a few times. It is amazing. Maybe it will help you."
"I don't care what it is, if it could help me - I'll give anything a try."
Her craniosacral therapist was away, and so we phoned round and found out that there was a certain Mr H who lived in Haslemere. I booked an appointment the very next afternoon.

He lived in a stone cottage and welcomed me into a small room with a couch. We spoke about what I had been going through and then I climbed onto the couch.

As I lay there looking up at the wooden beams of the ceiling, he laid his hands gently on my feet and rested them there for a while. After a moment I started to feel a pleasant, tingly feeling running up my legs. Then he put his hand under the base of my spine on the sacrum and a gentle movement started up which felt really comforting. Suddenly a layer of pressure that I didn't know was there gave way, and my back dropped more comfortably onto the couch. I found myself sighing, and noticed my back stretching out all by itself. Still with his hand under my sacrum I felt a gentle pressure moving around my head. It was extraordinary.

"How can such a tiny movement down there make things move around in my head?" I asked, in surprise.

"That's Craniosacral Therapy for you. It's the membranes that are moving, not me. They are readjusting themselves."

"What, you mean that you are not moving your hand?"

"No." He smiled.

"Well what's moving then?"

"That's your body unwinding," he said in a matter of fact kind of way.

"Gosh that's amazing. This is so relaxing." I found myself yawning and the racing thoughts inside my head started to slow down.

I then became aware of an incredible tension in my neck. It felt like it was held in a vice. It was actually painful. And yet, slowly, but surely, it started to release and let go. The relief was almost overwhelming. To my amazement my body grew floppy and heavy, and sank into the couch like a melting marshmallow.

Then he went to my head and put a clump of fingers just in front of my right temple and another clump behind my left ear on the bony protuberance.

My eyes were closed at this point. Suddenly I saw a bright green flickering in my eyes.

"That's amazing," I said out loud. "It's like there is a bright green light going right through my head! What on earth is that?" Then it happened. My tinnitus started changing pitch and tone.

I gasped, and in shock I grabbed the side of the couch.

"Are you alright?" he asked, slightly concerned.

"Ah, um, I don't know." I gasped. "You've got my tinnitus! You have just changed my tinnitus! How do you do that?!"

"I'll tell you at the end," he said settling his hands lightly back into position, barely touching my head. "Just try to relax."

Then it happened again. It felt like he was twiddling a tuning dial on a radio and was changing the sound of my tinnitus. I gasped again. He took his hands off.

"No no no. Don't stop, please. That's it! You've got it in your hands."

For the next five minutes I felt like he was loosening and adjusting tightness that ran right through the middle of my head and was somehow getting it to slacken and release. My head started to relax and feel more comfortable inside. My tinnitus was getting a bit quieter. My mouth fell open.

"I don't believe this is happening!" For a moment I dared to think the nightmare was coming to an end, but found myself holding my breath to disallow that thought. I wouldn't be able to bear the disappointment. No surely not. This is just a dream.

"Just relax," he said. "You are doing really well."

"No you are doing really well. This is incredible." My head felt literally like it was expanding and becoming more relaxed. I had no idea that I had been walking around with tight membranes inside head, probably for years. My eyes filled with tears and then before I knew it I was crying. I felt a bit embarrassed.

After a period of time I realised that Mr H had sat down and that the session had come to an end. I lay there motionless and relaxed and had to gather myself together enough to sit up.

I felt incredibly heavy, almost drunk. I started laughing.

"God that was extraordinary. How do you do that?" I asked.

He smiled.

"What on earth was that green light in my head?"

"You saw a green light, did you?" He laughed. "That's amazing I was doing a power drive across your head and was visualising green light while I was doing it."

"Really?" he lost me a bit there. How was that possible?

My head felt more spacious and really heavy and I needed to make an effort to hold it up with my neck and keep it in place. I swung off the couch onto the floor and stood up and felt distinctly wobbly through my middle. My feet felt like they were being anchored deep into the ground by big magnets. I also felt like I was standing up taller.

"Ooh, that's weird. I feel completely different." I laughed out loud. "Gosh, that's amazing." My voice sounded a bit slurred and slow.

In a bit of a daze, I thanked him and paid him for the session.
"I swear my tinnitus is a bit quieter. I don't know how you did that but this is amazing!"
I walked out to the car feeling drunk and a bit emotional. I had to walk slowly and take care that I would not fall over. "Gosh! How is that possible?" I kept thinking to myself. "It's such a light contact."

The drive back through the hills and woods to Rudgwick was slow because I was incredibly relaxed. I actually had to pull over into a layby along the narrow forest road because I started laughing uncontrollably. Thank God nobody could see me there, all alone in the car in the middle of the forest in the dark. I kept on laughing and had tears of relief flooding out of my eyes. I felt incredibly relaxed, everything felt very slow, loose and chilled. I honestly don't think I had ever been that relaxed before. I felt like I had been drugged.

I got home to find Grandpa and Mum engrossed in a soap on TV.
"How did it go darling," mum asked without taking her eyes off the screen.
"It was amazing. I feel just so much better."
"Really?" She turned around. "Gosh, your face. You look much better. Oh come and give me a hug. That's really good to hear, dear," she said.
"I swear my tinnitus has got quite a bit better. I can't believe it!" I said, beaming at both of them.
"Thank Bloody God," said Grandpa. "About time we had some good news. I'm really pleased for you." He reached over and shook my hand tightly.

I flopped upstairs and slumped into bed feeling intensely comfortable and released. To my total amazement my head was still noticeably quieter. Mr H had turned my volume down. I was too relieved and relaxed to give it any further thought and fell into the deepest sleep I had had for years. I slept for ten hours without stirring once, and, in the morning I woke up inside a slow, calm and deeply relaxed body. I climbed out of bed and walked heavily to the bathroom, feeling how weighty my legs were, and noticing the shape of my chest and shoulders. My back felt slack. It was like I was able to feel my body properly for the first time. I could feel my chest expanding and contracting as I brushed my teeth. It felt as if an anaesthetic had lifted and now I was walking around from within my body. I felt incredibly clear inside.

I walked down the stairs feeling how the body manoeuvred itself with greater ease. There was more bounce in it as I bounded down each step. I felt like I was completely stoned. I couldn't stop laughing. There was much mirth over breakfast watching me get my new bearings.
"I swear my head is better. The tinnitus is definitely quieter. I can't believe it."

The sense of relief was delightful and kept catching up with me over the next few days. I kept on dreading something automatically and remembering that there was no need any more. I kept bursting out laughing or crying and it felt good, like I was letting go of something. I felt like a spell had been broken and just found myself in a good mood. I started sleeping like a baby and eating for England. I felt a thousand times better. The mood in the cottage lifted too.

I went back to Mr H and had a few more cranial sessions and although the reactions weren't nearly so extreme as the first, I dropped into states of calm I had never experienced before. I had definitely turned a corner and started to feel more hopeful and happy again. The noise reduced back down to the sound of a gentle pressure-cooker hiss in the same room. The sound was much more constant now which meant that I could start to stabilise around it instead of being flung about at the mercy of any terrifying new sound. But most of all, the wincing pain in my head stopped. Sound no longer hurt me. For the first time my mind dared to consider that maybe I would not have to spend the rest of my life in hell.

I was fascinated in how such a light touch on the body could bring about such radical and long-lasting changes. I heard that a teacher called Thomas Atlee was offering a week-end taster session of Craniosacral Therapy in Oxford. I decided to go along. It felt good to do something practical.

Thomas welcomed us in and gave a brief introduction to what cranial work is. He showed us the anatomy of the membrane system, three layers of skin that surround the brain and spinal chord which act like balloons containing cerebro-spinal fluid. It was quite surprising to hear that the fluid moves up and down the central nervous system over the course of a couple of minutes in a hydraulic system. Nobody to this day can explain what drives this movement of fluid. The really big surprise was that the bones of the cranium and sacrum move quite a lot to accommodate this flow of fluid. Craniosacral Therapy was principally based on palpating and working with this fluid movement.

"Ok, so that's enough of me explaining this system to you. Now it's time for you to feel for yourself. Your desks are really couches so why don't you find someone you would like to work with and one of you can lie down and the other can get in touch with the Craniosacral system."

Before I knew it, a woman was lying on the table in front of me. Thomas told us to take a deep breath and start focussing on our own bodies and how we connect down to the ground.

"The most important thing is to make sure you are all comfortable and relaxed. The calmer and clearer and more relaxed you are, the more you are likely to feel." He showed us how to take up contact.

I found myself checking out my own body and what felt good inside me and then I rested my hands very gently with a butterfly touch onto the sides of the woman's head lying in front of me.

"Be careful just to sit back and let the information come to you. You don't want to go rushing in, just rest your hands there and wait and see what happens. Keep it light and spacious and wait for any movement to show itself to you."

I sat there and felt slightly nervous. I let the hands rest in the contact for a minute or so, and then, to my amazement I felt a very slow, gradual expansion and contraction. It was like the bones were floating very gently on liquid. I was fascinated. There was a distinct feeling of a balloon filling very slowly with water and then very slowly starting to go back down again, pretty much like the tide coming in and going out. It felt really calming to be doing this and after about half an hour we stopped and the woman seemed to be asleep.

It took her a while to come round and then sit up. Then she turned to me and said,
"Thank you. That was amazing. I feel so relaxed. I felt like my whole body started to float gently and my head feels so much better. Thank you."
"A pleasure," I said, now knowing what I had done. We all shared our experiences together, some reporting a clear sense of movement, some picking up vibrations, and others feeling a sense of settling and dropping into stillness. We were all amazed just how much we could feel and how much we all benefited from the experience.

Later Thomas asked for someone to demonstrate a hand hold on. My hand flew up into the air before I had time to feel shy. I found myself lying down with the group sitting all around watching intensely. I closed my eyes and began to feel a very light touch, which started to wake up subtle movements inside me. After a few minutes Thomas put his hands on my forehead and rested them there for a moment. Suddenly I had a feeling of being pulled from the bottom of a dark pool up to the surface. My body felt like it was expanding and became much lighter and more relaxed and strangely full of light. I gasped. I had never experienced anything like it before.

After the demonstration I sat down and felt very still and clear-headed. I could feel clearly the insides of my body still expanding and contracting like they were made out of elastic. Cranial work was opening up a whole new world to me. Before my body was like a house where I had been living in the attic. But now a door had opened and I was discovering whole rooms downstairs that I had never been into before. I literally felt like I had dropped down into my body and was living closer to the ground.

The introductory day blew me away. I was in awe of strange new experiences that I had never felt before. Feeling calm and relaxed was still such a new territory for me. I walked back to the station in my belly, legs and feet, and felt like my head was something that was up there somewhere. I sat on the train seat and could feel inside every cylinder of my body that was still expanding and contracting gently. It felt very odd.

I quickly enrolled in the next Craniosacral Therapy training course at the College of Craniosacral Therapy in Primrose Hill. On each training week-end we learnt about different bones of the cranium and how to work with them. I was most interested in the temporal bones and how to engage with the ear and the auditory system. We were told how this part of the body is an emotional store-house and how working on the jaw and ears could release strong feelings and help people really settle into a much better state psychologically.

My tinnitus started changing dramatically. Often after practice sessions it would feel slightly fizzy like a brand new bottle of Coke had been gently opened up to release pressure. Then over the next few days the sound would come down and start settling to a new lower level. It wasn't a massive drop, but more of a gradual decline, which was very, very welcome. I became really interested in the body and learning about how certain life situations tended to affect certain parts of the body. I discovered a new-found enthusiasm and positive focus that was just so completely different to listening to my tinnitus. This body-based distraction was turning out to be a very good antidote to tinnitus. I felt like the more I focused on my body the more energy I had.

After training week-ends I would get back to my mother's sitting room, sit down and feel whole new areas of my body still reacting from students having practicing on me. It felt like something was waking up inside me more and more and, at times, I felt like I was literally glowing with light or energy in each bit of my body. The further I went into the course the more I felt, and the more this internal world came to life.

One evening I was sitting watching television with my mother.
"What on earth are you doing, darling?" she said looking at me as if I was some kind of a weirdo.
"I can feel my liver doing strange things. We were working on the viscera all week-end at the college."

"But why are your hands moving around off your body?"

"I can still feel the liver kind of floating around gently inside. If I move my hands near it, it seems to cause the feeling to change, a bit like a magnet pulling iron filings in a different direction."

"How weird, darling! Gosh you're learning some interesting things. Can you give me a treatment later? I've got a sore neck."

"Sure."

I converted the back room of the cottage into a treatment room and now friends and family were queuing up for sessions and were providing the perfect guinea-pigs for me to practice on. I started getting good results almost immediately, and still couldn't quite explain how I was doing it. All I knew was the simple practice of sitting and feeling deeply into the subtle movements of the body caused it to release and let go deeply and in an incredibly positive way.

My body was waking up after a life time of being shut down, and I was feeling more and more alive and responsive with every step. I started to discover that I was far more sensitive than I ever thought possible. For decades I had been horribly unaware of my feelings that had been buried away deep inside. Now, I was starting to experience things in real-time, in a much more direct kind of way.

So instead of thinking about sadness when watching a film or listening to music, I felt an immediate pulsating in my heart and a direct emotional expression that came flying out of the centre of my body. It seemed for years I had been relying on my head to make sense of the world, but now my body was telling me something very different. In fact it started responding to situations immediately, of its own accord. My heart starting feeling happy or afraid before my head did, and I didn't need to work out what was happening in my head anymore because the feelings just showed me.

Meeting someone new, for example, instead of trying to suss them out mentally, I would feel an immediate push/pull feeling in my guts and chest that would give me direct feedback before I even had time to assess them. Of course I still looked at visual clues or noticed their manners and way of speaking, but it was like discovering a deeper, body-based intelligence that was opening up. This body-based awareness was there to help and revealed me things that were more reliable way than my head.

At times this new awareness really challenged my world-view. I had to study anatomy as part of my training. I remember once, when I was examining the liver, feeling an immediate reaction inside my body as if it were responding to me directly and saying, "Yes, this is me. I'm really here and of course I'm going to react to what you are exploring!" There really is a wisdom in the body giving direct feedback all the time if we learn to focus clearly enough. My awareness was starting to open up and I could feel if someone was an energy sapper, wanted to snuff me out, or instead, was actually calm, safe and let me be.

It seemed that the key for this to happen was to enter into real-time, direct relating with someone who already has this kind of awareness. When someone is there with their hands on your system and is genuinely curious, and tending to you with a fresh, heart-felt interest and intention to help you, almost like magic, an awareness comes into being and starts to permeate you gently, almost imperceptibly at first, but builds gradually over time until it becomes second nature.

Awareness needs to be there first, and we are introduced to this directly by another person who already has it. The more awareness comes into our own experience the more present and alive we feel. For years I had been walking around like an out of touch and invisible ghost. But now here I was, starting to flesh out into a real-time unfolding experience. Of course my experience and awareness of my body was still very patchy but Craniosacral Therapy was starting to fill in the gaps. I was changing from a thinking person who lived in a made-up world of ideas into a feeling person who could navigate through real interactions. Life was turning into a very palpable and constantly renewing experience. All I had to do was stay focused and learn to sustain my attention in a particular kind of way. This kind of awareness can flick on and off in the spur of a moment, and is a body-based thing. Thinking about it doesn't work.

I started to realised that I needed to be in touch with the heart to know what was real and what was bullshit. I felt like I had been lost for years because I had been relying on my head to make sense of the world.

The way our hearts feel is everything. So when we are looking for therapists to help us, if they don't really care and have seen it all before, this won't cut the mustard. Every interaction needs to matter otherwise we can never drop into a deep stillness and sense of peace with someone else. Some of those first Craniosacral experiences in Oxford were some of the most powerful ones I ever had, because I was totally there, fascinated, mouth wide open with the amazement of how incredibly beautiful and unbelievable a human body and mind is. I was in awe of what is possible between two people. We were blessed with fresh, untainted minds that could see and experience things clearly without being distorted by expectations or agendas that come flooding in and ruin things.

The clear heart space of: Gosh, what is this? What's happening now? How can I help this person? What is their body trying to tell me? What could possibly happen next? This is simply the most powerful way we can interact with another. We enter into unbiased, genuine relating with another, which depends on us being open to whatever emerges.

The moment we are exposed to a heart that is saying: "You are not the way I want you to be. I need you to change. Stop being the way you are. I want you to be like this," then something in us shuts down. We retreat into our head, stop being alive, and the flow of being open to whatever emerges closes down again. For me it was such a big surprise to find that we can enter into an alive, flowing process that is constantly presenting itself as something new, with fresh potential in every step. My sense of "me" found this strange.
I thought I had my usual way of reacting, I thought I knew who I was, but actually, something else was opening up and revealing itself to me. It seems that we are really receivers of a larger life at work that is happening through our sense of "me." The way we think we are just gets in the way of this.

In short, the power of a simple human contact with its genuine, heartfelt wish to help and be there for another is where the power lies. This is the key. When someone is there for us, we can drop into stillness, and the real mind can start presenting itself to us through our bodies. Our heart knows this and recognises this for us. Our heart knows what the head doesn't.

On my Craniosacral Therapy training, I was basking in treasure of the open and unclouded minds of fellow students offering me space and some of the most allowing treatments that I would ever receive. Just being allowed to be here in all our glory with no spin, no requirements, and no pretence, no games or bullshit finally helped my head quieten down. The charades could stop. For a moment that person and I could just find ourselves there on the couch with a clear head, feeling peaceful and neutral.

It was the direct contact with this invaluable interaction that brought me alive and into the present moment for the first time in my life. This left me feeling incredibly open sometimes. Walking down the garden I could close my eyes and feel different parts of the body reacting to trees around me as if the normal boundaries had melted away and I could feel more connection. I would come into contact with people and feel an immediate push/pull. I starting learning how to pick up information on a different level. In short this whole new language of direct communication or transmission was like discovering a secret door at the bottom of the garden, and stumbling across a whole new world.

One day I had a headache and I couldn't organise a treatment from anyone. So I walked down to the woods and stood next to a tree. I approached it and then stopped. I looked at it and felt its strong vertical energy in front of me and wondered if it could in some way help me. I stood motionless for a moment and then noticed a gentle pulling feeling. I walked up to the trunk and stood with my back resting against its strength, and tuned into it. Immediately I could feel this very powerful up and down energy, which started to interact with my body. As I let go it felt as if I was being recalibrated somehow. It was fascinating. I literally felt like the top of my head and the base of my tailbone opened up and tension or blockage that was causing discomfort started being tugged gently up and out of me or down and out of me. I stood there amazed. A tree was getting rid of my headache. I felt it as clear as pie. It took about ten minutes for the pain to shift, but I walked back to the cottage feeling much better. I had become a tree-hugger.

I remembered Thomas Atlee saying that we are not just flesh and blood, but also bundles of energy. So if I am aware of my own system as a bundle of energy I can be aware of a tree as a bundle of energy too. All energies interact with each other.

This is a basic law of physics. But it seems awareness needs to be open to this for shifting to occur. If we stay stuck in a mental version of what we think we are then this seems to narrow down the possibilities. But once awareness opens up, whole new potentials become available to us.

I could close my eyes and feel where people were in the room. I could feel my energy changing in response to our thoughts, feelings, interactions. I could lie in the bath and feel the water around my body as an interactive field, where the buzziness of my nervous system could release and then go calm. Each day seemed to bring new surprises and the world became a much more communicative place. I started reading fascinating new scientific discoveries on water having consciousness, about the impact of coherence and order on health. Finding that I was alive inside a body that was displaying its own interactive intelligence in an interactive field was utterly extraordinary to me at the time. This period of awakening filled me with great enthusiasm and motivation to learn more and to meet with others who had much greater awareness than I did. It seemed that life had switched itself back on again, but this time, it was glowing in glorious technicolour.

But the most extraordinary thing happened six months after starting my Craniosacral Therapy training. I came back to my mother's house one evening in the early summer and went to bed feeling well. In the morning I woke up and had a life-changing experience I will never forget.

I was having a strange dream. I dreamt I was asleep at the bottom of a gigantic yellow tulip. It was warm, bright and very comfortable. The petals I was resting on felt soft yet firm and everything felt really light and peaceful, as if it were floating in space but gently supported. The sun was shining onto the soft yellow space, which was rocking very gently in the breeze. A puff of air wafted in through the window against my face bringing a smell of roses in from the garden outside warming up in the sun. As I came round, and opened my eyes, the brilliant sun was streaming in through the window of the small bedroom at my mother's house. I could hear a woodpigeon cooing in that wooden pipe kind of way. It is always such a lovely, relaxing sound. "Tut tuuut tuuut tuuut, tut tut." Then it stopped for a moment. The room fell silent for a moment. Then it started up again, "tut tuuut tuuut tuuut, tut

tut," then the room fell silent again for a moment. There was a longer silence. Then it started up again, "Tut tuuut tuuut tuuut, tut tut," then it stopped and the room dropped into silence again.

I sat up and listened. Silence. I was sitting in complete silence. I got out of bed and looked out of the window across the Pennyfarthing weathervane on the top of my mother's garage to the trees in the next door neighbour's garden. Silence. There was no sound at all. I sat and listened, transfixed. Nothing. I could vaguely make out some rustling leaves and country-sounds hanging in the air as a backdrop, but there it was, a magical and entrancing silence. My life had gone quiet. For the first time in twenty years my world had dropped back into stillness and quiet. It was like a dream come true.

I sat back down on the bed and felt absolutely elated. The woodpigeon started up from time to time, but in between, in the quiet, I sat there waiting for the tinnitus to come back, but it didn't. Instead, there it was: silence lying all around me like a shimmering expanse of stillness hanging in the summer morning air. It was like a reward sent to congratulate me. The whole space was shimmering in silence, and I was sitting inside that space. I felt like the silence went right through me. I felt like I had won the lottery. My hell was over. My deepest wish had been granted. I sat still again and listened. Yes. Silent. Still there. It was like the whole room was smiling at me. Full of energy I ran downstairs to meet Mum and Grandpa already at the breakfast table.

"It's gone. It's gone! Can you believe it? It has gone! The ringing in my ears has stopped. It's gone away. I can hear silence."

"No!? Really? Oh come here!" Mum stood up and gave me a long, hug. "I'm so happy for you, darling." Grandpa was seriously ill now and needed help getting around, but he managed to stand up and give me a hug too.
"Well done Cowboy Hill," he said. "You deserve it after all the hell you've been through. Crikey!"

I was so happy I ran outside to the bottom of the garden and caught my breath underneath the pear tree that was covered in white blossom.

"My tinnitus has gone," I yelled at the field. I waited one moment and listened out, just to double check, and yes, it was still silent. "I can't bloody believe it!" I yelled across the gardens. "It's goooooooooone!" I cried out stretching my arms out and looking up into the deep blue sky.

Then a penny dropped. It was one of those moments when suddenly something came to me and fell into place. An idea came to me, out of the ether. I didn't have the idea. It came to me. I remember it was that way round. It entered my space. I found myself with hands in praying position, saying out loud:
"If I can do it, then so can others." I stopped for a moment and let this surprising idea sink in.
"If I can do it, then so can others," I said out loud again, daring to make the thought seem more possible.

My voice started taking on a serious tone.
"I vow to do my best to help others let go of their tinnitus." I took a breath.
"I vow to help others let go of their tinnitus. I vow to help others let go of their tinnitus! If I can do it, so can they!" Although my audience was made up of trees, grass and the warm summer morning, my message was for tinnitus people.

"It IS possible. I knew it!" I started yelling defiantly.
"Sod them! They are wrong. I knew it. It IS possible to let go of bloody tinnitus." I had tears streaming down my face.

In my body I felt something aligning with the top of my crown that went right through my spine and down into the ground. I felt centred and in the right place at last. My feet stood firmly on the ground. It was one of those alignments that would hold sway and form a fulcrum for years to come.

Chapter 10 The Sound of a New Life

Autumn Cottage, West Sussex, 2000

Thirty spokes join one hub.
The wheel's use comes from emptiness.

Clay is fired to make a pot.
The pot's use comes from emptiness.

Windows and doors are cut to make a room.
The room's use comes from emptiness.

Therefore,
Having leads to profit,
Not having leads to use.

Lao-Tzu
Tao Te Ching 11 (Addiss & Lombardo)

I put small fliers in the village shop saying that I was a student looking to work with people who had tinnitus. I wrote that I had cured my own tinnitus with Craniosacral Therapy and was interested in helping others do the same. My practice became full almost immediately. Although I was charging student rates, it was such a relief to start earning money again. I loved working from the little room at the back of Autumn Cottage looking over the rose-bed down the long garden to the field and woods beyond.

Being a Craniosacral Therapist turned out to be calm and peaceful work and often left me feeling much better too, as well as the client. It was extremely satisfying and a great privilege to feel people letting go and dropping into a deep stillness.

At the start of the session, I would take up contact with the body and feel agitation and buzzing in some places and numbness in others; there would be a general sense of disharmony with lots of different things going on, all at loggerheads with each other. Then, very much like a conductor working with an out of tune orchestra, I would provide a steady hand and leave it there. Over the course of a few minutes this would call all the different body parts, with their chaotic pushes and pulls back into one point of unison and focus. Sitting with the contact and deepening over the course of an hour, much of the wrangling and buzzing between areas of abrupt contrast would slowly start to melt away and harmonise, coming together into a more coherent shape.

Sometimes there would be a sudden release like several bubbles giving way at once, leaving a much freer and more comfortable feeling with greater elasticity, ease and balance. Once everything joined up into a unison hum of body co-operation, sometimes the whole system would drop into stillness. When this happened it was like magic. A resulting sense of peace would radiate through the client's body and permeate the whole room, filling it with a palpable sense of stillness.

After all the stress and disturbance I had been through over the last few years, to find work that dropped me and my clients into a deep state of calm was awe-inspiring, and like daily nectar. I found myself looking forward to meeting the steady flow of interesting people who arrived stressed out and tetchy, and under my hands felt like jumpy electric jelly. After an hour they would then floated off, smooth and calm inside with a big smile on their faces and really grateful. Giving cranial work was really satisfying and it was a great pleasure feeling health radiate out of people more and more. Over the weeks people would come back stronger and more centred, and then they would pay me for this! I felt very lucky to be doing this work.

At first I was eager to please and enthusiastically went the extra mile, wanting the people on the couch to benefit as much as I had. But with experience I dared to sit back and relax, and let the work do the work. Doing less really is more, it turns out. Learning to be a good Craniosacral Therapist in the first few years involves not interfering with a person's system. The more you understand that the natural organising force of health is there, the more you can let it radiate through. Hard as it is for the mental self to accept, if you give space to someone by taking up an allowing contact, spines straighten themselves, minds go quiet and aches and pains subside. Experience teaches you this. It took me years to come to terms with this. Bodies are the greatest teachers for the people they contain within them. Bodies reveal, day after day, that there is a force of health at work and it knows what is best.

I started to learn that coherence is stronger than chaos. For hours every day, bodies of all shapes and sizes kept revealing this to me over and over again. All I had to do was just relax and let go and, between my hands, the weaker forces of chaos would let go back into a larger pattern of coherence and health. Over time resistance starts to gently melt away leaving us feeling more open and connected.

It took me thousands of hours to learn that it is the body that turns the head off, and not the other way round. Thinking won't turn off thinking. A head cannot turn itself off. It is the body that turns off the thinking. Learning to hang out inside the body and sustain attention there, spending time noticing the feelings inside our own skin-bag of experience, this is what allows the wretched twitter of the mind to switch off. In turn, as my own twitter started to slow down and switch off, it was wonderful to realise that I could spend longer periods of time with no particular train of thought rushing through my head and taking over. Instead I could just stay in touch with body sensations and surf through on the top of them in quite an awake and relaxed state of mind. I could just walk down the garden and feel my feet on the grass, smell the smell of roses, feel the sun on my face and see the trees around me without getting lost in thought. There was a body there experiencing all these things, and I was there too, but I was learning gradually not to put too much of a spin on things.

At the end of sessions, either giving or receiving, I would come round with no drama going on in the head. The usual "Julian programme" was not running. The stage was empty. There was no show on. For a few precious moments as I was standing there with my hands on the client's feet and he or she was lying peacefully on the couch, there was nothing much going on except awareness. There was awareness of being in a room, in a body, someone else was there too; there was nothing to be careful of. There was nothing to defend against or be wary of. Things felt safe, open and connected. Awareness was sensing openly through the hands, through the bodies, through the eyes, through the feet. Nothing needed gathering together and turning into a sense of "me." Experience was relaxed and open and gently all encompassing. There was a sense of being there and being alive but there was no need to apply an internal dialogue and interpret and comment on what was going on. A much more bare mind was there, not getting covered over in too much thinking, and this seemed to give both me and the person I was treating a sense of peace. The openness of this experience was calm and still, and spread out gently into the room. And then I would look at the clock and need to bring the session to an end.

And there we both were again. Out of an open interconnected awareness where self has melted away, within seconds we had rebooted our "me programmes" and the twitter had restarted and we were easing back into behaving and thinking in the usual way again. By the time I took payment and walked whoever it was back to the car, the mind was once again buried back in show time: the Julian show: "Gosh I hope that session helped them. I should have spent more time around the sacrum. Did I bring them round too abruptly? Will the next client arrive on time? Maybe they have got lost." Once again I was back to spraying the neutral world with the same old shit.

After nearly two decades of this work I have developed a fascination for this deep state of peace at the end of sessions where no trains of thought are taking over. There is a blissfully empty mind, a calm body and no apparent stress anywhere. In this calm there seems to be an awareness of something going on in an open space, which is not attached to anything in particular. It is not empty like a void, but full of presence.

It's a little bit like waking up and finding yourself hanging in the middle of a vast sense of stillness radiating out in all directions. This is not a dream. It is there, palpable like a heavenly balm. We all know this experience. And yet, for some reason, we choose to abandon this big, sky-like feeling floating through us, and, shrink back down to a small body again, finding ourselves sitting up, on the edge of the couch, and turn back into me again. Before we know it, we trundle back down Same-old Same-old St. and produce the same thing all over again, for the millionth time.

Haven't we all had enough of this stuff? Don't we know what the next sentence is likely to be? Why do we leave the open fields and clear blue skies of an empty mind to turn back down into the terrible cul-de-sac of me? It's like watching the same soap opera again and again every day. Who in their right mind would go to a show in the West End and watch it ten thousand times? Do we really have to become "me" again every moment of every day?

Thoughts come along and pop into our heads like trains pulling into a station. What happens if we sit back and let these thoughts arrive without jumping onto them? So there I am standing at the gate, wondering where my next client is. Along comes a train of thought that is worried that maybe they have got lost. This thought appears. The doors open. For a split second I have a choice: either I can jump onto the train of thought and get carried away with it, imagining clients flying into a rage as they get more and more lost or maybe missing the session completely. Alternatively, I can just take a breath, and come back to my feet on the ground and look around me and get my bearings back. The extraordinary thing is, that if I stay with my immediate experience, the train doors close and the thought just pulls off, out of the station. I have a very real choice. I can get hijacked by these thoughts or I just stand back on the platform, take a breath and see that the trains of thought just go by themselves.

My teacher repeated this over and over again for years before I finally got it. Just come back to the breath, be aware or where you are, relax and the thoughts go all by themselves. We don't need to do anything. When a thought comes along and the train doors open, don't jump in and get lost, just come back to where you are. It is really that simple. So, in a calm state, standing next to the gate of Autumn

Cottage, instead of fretting about clients wrapping cars around trees or arriving late and yelling at me in a fluster, or worrying about them not being able to pay, and my body correspondingly tensing up and bracing itself, I learnt slowly to just stand there and look at Church St gently sloping up through the village, enjoy the smell of the honeysuckle and feel the warm sun on my face. As I did this, not surprisingly, my body relaxed too.

In the small garden room by the roses, watching the wrens and blackbirds jumping from branch to branch, I was able to sit back and notice how thoughts pass by like distant trains rattling across the countryside. They just appear out of nowhere, disturb the peace for a few moments with their clickety-clack before disappearing out of sight, letting peace re-establish itself once again.

To be honest, before I did the Craniosacral Therapy training, I had no idea how lost in "me" I was. I had no idea that there was any alternative. I had never experienced calm before and quite literally had spent most of my life locked inside a hurricane of thinking. My head was trapped inside its own circular drama and my body was numb and shut down. So discovering that the mind was a big, still, empty space with no thinking going on inside it was a big shock for me.

There are a million different ways to access this sense of stillness or vast calm, and my own particular path took me down the Craniosacral Therapy route. However, most body-based therapies and meditation practices can help the mind open out and access the big stillness that is sitting with you and me right now, waiting here for us to recognise it. For you, it could be walking in the woods, or going on retreat to a Zen monastery or dropping into a deep state of calm during a wonderful tai chi session. For someone else, their enclosed bubble of self could burst while painting a beautiful oceanic landscape or tending a baby and sensing its heavenly energy. When we are very aware and connected, and engaged in a peaceful state, we can access a much healthier mind here waiting for us.

This new job as a Craniosacral Therapist was specifically forcing me to slow down and focus on the body. The more I did this the more I discovered space inside my body. I was spending hours feeling the client's body space too. These spaces were constantly changing shape and quality. Sometimes the body feels long and thin, other times it feels short and wide. A big revelation to me was that internal experience is constantly shifting and changing shape all the time. When we focus on this internal experience, thoughts can fall away. When thoughts fall away, and the head clears, there is just a sense of space.

Once in a while something truly awe-inspiring happened. At times, when both the client and I had dropped into stillness, the resulting calm in the room seemed to become unusually strong and palpable, as if the whole space around was starting to join in. This tended to happen when both of us were deeply relaxed and were focussing gently on our bodies. The more we settled, the more an experience of presence would fill into the room. When two bubbles of awareness burst into a larger one, sometimes something much bigger would then coming into play. Instead of feeling locked up inside a separate body, a shared experience opened out and there was a palpable sense of much more being there than just us in the room.

From this joint-experience the larger space would very noticeably start to join in, ebbing and flowing gently yet strongly, interacting with our bodies and minds like a powerful, interactive field. At times it felt like giant magnets had settled over the crown of the head and beneath the sacrum, and were reorganising our midlines like iron filings falling into place. A heightened sense of awareness would gently switch on bringing with it a new level of awareness, like accessing to a highly interactive matrix. We started being able to sense each other's state incredibly well, sometimes with breath-taking clarity.

If one of us moved an arm gently, a sensation would ripple through the web of awareness that the other could sense directly. This presence caused us both to sit up and pay more attention, and was immediately humbling. We both found ourselves being fascinated and wanting to go stiller and see more. As things went calmer still, if we each had a deliberate thought or intention this felt like it was interfering somehow and sent jarring ripples through space. So we spontaneously found ourselves letting go and simply allowing things to unfold with less and less resistance.

The more we relaxed into this now quite powerful organising force, the more the experience intensified. I was not able to read the client's mind, but I was able to get a strong sense of him or her. I could directly sense a shared body-experience and quality of mind that was immediately reciprocated and completely mutual. So if my client felt tightness in her chest, I too felt it in mine. If we both hung out with this experience for a few minutes then somehow it lightened and then dissipated altogether. It turns out that a problem shared, when there is open awareness, really is a problem spared. This forms the basis of Eugene Gendlin's work on Focussing, and provides a transformational way of working that brings about real change.

Entering into joint experience, the mind starts to make itself aware to us. It is not "My Mind" that I am aware of, maybe it is more the "big mind" that is aware of me. This awareness gently makes itself known more and more to whoever is open to it. This is not a cognitive, thinking thing. This is awareness itself that is there anyway, irrespective of what we are creating in our made up theatre of thought. The big mind is the subject and we are the object. If we sit and wait for the wretched thinking to stop taking centre stage we can discover that awareness has been there all the time, with or without our thinking getting in the way of it.

So in this way, sometimes when I sit with clients, and we both settle and let go, there is an increase in potency like a stronger magnetic field that passes right down our spines. It is like we are both being spring-cleaned, or reconfigured in a really healthy way. This happens effortlessly like it has been waiting to happen for years. An increased vital energy fills the vertical midlines and feels bright and clear like we have plugged into a potent healthy force. When this is strong enough, the light or energy arcs from one crown of the head to another like interconnecting aurora borealis. Sometimes there is a sense of this energy spanning out into a space quite a long way. A most wonderful depiction on this state can be seen in the breath-taking work of Alex Grey, "Sacred Mirrors: The Visionary Art of Alex Grey," in particular The Universal Mind Lattice, which you can also see on-line.

When we are sitting together in this very energetic kind of way, the moment we even think about bringing the session to an end, this interactive energy field gently fades away, and the space around us starts to feel emptier again. But we both leave the space feeling stronger and clearer in the body with a better connection to the ground, and a spine that feels like it is standing taller. Knowing that this experience is possible means there is the possibility of it happening again.

Working hands on, when the movement in the body settles, and the space opens up into a larger holding field, we drop into the Long Tide, an almost mystical experience where the sense of self melts away and the awareness moves from the body out into the field beyond. These organising forces bring a sense of great energy, and clarity, and the body has what can only be described as sort of energetic purge and realignment at the same time. This is where the Breath of Life manifests and makes itself known to the body and mind. The Tibetans call this the "Unconditioned Winds of the Vital Forces."

As a Craniosacral therapist, to get to the long-tide, you shift the focus from local body-based awareness, where the practitioner may be palpating a body part, such as the lower leg or the liver, out into an awareness of the entire body, where the shape of the whole body can be felt to expand and contract gently. Then, the practitioner needs to be aware of his or her own body, and that of the client lying on the table. Then, from this whole body awareness, we need to open out to include the larger space by sensing the atmosphere in the room, for example. If both systems are close to stillness it becomes much more likely for the long-tide to emerge. The mind needs to be calm and clear enough to detect it. If it is full of its usual, daily twitter, then it is easy to miss. In the Long Tide there may be a very subtle, slow expanding and contracting of the shapes over the course of a few minutes. The experience of movement almost shimmers in and out of the stillness like a mirage. Sometimes the whole room may feel like it is expanding and stretching very gently, as if space itself were moveable and was being breathed very, very slowly. Sometimes the very bedrock we are sitting on, or the building of a sacred place we are meditating in, or the room in which we are doing cranial work can open up and feel more like a vast empty space full of evanescent form floating in space.

Whenever the long-tide arises it is utterly humbling to witness and deeply revitalising and pleasurable to work with on so many levels. There is a sense that whatever these forces are that exist both within and beyond us, they work way beyond our ken. Our work as Craniosacral Therapists is to become aware of them, get out of the way and let them take effect. When this happens, the mind slows down, the resistance falls away and the body becomes incredibly comfortable. Things just feel in the right place.

For me, the first few experiences of the long-tide gave me a direct experience of feeling like I was on the right track at last, and acted like stepping stones of peace carrying me through the turbulence of life on a journey towards stillness and then silence. The more I experienced moments of deep peace that first manifested through the long-tide, the more a sense of calm seemed to take root, and the harder it became for the tinnitus to make a come back. Quite literally the Long Tide reveals that the world is hard and physical and measurable, and yet, at the same time, energetic and immeasurable at the same time.

At first these experiences were extraordinary for me, and left me in complete awe of the body and mind, and what is possible. But over time I learned to accept that what was happening was absolutely normal and part of our nature. If only we could all just sit safely and quietly together and put our hands gently on each other's heads or sacrums and wait. This would allow us to settle, drop into stillness and let the bigger awareness manifest through us and connect us to a deeper state of well-being. You can try this for yourself. You can have a couple of Craniosacral Therapy sessions and really note how the practitioner takes up contact with your sacrum. Then lie head to tail with your partner on a bed, when you are both in a good place, and with your right hand, take up contact with each other's sacrum and wait. After ten minutes you may feel much calmer, clearer in the head and far more comfortable in the body. If you let go, deepen and allow the natural forces to work through you, you may reach the Long Tide. I hope you do. It is amazing. If we all allowed this to happen, our days would become much more peaceful and pleasant.

To help ease Tinnitus in clients I learned to place my hands on either side of the ears and become as calm and clear as possible in myself first. Then I would wait, sometimes for ten minutes or so for the buzzy vibrational charge to show itself. Literally I would start to detect a high frequency pulsating more and more clearly between my fingers, because if you pay attention, you will find that the tissues, bones, and structures between the hands are literally vibrating and pulsing. Once I had tuned into this vibration and allowed it to engage with the calm of my hands as directly as possible, the buzz would gradually, over another ten minutes or so, discharge and become less intense. It is a bit like your hands functioning as low-grade, lightening-conductors and the client's activation or charge dissipates into this hand contact. Another description is that you drop into stillness and let the buzzy charge of your client dissipate back into this stillness.

When this buzzy charge between the ears calms down, clients frequently report the sound of tinnitus backing off or becoming less intense or sometimes going away completely. It was immensely satisfying to witness. Ten minutes doesn't sound like a long time, but it is important to bring a lot of present-time awareness into the contact. Only years of practice as a therapist or meditator helps you develop the important skill of learning to stay in contact with experience with sustained attention without being distracted by analysis, judgement or diagnosis. The mental really gets in the way of this kind of work. We need to stay with the experiential.

With practice I learned to hang out with finer and more sensitive levels of body-based awareness until it felt like the focus was dancing on tiny nerve endings, or along membranes or on the unchanging stillness that underlies all movement itself within the body. I was often mesmerised by the unfolding process and couldn't believe what was being presented to me for hours every day. As thousands of hours or practice started building up I found that there was a stillness there that acted more and more as the main resource and true fulcrum and ground for this kind of work.

Of course an occasional session came along that didn't go quite so well. I remember asking one man to relax his head. He was lying down on the couch.

"This is the most relaxed you are going to get me," he replied. His head was sticking out into the air and was rigid like a statue. "Please can you lower your head onto my hands... I need to feel a sense of traction against the back of your head to do the work."
"Oh, ok then," he said, pushing his head down onto my hands abruptly. "Is that better?" he asked.
"Yes," I replied, feeling him forcing his head into my hands. Then, a moment later, to my surprise his head lifted off my hands and sprang back up into the air again.
"Are you relaxed just now?" I asked, marvelling at the acute level of tension in the body.

"Very relaxed, thanks," he confirmed.

"Oh! OK then," I replied, collusively.

Suffice to say that the cranial contact didn't do much good, and I referred him on to a deep-tissue masseur. Thank God for Rolfers or stronger handed therapies when you need them.

My practice filled with a huge variety of aches, pains and emotional upsets. People cried, shook, coiled up into balls, snored, dissociated and mostly just relaxed deeply. Some turned up in posh cars, on bicycles, or with walking sticks; others arrived with dogs, and kids. Some were immaculately dressed and wore the finest colognes; others were scruffy and a bit smelly. But I just threw the windows open and changed the couch cover and ploughed on through, quite happily.

After graduation I set up a practice in London and sent an article "The Sound of Silence," off to the Standard talking about how Craniosacral Therapy can help tinnitus back off. To my amazement, they published it, and paid me £350 for the privilege. Over the next few months I was inundated with nearly a hundred and fifty new clients. It was far too much to manage, but served as a baptism of fire for my practice and provided a vertical learning curve. Incredibly that one article still produced clients even ten years later.

The only clinic that had space for me to work in was on Harley St, in central London. There I worked with people from all walks of life, including the rich and famous. Most people felt very relaxed and much better after the sessions but not everyone's tinnitus backed off soon enough for them to continue with therapy. Consequently an impatience for immediate results led them elsewhere. Let's hope they eventually settled with something, instead of flitting from one thing to a next, which a lot of people in fight or flight tend do to.

Most tinnitus people seemed to be looking for a quick fix. I soon realised that that was not what I was offering. Fortunately a natural vetting system takes effect in one's practice, and people quickly sense if an approach is not right for them.

One man came in, sat down, and immediately started grimacing at me with wide staring eyes.

"How can I help you?" I asked.

"I hate therapists," he declared. He was breathing quickly and his face was red and sweaty.

"Oh really? Um. That's a shame."

He stared furiously at me like a wild boar that was about to tusk me.

"How can I help you?" I asked innocently.

"Help me? Do you really think you can help then?" he challenged.

"Er yes. Cranial work was the thing that most helped my tinnitus back off."

"Well I think it sounds like a load of old bollocks!" he said, looking like was enjoying himself suddenly.

"Um, look… Do you really want to have a session here?"

"No, not really."

"Well maybe we should leave it then," I ventured.

"I think so!" he said, with a downturned mouth like a shark. With that, he got up and stomped towards the door. Then he turned around and shouted: "I sincerely hope you don't think I'm going to pay you!"

"Please don't worry about that. I think I'll take a lunch break now. OK?" I offered, wishing him out of the space as quickly as possible.

"Fuck off!" I heard him boom from beyond the door.

For a moment I wondered what abuse, neglect, or misfortune must have befallen that man to lead to this kind of behaviour. It was such a shame we couldn't get to the table. Sometimes calm hand-contact can by-pass all the drama and directly drop people into calmer states. Bodies are often better at sensing safety than thinking minds.

Sometimes opening a practice to the general public can be jarring, even shocking. Answering the door a bit too abruptly, or getting up to let a delivery in, or opening a window can bring up deep-seated feelings of rage, resentment or rejection that can end the therapeutic relationship on the spot. I have been taken completely off guard a few times when, out of nowhere, hatred has appeared, bashing down on my head like a broomstick, leaving me trembling and with no idea what on earth I had done wrong. Having a good emotional dump and then scarpering helps us all find our boundaries.

If someone arrives like a grenade I have learned to shut down to avoid going into shock. Being energetically open and aware can be very hard work, especially when I have to spend hours processing my reaction to the uncontained blast of baggage afterwards. Fortunately this is rare, and most people find great benefit from the work.

The upside is that some people have walked through the door to have life-changing experiences. Eye-sight has improved so much so, that, clients have seen their partner and home in a completely new light. Stutters has vanished in one session, intense long-term pain has lifted and nightmares and fears that have bugged people for years just fizzle out.

I started encouraging taxi-drivers to do body-based focussing in their taxis in their lunch breaks. Sometimes clients of mine who were wives relaxed so much their husbands made complaints when their homes fell into disarray. I wasn't going to apologise for that.

In my growing confidence I started giving talks on Craniosacral Therapy at local tinnitus groups. I learned that tinnitus was directly linked to the fight or flight response and that when we run on too much on adrenaline, fear or exhaustion, our hearing starts to listen out for danger and becomes far too switched on or hypersensitive. Eventually we end up listening out so acutely that we not only hear the noise of the external world around us, but also tune into the buzz of our nervous system. Quite literally our ears are so hypersensitive that we end up listening to the noise of our nervous system. It all started making sense and falling into place.

I learned that when we are well, calm and settled, our hearing switches off and becomes extremely good at ignoring things. We can stay at a hotel and ignore the air-conditioning, we can fall asleep at a party despite the loud laughing and dancing around us. But if we become anxious or terrified, our ears can open out like giant antennae and listen out for danger. If we stay stuck in this super-alert state of hearing for too long, we will often end up tuning into and detecting the nervous impulses along our own auditory pathways, or other sounds inside the body.

I found out that Heller and Bergman in 1953 did an experiment where they put a hundred people individually into a silent room and asked them to report any sound they heard from a speaker. No sound was played, and yet ninety of them developed tinnitus just by listening out more acutely. They inadvertently ended up hearing the buzz of their own nervous system. This reminded me of my father taking me out to the silence of the Saudi Arabian desert and how I first heard tinnitus there because I was desperately trying to hear something out in the silent desert.

Once I was starting to understand how tinnitus worked I phoned up a local tinnitus researcher to confirm various hunches that I had been following. I guess I was looking for validation at the time.

I asked her, "If tinnitus is just a fight or flight response in our hearing then surely if we lower our adrenaline levels then tinnitus well get better. I believe tinnitus is directly linked to the fight or flight response."

"Yes that's right," came the reassuring reply. She talked for a minute or so confirming what I had felt for a while.

"Gosh, that's great. Thanks so much for talking to me. That explains why all the Craniosacral Therapy work I've been having has made me much better."

"What therapy did you say?"

"Craniosacral Therapy. It's a gentle hands-on therapy. It has saved my life."

"Oh is that one of those alternative practices then?"

"Yes. It's been an amazing."

"Oh I see… Well, all the best then," and with that she rang off.

I was really encouraged by this acknowledgement. At a talk I was giving near Brighton I was enthusing about how the treatment worked and how it had helped me. And at the end of the talk I mentioned this researcher's name and said that she had agreed that lowering the levels of adrenaline would help tinnitus back off. At that moment a man raised his eyebrows, got up and stormed out. The next day I received an irate phone call.

"Is that Julian Cowan Hill?"

"Yes."

"I hear that you were quoting me at a talk you gave recently." It was that female therapist again.

"What? Er, I just said you agreed that lowering the adrenaline levels helped tinnitus."

"Well I am really not happy about you doing this without my permission. You have confirmed all my worst fears about alternative practitioners. You are unprofessional and unscientific!"

"What? I'm sorry. I had no intention of causing any offence."

"Well you have. I want you to write to each one of the members you gave a talk to and tell them that you did not receive my permission to mention my name, and I want to be in no way professionally associated with you, do you hear? Tell them that we have no connection with each other and apologise to them. Do you understand?" and with that she slammed the phone down.

I was gobsmacked. I had no idea that alternative practitioners had any kind of reputation at all, and I didn't realise that I needed permission to mention anyone's name when being positive about what could help a symptom like tinnitus. In my mind we were all trying to do our best to help people with tinnitus and that was all that mattered. But I understood where the researcher was coming from and took the appropriate action. However I felt a bit shaken for a few days.

Cranial work is hard to get your head round at first, as it is primarily an experiential body-based practice rather than a cognitive mental science. Instead of trying to explain the work scientifically to a heady critic who may have read a few things off the internet, it was much easier and far less time consuming to say, "Just lie down, please, and let me show you." Often doctors and audiologists had really interesting experiences when I gave them a demonstration. However, if this work did not fit in with their paradigm then it was quickly forgotten about or dismissed as unusual or esoteric. I had to remind myself just how long it took me to get my own head around this natural and albeit very human way of working, simply because it was not in the mainstream of health care or medical education yet.

Given the extraordinary advances of Western Medicine with each decade, it is mind-boggling how much the power of safe hands-on contact is still underrated in health care. I remember reading about an two orphanages in Romania where one lot of babies survived and the others died. The only difference was that the former group of babies were picked up and cuddled regularly. Babies can die with no hands on contact. Adults relax and calm down deeply with safe, careful touch. Finding safety in contact can cause our anxieties to drop down and for our way of relating to people to soften and feel more comfortable. The NHS, however, would rather spend millions of pounds each year on expensive, long-term medication.

The conversation with the researcher came as a bit of a slap in the face when I was still a novice. At the time I was planning on setting up a research project with the Craniosacral Therapy Association of the UK. I had been looking into the complicated and intricate process of setting up our own medical research project. But because I had literally just graduated, I decided to knuckle down and just stick to helping people get better. I needed to get more experience under my belt first, before standing up and sharing my experience with the powers that be in the tinnitus world.

I was very busy in Harley St and wanted to open up another practice to accommodate the many enquiries coming forward for help with tinnitus. I spoke to the manager of the clinic where I worked and asked if she minded me working somewhere else on Harley St too. She said she didn't mind, as long as I didn't take the clients in his practice elsewhere. But when she found out that I was renting a room within a mile of her practice she took umbrage and confiscated all my client files and refused to pay the outstanding £600 she owed me. Most of my practice was hijacked and confiscated overnight. She farmed those clients out to another practitioner and I moved elsewhere. But I was glad to get away from her money grubbing hands, and constant demands for more clients and me putting my price up.

Gradually a high-pitched squeak crept back in to my life again. At the time I thought it was the stress of setting up a new business, and coming up against professional bullies and greedy thieves, or having too many clients early on in my practice that brought the tinnitus back. However, it turned out that I had to solve two more pieces of the puzzle before knocking tinnitus on the head for good.

For a while now I had been dealing with quite bizarre symptoms. If I ate any sweets, cheese or mushrooms, or drank alcohol I would feel incredibly tired. I would often get white spots appearing on my tongue and often felt sluggish with tingling hands and feet. On holiday in France, after a particularly fantastic bottle of Gigondas and a tangy and delicious lemon tart with raspberry coulis, I nearly feinted and had to lie down. I could barely move. I had become sluggish, and felt like I couldn't think straight and kept falling asleep all the time. Something was wrong.

I went to see a nutritionist who told me that it was very likely I had candidiasis. As a child I had been put on antibiotics practically every winter and ate an endless supply of chocolates, biscuits and cake.

"Why don't you get rid of your Candida? I am sure this will help. If you think tinnitus is linked to the stress response in the body, surely constantly fighting off a permanent yeast infection the whole time will keep your tinnitus there."

Another light bulb lit up in my head.

"Do you know, I think you are right. Can you really get rid of Candida?"

"Of course you can," she said. "You have had far too many antibiotics in your life and are clearly addicted to yeast promoting foods to keep feeding the yeast overgrowth. Starve the Candida of these foods and it will die off."

"Really. I thought it was a long-term condition."

"It is if you don't deal with it!" she said frankly. "You won't like it at first. There are quite strong side effects. But keep going and I bet you anything you will feel much better, you will have much more energy, and your ringing will stop."

I took heed of what she said and went on a strict Candida diet cutting out all sugar, yeast, fermented foods and drinks, sweet fruit and processed foods. I bought a Candida cook-book which made the whole process just about bearable. I learnt to do all my cooking in the morning, making a giant stew in winter or a giant salad in summer and ate it throughout the day. I didn't even eat cornflakes because they contained sugar.

It was hard work. After a few weeks I started to get really strong withdrawal symptoms and started craving sugar like it was a drug. I read a book called "Poison," and another book called "Lick the Sugar Habit," which shocked me with devastating facts about how damaging sugar was for the health. I had no idea that sugar messes with mineral uptake in bones, and is highly addictive and damages our immune system. I was encouraged to hear that giving up sugar causes your immune system to strengthen by 16 per cent in just 24 hours. I had been a sugar-junkie all my life.

I got off to a flying start with my new sugar-free life. But after about four weeks I went through a mini-hell. I hit the Candida die-off period when all the yeast overgrowth started to be leached out of the body. I had terrible headaches and woke up in cold sweats every night for a good week or so and started shaking and trembling for days on end. I was irritable as hell and horrible to be around. Then one day the inner struggle stopped. I felt calm and clear inside and I started being nice to people again. As the sugar craving subsided I developed an aversion to sweet things. I remember tasting lemon juice on pasta and thinking how sweet the pasta tasted.

But the best news was that the low level tinnitus that had seeped back into my life faded very gently over this period without me really noticing. It had become such a non-issue that it was a bit like being able to feel my socks. If you asked me if I could feel my socks, I would probably have said yes.
If you asked me if I had felt my socks all day, I would have said no. If I focused on the tinnitus I was able to find it, but it was so low, so why would I bother. I had better things to do. But a few months into the Candida diet, one day I realised that it had gone away completely and that I couldn't hear it even in a totally quiet room.

The Candida diet definitely helped knock my tinnitus into orbit. It released a layer of stress in my system and left me feeling much more awake, clear-headed and with more energy. The constant tingling feeling in my wrists and ankles fell away, and the brain fog, that I had been living with for years, cleared. This was the beginning of the prolonged period of no tinnitus at all that I have lived in ever since. Of course a bad cold, extreme stress or loud-noise exposure can bring it back briefly, but for all intents and purposes my tinnitus had gone. By gone, I mean silent head in a silent room.

Chapter 11 The End of Sound

London and Dartmoor, Devon 2004

I have come here
To lay my head at your feet,
To ask forgiveness,
To sit in the rose chair
And burn my thorns.

Whatever I thought to do,
When I am here with you, is nothing.

I come to weep.
There is no escape from grief.

Rumi
The Talking

The term scapegoat is applied to individuals and groups who are accused of causing misfortune. Scapegoating means finding those who can be identified with evil, blamed for it, and cast out from the family or the community in order to leave the remaining members with a feeling of guiltlessness.

Sylvia Brinton Perera
The Scapegoat Complex: Toward a Mythology of Shadow and Guilt

I stayed on a strict candida diet for two years and my tinnitus went away completely. I thought it had gone forever. My body grew stronger and the cloud of tiredness that followed me everywhere started to clear, leaving a brighter mind that seemed to work better! I got so used to not eating that hideous and highly addictive hormone called sugar that my regular treks across London to Artisan du Chocolat, Charbonnel & Walker, and Rococo dwindled to a lonely tasting of bitter cocoa nibs or a very infrequent chunk of a 100% pure cocoa bar with no sugar.

I lived in silence all the time and when I remembered my tinnitus it seemed like a bad dream. Strangely at first I almost missed the tinnitus. Living with a baddie for so long meant that I had got very used to this part of my life. To find it gone left me feeling a bit bereft, like something was missing. My life definitely felt a bit empty without this constant companion. For a while I went through that strange yet lovely phase of mental convalescence where you find yourself checking out on the tinnitus to see how it is, only to find is gone, over and over again. It was like waking up after a bad dream several times a day. I kept on rediscovering that life was good again. But as the months eased by, even this pattern started to peter out and I stopped checking. I had got used to it not being there. There was nothing to hold onto any more and I just started to get on happily with my life.

Working with clients meant that I dipped back into memories of tinnitus all the time, but this felt like it came from a previous chapter of my life. I was no longer a tinnitus person. In fact there was very little of the tinnitus Julian left. These days I would walk down the street and my feet would be walking along the street too, feeling the feet on the pavement. My spine would walk down the street too, sensing the world from my centre with a chest moving along facing the world, and limbs rocking and swinging along enjoyably, carrying me through space. Somewhere up there, at the top of the body, the head would move around, smelling, hearing and looking at the world too. As I walked along, the world changed around me and my inside reacted in tandem. It was a real-time flowing experience with only a bit of chit chat going on in my head.

Tinnitus Julian would walk from one end of the street to the other locked inside his head and thoughts. If you had asked me anything about that street, most of it would have gone by largely unnoticed. However, I would have been able to tell you all about arguments I was having in my head, or no end of negative dialogues about how shitty life was, or mistakes I had made, or endless grumbles about the people I lived with. I was locked inside a prison of thought that was almost entirely cut of from the street along which I was walking.

That half-empty, imploded-in, victim-Julian had gone. These days a happier, lighter, body-based Julian was there, moving from one experience into another, surfing through life's changing vistas and interactions more freely, not knowing what was coming, but ready to respond. Things felt much more immediate, interactive and alive. Of course I had moments when I would get stuck, feel sad or down and fall back into my family default position: its my fault. But the periods of being emotionally bogged down would clear after days rather than weeks. When the blues pushed in it was like a bank of fog that I knew would lift.

Work was going well. In my practice I was busy and was attracting a lot of traumatised clients. So I signed up for a training for Craniosacral Therapists working with shock and trauma. Before I knew it I was on the train rattling past the beaches of Devon and in a taxi heading up onto the open space of Dartmoor. I went onto this course not really expecting to have any big surprises. But I would find out that there was one last piece of the puzzle that needed to fall into place before I could say I had finally cured myself of tinnitus.

The Karuna Institute is a Psychotherapy & Craniosacral Therapy Training Institute and Kum Nye Retreat Centre run by Maura and Franklyn Sills. They were both part of the Theravadin monastic Buddhist tradition and served as a monk and nun for years under Taungpulu Kaba Aye Sayadaw of Northern Burma. They learned a wonderfully body-based approach to the mind, which I was fortunate to have passed on to me. This grounded approach formed a firm foundation of Buddhist practice that has helped them both become the great teachers that they are today.

The Karuna Institute lies at the top of a long windy road that runs higher and higher through woods into the more remote parts of Dartmoor. A path just above the institute gardens trails along a trickling stream, past some woodland before rising past sheep and wild ponies grazing on the steep hillsides before opening out onto the vast, lonely space of the moors.

Walking into the manor house of Karuna is like walking into a deep, deep stillness. This stillness hangs in the air like a presence that means pretty much anything you think, say or do is somehow noticed. Even the cook in the kitchen takes care to chop quietly. There is a Buddha in the broom-cupboard and wise words written on the wall next to the toilet. This is the kind of place where intentions matter. Walk into Karuna and you meet your stuff.

As much as I loved the place, and took to lighting the fire, or gazing out across the garden to the shrubs and trees next to the pond at the bottom of the large lawn, for me Karuna was like walking into a hall of mirrors. My baggage kept on bursting open all over the place exposing childish needs, controlling behaviours and anger or rage I didn't know was there. People were really mindful of everything they said or did. They were really self-aware and accountable for themselves, which meant everywhere I turned I would walk straight into my own issues and find something really difficult about my life. For the first few days on each training, I would run into my undigested life experience and quickly feel emotionally bloated. Often I would head for the moors with a need for space to clear the air. For all these years I had been running away from my shit, and now it was time to face the music.

I was intimidated by Karuna at first, but gradually I saw that other students were meeting their stuff too, and that the people holding the space and looking after us were doing so with a strong, clear intention to help. They had plenty of compassion and personal experience to draw from, and this challenged me to take interactions and awareness to a new level. Although it was hard, and I struggled a lot, I had a sense that Karuna would provide the best kind of holding possible and was one of the best places in the country to go through this kind of training.

I was so locked up at first that I found it weird to even own that I had problems of my own. All the body-work had left me feeling so much better, but coming to terms with the kind of person I was, and to acknowledge what I had been through, this was a big jump for me. The first shock and trauma training I did at Karuna moved me from: "I'm fine, I am a good person, there is nothing wrong with me!" to a more wobbly: "Oh my God, I am not fine at all. I can't believe how in denial I have been. What am I like!?" Before I was a shiny Christmas bauble that presented well to the world, but this was in response to a horrible empty inside which I used to avoid at all costs. Now I was turning into more of a transparent mush that had a lot of pain and trouble inside, but there was some sense of change taking place.

The painful truth is that we all have to get in touch with what is inside first before we can let go of it and genuinely move on. We cannot let go of what we don't know. So the beginning of therapy can be hard because a lot of it is starting to see our own shit and hopefully, with the therapist's skill, being able to say, "OK shitty stuff, lets try and make friends with you!"

The shock and trauma training course I did at Karuna took place during the foot and mouth disease outbreak, which meant that we were not allowed to leave the institute and walk about on the moor. The tutors were very good at tending to our needs, and listened to us in that unusual, full-on, head to toe, open-hearted kind of way, which was a bit disarming at times. They responded to things that came up in a calm and respectful way creating a sense of safety that I just had not experienced before. Being safe with others in relationship was something mysterious and new for me, and brought my feelings flooding up to the surface.

I had grown up having to tip-toe around moodiness and anger, or trying to avoid being swamped by depression or a deep sense of dread and despair that hung in the home for years on end. I had learned that engaging with people meant either obeying them with a smiley face in order to avoid being told off, or cutting myself off into a bubble to protect myself from overwhelming demands. I was a lonely and invisible person that had no self-reference point, so consequently I needed constant validation and feedback from anyone or anything because there was very little else to go on.

So suddenly being with a group of people that acknowledged me, gave me space and let my feelings and responses just be there equally alongside everyone else's, was so revealing that my insides and their emotions felt like they were tipped out onto the table like a bag of unwanted viscera for everyone to see. Everyone else was fine and just let it be there.

Because I had grown up like a satellite floating around the orbits of my parents, much of my tendencies were only in response to someone else. So if nobody was making demands on me, there tended to be nothing there. My father was the sort of man who was always right and his mood held sway in the house like a prevailing weather system. God help you if you got in the way. I remember daring to challenge him for the first time, when I was 16 years old.

One afternoon, in our house on an RAF base-camp in Cranwell, Lincolnshire, Dad was doing a crossword. He had got stuck. I peered over his shoulder and offered:
"Transylvania is in Romania, I think."
"No it isn't, it is in Hungary."
"No its not. Its in Romania."
"I tell you, it is in Hungary."
"Dad, I know I'm right. I promise you, it is in Romania."
"Julian just shut it, will you."
"Dad, this is a crossword. Look it fits... They speak Hungarian in Transylvania. That's probably what you are thinking of, but I swear to you, it is in Romania."
"Don't you dare tell me what I am thinking. When are you going to learn?" Dad signed sanctimoniously, and picked up the paper and started reading it with pursed lips.
Like a dog with a bone, I walked over to the bookshelf, picked up the world atlas, opened it at the right page and then banged it onto the table where my father was sitting.
"What does that say, huh?" I said, pointing defiantly at the word: "Transylvania."
Dad looked down, grabbed the book and slammed it shut.
"I will NOT be spoken to like this."
"Dad! That's ridiculous! Can't you..."
"SHUT UP SONNY JIM. Just leave it!" he yelled.
Seething, I went back to my chair and realised that some people just have to be right, no matter what the cost.

Dad was very outspoken about his views and expected me to pay attention to the way he wanted me to think, how to speak, who to have relationships with, the kind of clothes to wear, what to do with money, and so on. It was often a bit of a shock for him if I dared do our own thing and live my own way.

The family dynamic was clear. There were those who tended to fall into the bossy, bullying camp, and those who tended to fall into victim mode. The bullies tended to

205

do things on their terms and ascended to the land beyond reproach. They were allowed to criticise, tease to your face and hand out requirements. The victims tended to tiptoe around them to avoid their wrath. I grew up in victim mode and learned quickly to sit quietly and fit in. If I acted out of line there would be days of moodiness as punishment, and I would feel deeply guilty, like I had committed a crime. If I spoke out then all hell would break loose. I often got steam-rolled, or if I disobeyed or exposed negative behaviour I would be ghosted or excommunicated for years at a time. So my whole being gently learned to sit pretty or fly beneath the radar to avoid conflict. As a coping strategy, I went invisible.

For years Granny was Dad's scapegoat and would receive a never-ending tirade of criticism. Then the buck was passed onto mum who received the relentless grilling and scathing attack. For a while Dad took it out on the God channel, and the TV received the ranting and eye-ball rolling incredulity, before, finally, the buck passed to me and I was placed in the unenviable position of being the family dumping ground and receptacle of disowned and unprocessed rage.

Years of therapy changed this dynamic. As soon as I was given equal rights by the therapist and provided with a safe and even playing ground, my rage surfaced like a volcanic eruption, needing years to process before finally simmering down to a cooler place. I stopped thinking everything was all my fault, and found a less distorted view of myself. Slowly I started believing in myself, and stayed firmly on a level playing field, which, of course went down like a lead balloon with the bullies. When one of them came along and started making demands, I found I could sit back into a delicious armchair of choice, put a finger onto my top lip, roll my eyes up to right and ask, "Errrrmm, do I really want to jump on a plane and be shouted at, ordered around, humiliated, torn to pieces, teased, or insulted?" I could simply take a deep breath, and ask that incredibly important question, that literally took me decades to learn to ask: "Mmmm. Do I want to or not?" "Errrrr let's just think about this for a while….." Finding that I actually did have a choice and didn't have to jump when I was told to, was a massive landmark for me. "Errrr no thanks. I'm not coming to the party. Bye."

Saying NO is not being selfish, as bullies would have you believe. It is simply being a different person, a person who is not doing as he or she is told. We all have our own unique viewpoints, needs and opinions, and they are all equal. Nobody is more important than another. When requirements are thrust upon you, take it or leave it, think about it, there is always choice, but please, never obey anyone. Obeying is power, not love. When you obey someone, you disappear. You stop loving yourself. Power and love are opposites.

Disobeying bullies brings a downside, unfortunately. If you don't do as you are told, then you risk being cut out. Either you fit onto their view of the world like a prosthetic limb and walk the way they want you to walk, or war breaks out. When I gave my own viewpoint, this was called: "answering back." If I complained, I was told I was being unbelievably petty, or if I tried to fight my corner to get some sense of fairness I was punished with relentless attack. But God help me if I pointed out a bully's fault or misdemeanour, for ended the relationship. Once, when I stood up to my father, we didn't speak to each other for seven years. For seven quiet years the finger in the South of Spain pointed at me. In London it didn't quite reach.

I went into the first training at Karuna largely unaware of all these patterns. Behind the shiny surface that I presented to the world I was terrified of people, and I found it incredibly hard to trust anyone. I was permanently bracing myself against attack. As we started working on each other my body could sense that I was in safe, good hands and to my great surprise started releasing shock. By shock I mean the undigested life experience locked away inside, started coming round and responding like a waking giant. My body literally started vibrating and twitching unnervingly.

On the second day I hit a wall of strong shock. I felt like my nerves were plugged into an ACDC current. I couldn't sit still I felt electric ants crawling and sparking over my head, down my spine and basically down to the end of every extremity. My legs were trembling and twitching and I could not focus or concentrate on anything. The only relief came from getting up and moving. I wanted to bolt.

"Excuse me, I've got to get out. I need to run," I said hastily, interrupting the lecture. Nobody minded. A couple of faces smiled back at me encouragingly.

I didn't care what the others felt. I had to escape. I shoved the door open and ran up the path that led to the moor. Some red and white tape was blocking access and reminded me: "Danger, keep out. Foot and mouth disease." So I turned around and ran back down to the institute in great frustration. I was buzzing inside and I couldn't keep still. Fortunately there was a fairly large garden around the main building, so I took off as fast as my legs would carry me. I leapt off walls and tore up stairs and raced to the bottom of the garden and shot through the thicket beyond the pond. Out of breath I would sit down. The moment I started settling another surge of energy would rush through me like a wave of electricity propelling me back onto my feet and up the hill again. I felt like an athlete. I was an enraged one. I felt an overwhelming surge of anger seethe through me. I had no idea where it was coming from. All I knew was I needed to run. I also wanted to kick and stamp and lunge. I stampeded down to the copse of trees as far away from the house as possible and yelled: "Fuuuuuucccccckkkkkkk!" I raised my fists up to the sky, my neck bulged and my face turned purple.

The body work over the last couple of years and developing trust in the teachers and sense of growing safety and understanding meant that the part of me that had been shut down and frozen for decades was starting to thaw out like a giant Canadian river of ice suddenly meeting the warmth and kindness of the Spring sun. Suddenly this amount of care and consideration was causing the internal defences to start giving way, and huge spans of ice were starting to smash, snap and explode free. I felt like my whole internal world was starting to shift, and give way. It was on the move, and out of control.

I stopped for a moment to catch my breath. I was shaking and trembling from head to foot. My legs felt incredibly jumpy as if, at any moment, I would spring up into the air like a giant grasshopper and jump right over the roof. A layer of numbness I didn't know was there was wearing off like an anaesthetic and my body felt like it was starting to pop and explode. My limbs needed to burn off the steroids that were flooding my blood and nervous system. Strong electric fizzing and tingling started building up to an almost unbearable level. Thank God I was on a training course, which was explaining this process to me, and giving me some insight into what was happening. If this had happened home alone with no understanding I would have been terrified. Peter Levine's book on shock, called: "Waking the

Tiger," was one of the main works on the reading list for the shock and trauma training and was to become a mini-bible for me over the next few months.

At the bottom of the garden at Karuna, trying to sit still was just not possible. So off I shot again, round and round the manor house like a gazelle running for its life. Up ahead I saw a wall rising up at the end of the lawn and I found myself accelerating towards and then leaping like a ninja into the air I yelling out "Arrggghhh!" with arms punching the air and daggers coming out of my eyes. I wanted to punch a hole through something.

After a while I walked back inside and tried to join back in with the teaching, but it was really hard to focus. I was just sitting there and the trembling was hard to conceal. I lay on the couch during a practice session, which caused the electricity to build up until I literally thought I was going to shoot off like a rocket through the window. My legs and arms started convulsing and shaking. Then Franklyn Sills came over, and with a calm, knowing smile on his face, said, "Its ok. Don't worry. Just let it happen." He paused, and stood there looking into my eyes. He had that great combination of being kind, and understanding, and yet very strong too. The moment he said this I let out a furious yell: "Bloody hell!" A few tears started coming. "Arrrggghhh!" I cried out. "Go for it Julian," Tracy, the student working on me said, encouragingly. Franklyn continued to stand there watching as Tracy kept her cranial contact under my sacrum. My legs carried on convulsing. I was sweating.

The contact at the base of my spine felt like a mooring, and Franklyn's calm strength helped enormously. I sensed that he was okay with this. This helped the whole experience feel safe and manageable. After what felt like a long time, my arms and legs slowed down into more of a tremble, with judders of shakiness rippling through like aftershocks. Franklyn looked over and said: "It looks like you are moving towards completion, but it will probably take some time…"

It certainly did. For the rest of the training I tried to sit in for more lectures but had to keep on getting up and running off like my pants were on fire. Nobody batted an eye-lid. Karuna is the kind of place where going into process is part of everyday life.

The Shock and Trauma training week-end had brought a deep layer of activation to the surface and for a couple of months I felt twitchy and irritable and needed to escape, get out and run, burn off energy. Not surprisingly I had ringing in my ears again. It was low level and didn't bother me much at all because the irritability I felt in the body was far more of a problem.

The buzzy charge that followed me around from head to foot, wherever I went, was no longer acute like electric ants. For a while it turned into ferocious fizzing. My nose itched, my legs were restless, my arms felt jumpy, my eyes were sore. I often had to wear sunglasses as the light seemed bright and irritating. I kept on changing channel on TV. I couldn't settle or be satisfied with anything. I flew into arguments like a wrestler looking for a fight. I stood my ground on escalators like bloody-minded goat. I lashed out at the slightest challenge like a snake, and tossed and turned through months of fitful sleep and dreams of fighting off monsters. I became incredibly impatient and would fly off in a huff. In short I turned into a total arse and drove everyone round the bend for weeks and weeks on end. I hooted the car too much and hit the accelerator pedal at the slightest threat on the road. My libido went through the roof and for a period of time I bonked for England as a way of releasing the build up of too much energy. In this state it was hard enough to cope with what was going on inside me, let alone be aware of others, that I dread to think how it must have been for those around me. "Sorry, please accept my apologies," I write retrospectively from a much more grounded and peaceful future!

What really helped me through this intense period of processing shock was the swimming pool, where I would tear up and down at top speed. This literally discharged all the steroids and stress hormones racing around my blood stream. Going for run was essential too, where I would still need to have the occasional kicking and stamping session. I took to taking my frustration out on lifting weights at the gym and yelled out like the Incredible Hulk.

Very, very frustratingly slowly, but surely, with plenty of Craniosacral support, the buzzy charge started to release and settle, and the shock in my system started to subside. And with this, so did my low level tinnitus. Months and months and months later the charge in my body gradually started to soften, and then one day it was like the turbulence stopped. It felt a lot like one of those long-haul flights where I had got used to moderate turbulence. Then suddenly it stops, and the whole plane goes calm and clear, and you can feel it gliding like silk through the air. My body one day just went calm and still. My nerves switched off. My limbs relaxed and started hanging down in a comfortable way again and it was over. My life had gone smooth.

The tinnitus that reappeared while I was processing shock went away too. It happened in a rather subtle way. The sound gradually lost ground and gently started fading. I didn't really notice it happening. Sporadically I checked up on it, but I didn't really care. When I found it wasn't there I just quickly got on with other things. I knew it would go. The monster that had taken over my life like a ferocious tornado and that had hounded and terrified me like a demon for years on end, had just grown very weak and frail over time, like a spiralling column of dust, losing its momentum, and was now very easy to see through. When it eventually disappeared, it was like a small swirling cluster of leaves that had moved into a corner of the back yard, that finally petered out and came to rest without me even noticing. The tinnitus had gone. It really didn't matter any more. The spell had been well and truly broken.

My irritability stopped too. I became more bearable to be around. I slept better too. I thought more clearly too. I felt happier too. I started being able to relax and just hang out with things too. I started being able to sit back and focus on reading a good book or enjoying staring at some flowers too. I slowed down too. I started being able to meditate better too. I could curl up and fall asleep in the sunlight like a cat too. I could lie in a hammock by the river on a hot summer's day and just get lost in the shimmering, flickering green light of the leaves too. I knew the shock was over. Franklyn was right, I reached completion, eventually… I was able to ride the storm because my head had a handle on what was going on. The trainers at Karuna knew what they were talking about, and their confidence and understanding helped reassure me. It would have been too much to go through alone.

Not surprisingly my overall reactivity plummeted right down and I started feeling positive and robust like my nervous system had become strong again. So I started pushing the boat out a bit more and drank more coffee again, listened to music a little more loudly again, had the most hideously sweet looking pudding on the menu again and just started getting on with life.

The only time tinnitus ever comes back is when I catch a bad cold or eat far too much salt or listen to extremely loud music. But it quickly falls away again. Tinnitus has literally become an old friend. It acts like my own personal in-built healthometre that taps me on the shoulder gently if I overdo things or need to rest. It has moved from being the worst and most terrifying tyrant of my life into becoming a good friend. This is what prompted me to writing the book: "Tinnitus, From Tyrant to Friend: How to let Go of the Ringing in Your Ears." I decided to collect together all the constructive positive and practical advice I have learned from working with several hundred clients.

In 2009 I had one last shock, however, which knocked me out of all my complacency. I was on my way to a therapy session a few minutes walk away from my flat in Westbourne Park. Between my flat and my therapist's house was a flood of drunk, dancing people splurging out of control along the streets of the Notting Hill Carnival. I pushed my way through the sweaty bodies, bright colours, changing music, and smell of beer and barbecued corn. Suddenly I was thrust in front of a loud speak booming insanely loudly off to my right. In a split second I felt a sudden pain sear through my right ear. I panicked pushed my way feistily through another five minutes of crowds to Joshua's front door. I pushed the doorbell. No answer. Of course he would be away. The noise drives all the locals away during carnival. To my horror, I realised that there was a horrible muffled feeling hanging down the right side of my head like someone had strapped insulation over my ears. I had gone deaf. In a matter of seconds my world had changed. I pushed a finger into my left ear, which for decades had been the bad one. As I blocked that ear, my heart sank as the whole world went quiet. My right ear was damaged. I knew it. I sat down and kept pushing my finger in and out of my left ear hearing how horribly quiet the world was going when I just listened out through the right ear. I felt sick. Intuitively I knew that I was now inescapably hard of hearing or deaf.

My right ear has not been able to hear properly ever since. A hearing test revealed that I was severely deaf in my right ear and moderately deaf in the left. The day after the loud speaker damage a new tinnitus arrived with a vengeance and, for a week I felt like I had gone right back to the beginning again. Fear piled back in and grabbed the pit of my stomach, and I felt a complete fraud trying to help people with tinnitus while mine raged inside my head once again. The loud noise damaged my cochlear. This created a void in my hearing. A new tinnitus sound raced in like some phantom-limb experience to fill the gap with a new deafening din. I couldn't believe it. Loud speakers should carry warning lights and have an area of safety cordoned off around them. They are like assassins that can damage your relationship with the auditory world for life. This is auditory violence with no safety warning. Please beware!

I tried not to panic and went back to having weekly Craniosacral Therapy. I spent hours every day practicing yoga and tai chi to take my mind off the noise and settle the system. It was a struggle. I felt my adrenaline spike and for weeks and weeks I felt like I had lost my ground. The world outside seemed quieter and felt slightly dreamy. And my inner world was hissing and spitting and roaring and I felt crushed with disappointment. I was furious that I even let myself anywhere near those stupid, dangerous speakers that should have a health-warning attached to them. In Britain our weather forecasters tell us to wrap up warm if it is chilly, and our buses warn us to hold on when they start moving, and yet we are allowed to have our hearing blasted to destruction and nobody gives a shit? Even cinemas can almost pop our ear-drums for that all important adrenal, thrill factor that brings in the business, keeps us addicted and sends us away with tinnitus.

There was no way out except back into the body. I knew what I had to do: distract the mind away from the sound, and settle the nervous system. For hours every day I lay on my back and pressed into the tightly bunched up muscles around my shoulder blades. I did my best to pummel out the tension on the floor boards. I used flowing, smooth tai chi movements to calm my mind. Sometimes I would punch the couch in frustration, but eventually, I settled into a calmer state. I would lift up into a cobra position from the floor and with my face pointing skyward feeling my tight lungs and frustrated diaphragm slowly release and free up. Slowly the anger subsided, the fear came down, and tears of grief came through, as I was now pretty deaf and felt more isolated from people, friends and their banter now.

Because I knew how to heal this, I managed not to lose it. In the end it took me about six weeks to get rid of this nasty bout of tinnitus and return to the new normal. My tinnitus fell away, as expected, but I now lived in a much quieter world with no more sound of rain, birds, or the fricatives and plosives at the ends of people's words that helped me make out what they were saying. My life had changed for good and I had to get used to it. I will never go anywhere near a loud speaker again. If a fire-engine or an ambulance goes past I think nothing of dropping my bags and pushing my fingers firmly inside my ears. If I go to the cinema or a concert I have a box of musician's earplugs, which I use if I feel remotely uncomfortable with the level of sound.

All in all, it has been a long, arduous journey, and I dread to think where I would be, had I not discovered Craniosacral Therapy and Core Process Psychotherapy.

A few years later I was lucky enough to become a father. Having Oliver was like the sun coming out. Everywhere I walked with my little baby son against my chest in a baby-carrier or in a pram, women smiled at me, men opened doors and life became joyful. On Spring days we would picnic in the park where Oliver could just see over the tops of the daffodils. Toddling along the South Bank he would smile radiantly at everyone walking towards him, filling the space with joy. Everyone beamed back.

Becoming a father, a powerful protective force swept over me. Alone, I was prepared to put up with a tremendous amount of undermining, yelling and abuse by myself, but when my little boy arrived, I suddenly found it unthinkable to expose him to such behaviours. The last conversation with my father went like this:

"So when are you going to bring Oliver to visit me then?" he asked impatiently.
"Well Dad, it depends. I will bring him on one condition: can we both agree to be decent to one another and treat each other with respect?"
"What do you mean?" he asked abruptly.
"If you start laying into me as you usually do, and start shouting or criticising me I will leave. I do not want Oliver to see this. OK?"
"I don't know what on earth you are talking about."
"I don't want you to start yelling at me in front of Oliver. If you start being

offensive or disrespectful, we are going to leave. Do you understand?"

"Listen Sonny Jim, when are you going to accept that you have got it all wrong… "

"Oh don't start all that again. We all know what's happened. I am not going back into all that again." For years Dad had rewritten my story to suit his own needs, but now I found this intolerable.

A brooding silence greeted me down the phone.

"Dad. I am just asking us to treat each other decently. I do not want Oliver to be exposed to the usual. Can't we just make an effort to get on this time, and be civil?"

"Listen matey, you do not impose your rules in my house. So don't come. You are not welcome here!"

"What? Is that how you want to leave it then?"

"Yes. You are not welcome here. You really have got it all wrong. It's about time yo' realised that when your mother…."

"Oh just shut up, will you!" I yelled, and hung up.

He couldn't bear to be anything other than perfect. In his mind he was utterly innocent. So if tried stop invasive or offensive behaviour he just wouldn't see what I was referring to. He wouldn't know what I was talking about. Denial is frighteningly blind. The more we point it out the stronger it gets. In this way, my intention to create a space that was safe enough to take my young son to failed. Dad was not able to agree to treating each other with respect, so by force, the emotions had to turn inexorably back to Julian as the one who was mad, bad or sad. Dad needed this. He did not have the emotional strength to see his own part he was playing.

I never spoke to him again.

When he died 5 years later I was told I would not be welcome at his funeral. I asked to visit his house a few days after he had passed, but was told no. I decided to go to Agua Amarga anyway. From the mountaintop I could see down through the shimmering heat below to my father's house where my step-family were coming and going. It was extraordinary to think that what was left of my father's body would be sitting in a pot of ashes somewhere inside the house.

It was the height of the summer and all the hotels were stuffed to the nines with tourists and seafood, but no empty beds. So my partner and I decided to sleep on the beach. We climbed up the steep path leading west out of the village. High up on top of the rocky trail the late afternoon sun was still blasting the white rocks like an incinerator. Red faced, salty-eyed and with charred feet, we clambered down into the empty desert-like valley. We walked past scorpion cracks and razor-sharp cactuses down towards the cool of Cala de Enmedio, sparkling sapphire and turquoise before losing itself in the great expanse of azure.

Once on the beach in the swimming pool blue, buoyant and cool, we floated round to see the sun finally giving up its fight, dropping its fiery flares, and carrying its ember afterglow off behind a line of arid hills darkening suddenly with purple. On the other side of the sky a full moon was rising into one of the most perfect Mediterranean nights I remember. My father would have loved it. The warm sea shimmered pink, then orange, then yellow through to green, before finally settling into peaceful, silvery stillness. The moon was bright and the stars were bright too. My Dad adored watching the sky and "listening to the sunset." He was there in spirit.

I imagined that he could finally see how I really felt about him. He could love that glorious summer night alongside me and through me with no madness getting in the way. I felt close to him and had a sense of his spirit dancing there amongst the Andalucian hills as they radiated their heat far out into the night sky. Shortly after ten o'clock, the satellite that Dad and I had watched together from his balcony so many times, moved quietly and alone across the enormous expanse of sky. There we were, once again both watching it together and thinking of each other.

I thought about my father's spirit that would be leaving his body, in transit away from this world, reaching back into the eternal, leaving the distorted family relations behind. Surely Death is wiser and no longer gets tangled up in personal difficulty? His awareness would be panning back out into infinity now, so that his whole life could meet my whole life, and the arguments and awfulness of the last five years could fade back into a truer perspective. There was no separation between us now. Because he was dead, and at one with the bigger picture, Dad was now in direct connection. I thought death would make us more distant, but I felt close to him that night. Floating in the warm water that carried the humid scent of the night-time sea, I felt a deep sense of peace settle in. I was there for Dad. This is what he would have wanted. There were plenty of times when he saw what I saw when we were alive. And I saw what he saw. We both knew that. I looked down to my feet standing on the rippled, silvery sand beneath, and watched the small fish dart in between.

Months later I heard about the funeral almost by accident, while chatting to my mother one evening. She told me that the "whole family" were going. That said it all. I couldn't go anyway. My son was involved in a serious crisis and I had to make sure he was safe. Besides I felt I had already met him when he was transiting out of this mortal coil. So when I was told it would put too many people's backs up if I went to the village, I just felt glad that I had followed my heart and had already gone to pay my respects. I had connected with him directly in spirit, at the time that most mattered. So the funeral came and went in silence and my first connection to it came almost a year later when my sister kindly sent me a photo of the ashes being scattered.

There is an enormous price to pay when we stand up and challenge difficult or disrespectful behaviour. Therapy can help us gain self-respect and discover equal rights, but when we change in therapy, this changes all our relationships. When I was that invisible, over-tolerant people-pleaser, there wasn't really anyone there. No wonder I felt so lost. I was just a satellite of reactivity orbiting around others for decades.

When people become entrenched in hatred and are unable to apologise to you or forgive you, and drive you out like a piece of trash, the only option is to wish them well and let go. Pride is deadly, because it cuts people off from their own heart and removes the potential to forgive, repair and come back into relationship.

The scapegoats we use are never as bad as we make out. All we are doing is spraying our disowned stuff onto that person, and then pretending it is theirs. Then we ghost them. We annihilate them. We pretend that they no longer exist and hope that this will make us happy. But how can it? The trouble with annihilating someone is that we not only lose that person who quite often has things we treasure, but far worse, we end up cutting ourselves off from our own heart. As we rise above it all into the land of "me right, you wrong," down below, in our chest, something shuts down and dies. We shrink as people and become more removed from the very heart that connects us to our self and others, and the bigger picture out there. A scapegoat is always just another fallible person. We are all good and bad. We are all human. There is no such thing as being innocent. Me good, you bad, is not being aware.

I have said things I have regretted when I have got angry, just like any other person. I believe owning our shadow and apologising for acting out is normal, healthy behaviour. But some people refuse to see their own misgivings. Instead of apologising, they would rather drive you out. Instead of climbing down and seeing how awful they have been and saying sorry, they would rather cut you out of their lives. It is more important to maintain a sense of pride, being right and innocent. It's agree with this or die.

So with those that have cast me out and who have needed to scapegoat me, all I can do is reach back into space and take a deep breath. Instead of trying to get a line of Kalashnikovs to reconsider their position, maybe its best to take cover away from hearts full of hatred and confusion, and orient to peaceful practices. Whatever happens, we all have to learn to let go sooner or later. The growing number of dead people I know show me that letting go is the only way forward. The older we get the more dead people there are to remind us of this.

A lot of my tinnitus was caused by a relentless exposure to "auditory violence," hearing relentless criticism, complaining, and ordering around. I had to listen and didn't know I could stop it. This takes its toll on our nervous system directly through our ears. Our ears are permanently switched on. So the only way to stop the onslaught is by saying NO. We must say no for our own good. However, bullies, by their nature, find NO really difficult. So, living with bullies there is a very fine line to tread between disappearing to keep them happy, or being ourselves with our own needs and saying NO, risking losing the relationship. Somewhere in between lies a thin possibility where both parties can meet and find common ground. Whatever the situation, all healthy relationships are founded on mutual respect.

The way I recognise being with a bully is that my brain switches off and my body goes numb. Mysteriously, all the things that were clear in my mind just seconds ago, disappear. If I need to deal with a bully and have issues to go through I need to write things down to keep them in mind. Otherwise I may find myself floundering with a blank head.

One way of handling bullies can be to "agree, then go." When they are on their soap-box and are spouting forth, I can either throw my hands up into the air and obsequiously say, "Ooh I know….Yes. You're absolutely right…Ooh I know. Yes. Yes. Yes…" It seems to work best if I say this with a really nasally, Kenneth William's kind of voice. If I find myself being snuffed out and my mind goes blank, I can pluck up the courage and say, "Do excuse me for just a moment." If I unashamedly bow out, run to the loo, or find some excuse to escape the bullying vortex, almost immediately, the mind comes back and the feeling of the body returns. Once back, I can then ask: What is going on here? What's in this for me? I can either, go back and carry on being just a pair of ears and smile, or I can leave. "Sorry, I have to go. Bye!" Agreeing then leaving has to be better than standing up to a bully, and facing sulking, rage or instant ex-communication. I have been amazed working with tinnitus just how common bullying is with this condition and how often tinnitus people are exposed to considerable auditory violence.

The journey is to let go. But before we can let go of the self, we have to find one first. For years I had to fight for the right to have my own self and find my own story. I've got it now. My self is here and functional. It gets me through life without causing too much aggravation anymore.

At the end of the day, either way, therapy or no therapy, it all goes up in dust and returns to the stars. Dad shows this to me every day. He shows me that none of these family dramas really matter anymore. It is all going anyway. He has gone, and this morning, he is still gone. Finding peace is what matters.

Chapter 12 The Sound of Silence

Devon and London, 2004

Do you know this silence?
Is it not the same as in your room
When you have no one to talk to?

Rumi
Bridge to the Soul

Whenever you think or you believe or you know, you're a lot of other people: but the moment you feel, you're nobody-but-yourself.

E E Cummings
The Courage to be Yourself

Maura Sills from the Karuna Institute gave a talk at the Breath of Life Conference in London. This is a conference for body-based therapists who work at the fascinating interface between health, medical science and deeper energetic awareness. She was talking about the heart of compassion in Buddhism. She started to chant the Heart Sutra: GA TE GA TE PARA GA TE, PARA SAM GA TE, BODHI SVAHA.

I had an immediate and strong reaction stirring inside my chest that caused me to listen intensely to what she had to say. Then I went home and cried uncontrollably for about three hours. The next day I felt like a tonne of bricks had lifted off me. This came as such an unexpected relief, and left me feeling so much more positive that I decided the next training she did, I would do.

Very briefly, an amateur translation of this sutra could be: GONE, GONE, GONE BEYOND, GONE BEYOND TO THE OTHER SHORE, TO THE ENLIGHTENED STATE OF MIND. I interpret these great words to mean that awareness is not limited to our sense of self. It is something that goes far beyond our little bubbles of consciousness. If we sit and notice how awareness itself can be aware of our thoughts, our feelings and our experiences, it shows itself to be something much bigger than we are. There is something there that is aware of us. How can this awareness be something that is generated by a small biological brain? Maybe what we think is "me" is nothing more than a bubble of awareness floating in one, vast big mind? If we sit and wait for the wretched chatter to stop and settle into stillness, can't we all gently, quietly just let this bubble burst and become aware of this big awareness that is revealing itself to us? It seems like our sense of "me" is a contraction down from the big soup of experience that is available to us if we only allow ourselves to settle back into it.

It is easy to say this in retrospect, but when Maura Sills chanted at the Breath of Life Conference that day, I don't know why this teaching grabbed me by the heart, but it did. Something in the core of me was challenged and opened up. I felt something deep inside settle into a more peaceful state. A couple of months later Maura offered a foundation course in Core Process Psychotherapy for Craniosacral Therapists. Perfect. I signed up with the intention of learning a bit more about psychotherapy to help me hold my cranial clients better, but ended up doing the whole training.

On that training I had many extraordinary experiences that go well beyond the scope of this book. But suffice to say that this provided me with a grounding, and a practice and a profession that I have enjoyed alongside Craniosacral TherapY ever since. Karuna also put me in direct contact with the heart of Buddhist teachings in a very embodied way, rather than just thinking about it.

To put it simply, all wounding happens in relationship. So entering into a safe relationship with a therapist allows us to become aware of how we are relating to each other and work through to a deeper, more connected awareness. We can see how we are behaving and projecting and see that this is just a temporary learned pattern. If we both hang out in stillness and let the chatter calm down and the story soften, then much deeper and more immediate ways of relating can emerge.

Instead of getting lost in a fixed mindset, or shut-down, emotionless body, we can let the light of awareness soak in, freeing us up into a shared experience which is much less cut off from each other and at times quite extraordinary. The sense of separation can fall away revealing a shared experience, which has really challenged my sense of what "a mind" is. It seems more appropriate to say that "the mind" is there and we access it in our own unique, individual ways, but it is one universal thing at the core. Core Process Psychotherapy has given me direct experience of a shared field of experience and bigger awareness that comes into play if we only just sit back, relax and let the heart reveal this to us.

The more here we are, and the more in touch we become. The more in touch we become, the more awareness can take root in us. The more awareness takes root in us, the more we can see that awareness is something in its own right, something that is bigger than us, and something that can be aware of us. It is not just my awareness of me, but also, the Awareness that includes me in it. This definitely makes life far more interesting. It is no longer my problem inside this little skin-bag of reactivity. It becomes a big mind that is experiencing something locally in this little body. This for me is a much more spacious and comfortable perspective.

A lot of people with tinnitus I have worked with, just like me, have become stuck in a shut-down body. Their alarm bells are ringing because the central nervous system cannot handle the overwhelmed and overloaded mind and body. So having a good therapist is crucial to help open things out and re-establish a sense of safety in relationship. Or, as in my case, establish a sense of safety for the first time. The people that achieve a sense of internal safety get better. The alarm bells stop ringing. The anxious mind calms down and there is a palpable sense of being able to trust someone.

Being a psychotherapist has shown me that we need to experience this safety in relationship in order for awareness and presence to take root and settle in us. So my terror of bullies or being swamped with overwhelming baggage in others could, at last, finally find a calm, clear and spacious relationship with a safe therapist, who has no agenda than wanting to help, support and be there for us. Slowly, slowly I have dared to open and trust that they were not going to upset me or put too many demands onto me. It has taken me years to learn to trust another person in a heartfelt kind of way.

Once we can trust another person and enter into a calm, balanced relationship with them, then we can dare to open out further into a spiritual path or deeper awareness. Like a baby learning to trust and bond with his or her mother, we can become adults that can open to and bond with a spiritual path or a deeper meaning in life. As we get older we can wean ourselves off our parents and onto stillness/peace/God itself. Any spiritual or contemplative practice that invites awareness in, no matter what religion or path it comes from, can help the smaller mind in us come home to the bigger picture. When the smaller mind can rest in the sanctuary of the big mind, then we become calmer, more resourced and can finally find peace.

The Core Process Psychotherapy training helped me commit much more fully to Buddhist practice, which has become more beneficial as I have understood it, and practiced it more deeply, letting it massage its way into my system. Years of meditation practice, and input from teachers have helped me cope with life much better. Life is still shocking and full of suffering. When I have stared into the face of hatred and extreme behaviours in people close to me, when I have been cast out and rejected like a piece of trash rather than giving a simple apology, I simply would not have managed without meditation practice. In many ways extreme behaviours have driven me more and more deeply into Buddhist practice.

Some relationships have led down a blind alley to a brick wall at the end, with no way out, other than letting go. I have had to give up in the true sense of the word. I have had let go of my needs, my position and step back, take a deep breath and realise that all dramas come and go, and then, one day they go away forever. At the end of that blind alley, with nowhere to go, the only way is to see that all this stuff is just appearing out of a big empty, stillness, and then disappearing back into it. There is stillness. We are in this stillness. We are the stillness. Its just that, all too often, our the local disturbance coming from personal issues makes us feel the stillness has gone. But it hasn't. The stillness is here and has been here all the time. After the stone has been thrown into the pond, the local drama soon settles back into a big, still, unified pond. The Buddhist path, like any decent path has provided me with a vehicle to become aware of this. I don't know how I coped without Buddhist practice before. The truth is I didn't cope at all. How can a person manage alone without the wisdom of great teachings?

In particular I am very grateful to have met the excellent and clear teacher, James Low and the Dzogchen Teaching, which he received from the Tibetan Lama H.H Khordong Terchen Tulku Chhimed Rigdzin Rinpoche, also known as C R Lama. This line of teaching and James Low's deep understanding of it are directly helping me let go of my terror of death, decay and family struggle. You can find this great teaching on James Low's website: www.simplybeing.co.uk

There really are people and teachings and paths that help us find a connection back to source, back to the ground where it all begins. Surely we all need to remember where we come from? Before we stepped out of the eternal into the embodied and time-driven life that we find ourselves in, falling into the drama of life for another round, before all of this, wasn't there something else, something peaceful, something great, vast and still? Isn't it here now, at the same time? Can't we know this now, as all the ripples settle and the sense of self relaxes back into the big mind?

Why am I bothering to mention this here? You could say that this is a personal story about stopping tinnitus. But you could also say this is a story about a man who is essentially afraid of people, his mistrust of human relationship, and how this changes when he comes into direct contact with therapy. The safety of

Craniosacral contact brought me out of a traumatized state and helped me find a state of well-being inside my body for the first time. The more I had this work, the more I dropped into a stillness I didn't know was there. A calmer mind and greater awareness helped open up a whole new world of experience that had been completely unavailable to me before. Connecting to the Long Tide and finding a deep state of calm inside my body, the alarm bells stopped ringing and silence settled back into my life again. Silence seemed so important to me back in the dark days of sirens in my head. Now that I am really well again, I find that feel peaceful is far more important to me than hearing silence. A sense of peace is an experience extends out much further and includes more of the body.

If you have tinnitus or know someone who is struggling to get better, it is essential to enter into a safe and calming relationship with a therapist. This is one of the best and most direct ways to come out of fight or flight or the freezing response, and release and let go. I love cranial work because it is fundamentally a safe practice that gets sensed directly from one body to another without the head getting in the way too much. Bodies know how to do this and bodies know far more about life than we do! Peace is a very real state that we have to connect with directly to in order to experience it. Thinking about it won't get you there. Being clever, academic and philosophical won't make you peaceful. Peace or stillness is an experiential thing that is felt through the body and mind rather than in trains of thought.

Once we can sense a deeper state of peace, which tends to come from beyond the self, then the stresses and anxieties of being a little person in a scary, shocking life can relax and let go.

Finding a connection to the bigger picture has definitely helped me relax, switch off and access a deeper sense of peace. Whatever path you are on, I hope you can get a sense of something bigger that is holding you. Its so much easier to let go into something than into nothing. Connecting with others helps us experience the collective, interrelated states that go way beyond the self.

Many tinnitus people are locked inside fearful thinking and tend not to have much support or connection to calm, safe holding. They also come almost completely unable to self-soothe. Therapists can help provide this directly. Once we have settled into a much calmer place and have learned how to self-soothe, we can then open out and dare to face the big empty stillness which has been here all along, and which is arguably the true therapist or parent. Can we dare to sit with this?

Thankfully a lot of people respond well to Craniosacral Therapy. However, if you are one of those people that struggles to open up and let go, and easily falls back into a cut off, shut-down bubble of stress, I urge you to carry on with your therapist. Keep going, keep opening things up and let trust develop. I urge you to keep going with a contemplative practice or body-based practice like yoga or tai chi. This helps trust develop which in turn enables us to open more and more to the way things are. Setting up positive therapeutic relationships and body-based or spiritual practices to start undoing the legacy of difficult past experience will help you settle with time. Hopefully this will come across as common sense.

Why do some people get better quickly when others don't? Fear and trauma seem to be the greatest stumbling blocks that slow down the sense of progress in some people. This is why is it urgent that health practitioners stop dropping bombshells of doom on tinnitus people, and tinnitus people themselves stop traumatizing themselves by reading horror stories on the internet, or being exposed to negative messaging about this condition. The negative thinking comes from somewhere, most often our own head, and we need to calm the body down enough for this to quieten down too.

Sometimes symptoms hang around because people are stuck in tricky, frustrating or scary conditions at home, which means their nervous systems are constantly idling at a slightly raised, anxious rate. All too often clients get better with hands on work during the session only to bounce back into tinnitus as soon as they get home because there is stress there. Having cranial work and taking up yoga will very likely help the nervous system settle, but if you sneak back into bed with a threatening bully who quietly terrorizes the family or someone who drives you round the bend because they just don't get you, then the chances are your tinnitus may take longer to subside. In these cases psychotherapy can prove invaluable for helping people come to terms with intense frustrations or fears in their own home, which are often the main power supply for the alarm bells.

By far the biggest issue is the way tinnitus is handled by the mainstream health professionals. Messages put out by practitioners in a position of authority hold sway and trickle down to vulnerable people who feel disempowered and who are still terrified of their tinnitus. All too often the underlying message: "I can't help you and don't have a clue how to help you," translates into "there is no cure, and you have to learn to live with this for the rest of your life." I really want to share with all of us who are trying our best to help tinnitus people that these negative messages can have devastating consequences. People who are vulnerable, just like I was, are likely to believe you, particularly if you are in a position of authority. Please check for yourself. Call some of the clients you have spent ten minutes of their time with you and find out how they have reacted to bombshells of doom that you may have dropped.

I constantly pick up the pieces with clients who have been pushed over the edge by the very people they go to for help. If people with tinnitus fall into the erroneous trap of pretending there is no way out, this can result in triggering greater fear, depression and make symptoms far worse. To make tinnitus better we need fear to subside. Fear subsides when we have greater understanding and realise that tinnitus is principally a stress-related symptom. So de-stress with hands on help to bring in a direct sense of increased safety into the nervous system, increase support with therapy and the prognosis improves dramatically. Hopefully this should become common sense. I realise the medical model is tied up by strict medical research guidelines, but doctors and consultants should at least recommend calming, soothing therapies to help people settle, and direct clients down the psychological or therapeutic route.

If we tell people to learn how to come out of the fight or flight or freeze response this will not only help them take responsibility for their own health, and trigger a healthy learning curve, but also, will signpost them to health practitioners who can help and do know what to do. If consultants are hell bent on condemning tinnitus people to a sense of hopelessness and feel they must entrap clients with a sense of no way out, and refuse to inform them of things that are clearly helping already, then, at least tell people that they are eventually very likely to habituate, and that when this happens, they are likely to feel a bit better. Surely this is better than pushing desperate people off a cliff?

I know Craniosacral Therapy has helped me and many clients let go of tinnitus. Until recently my hands were tied and I was not allowed to share this information because all therapists are bound by confidentiality and cannot use case histories to prove the work helps. I have literally thousands of case-histories recording people saying, "Oh it went away completely after the last session." Or "It is definitely getting better." Or "That's amazing. The sound has gone away. I can't hear any noise at the moment." We are not allowed to use client information for research, or to prove Craniosacral Therapy helps tinnitus unless there are strict ethical guidelines in place to make sure they are kept clear of any untoward influences.

The good news is that I was delighted to discover that You Tube is a wonderful way of putting out information to help people in need, free of charge. This has proved to be a fantastic medium through which to share some of my findings with tinnitus people anywhere in the world. Once I had learned how to put a video together and publish it to You Tube, I started putting out a stream of videos in response to important questions that clients continually brought to my practice. There are now currently over one hundred videos helping tinnitus people get their heads around this condition and start putting things into place which will help them get better.

The best thing about these videos is that people can, at last, read about other tinnitus people's testimonials and success stories. It is all very well hearing me chiming on about how I did it, but when tinnitus people hear from an increasing positive bank of other people's stories, this is far more encouraging and motivating. The more people speak out about their positive stories and how they let go of tinnitus, the more the fear is likely to come down and others too will follow the same path to letting go of this condition. When the fear comes down, the adrenaline levels drop and the alarm bells stop ringing. The placebo effect, in the true sense of the word, makes people feel safe, which directly causes them to feel better and for symptoms to subside. Many people often write, "My tinnitus came down just watching your videos." This is not magic. This happens simply because we feel calmer, less overwhelmed, and safe which causes our hearing mechanism to stop listening out acutely for danger. The sound quietens down and we see a way out of this condition.
Go to my video, "Positive Tinnitus Stories," on You Tube and read what other people have done to get better. Here there is mounting evidence showing that cranial work helps this condition back off.

To state the obvious, when we find reassurance and comfort in reading how this approach has benefited others, this makes us feel better too. Taking my advice, setting up a support network largely consisting of hands on therapy, and learning a body-based practice to help distract the mind away from tinnitus and settle the nervous system, time and time again this helps people's symptoms get better. Its one thing to believe me, but it is far more convincing to hear how many other people have benefited from this body-based approach.

Putting my message out there has also incurred the wrath of a few suspicious people who accuse me of feeding off the helpless and needy, as if I am making it all up to make money. One man said I should be put in prison for telling stories. Another one referred to me as a baboon, which made me laugh until tears came out of my eyes, and has done so many times since. My reply to him is a big, "Ooh Ooh Ooh. Ahh Ahh Ahh!" But I understand where they are coming from: fear and mistrust learned from previous negative experience. Let's hope that they learn to trust more by meeting decent and well-meaning people. Thankfully the videos and the messages people write show that I am not making it up. I am very glad to see a large number of people are getting better, which is what this is all about.

We need to deal with the nocebo effect. This is the ability to harm people by giving them negative messages. I wrote to the ENT association in the UK citing the case of a person who became very stressed immediately after he was told there was nothing he could do to make his tinnitus better. Can you imagine believing that you will be locked inside a torturous sound for the rest of your life? This is enough to give anyone tinnitus. If the people going for help believe these messages of doom then this could cause fear, and therefore the sound, to remain. This is nonsense. This is not true. Please do not believe it. What the practitioner is really saying is that he or she has not got a clue how to help you.

In my letter I recommended that ENTs should tell people that if they take their minds off the sound by focussing the mind on body practices such as Yoga or Tai Chi and relax the body with effective treatments such as Craniosacral Therapy, Acupuncture, Hypnotherapy, Reflexology, Shiatsu, Reflexology, Osteopathy, Chiropractic and other body-based therapies or work through personal issues in Psychotherapy then the prognosis moves to "can get better." To date the ENT association has refused to answer my letter. I called the ENT association and was told that they have chosen not to reply to my letter. On a positive note however, the person on the phone conceded that it would make sense to direct people down the therapeutic or psychological route.

I realise that ENTs are bound by medical science, which can be hugely restrictive. A person reporting that therapy X made them better is often not proof enough. In order for ENTs and Western Medicine to be able to make recommendations, Craniosacral Therapy needs to prove under double-blind repeatable research-like conditions that it helps tinnitus get better. Personally I think it would be great to do a study of this nature. If the Craniosacral Therapy Association of the UK or elsewhere received enough funding I believe that we could prove scientifically, under strict, research-like conditions that Craniosacral Therapy has a significant beneficial effect on tinnitus. But this would cost tens of thousands of pounds to set up.

In a research project, to get a clear result, the sample group of tinnitus people would need to have no information or outside influences. They would need to experience just hands on contact in silence and answer some simple before and after questions to measure outcomes.

It is my sincerest wish that I can help spread positive and helpful information to health practitioners dealing with tinnitus. GPs are especially important as they provide crucial signposting that can direct people to those who can help. Instead of wasting resources on expensive MRI scans, it would be so much more productive and inexpensive for the NHS to point tinnitus towards calming body-based therapies to help settle the nervous system and take the mind off the ringing. If John Smith says: "I had three sessions of Craniosacral Therapy and my tinnitus got better," surely this is good enough and we should start paying attention to this.

Both scientific enquiry and experiential feedback need to be gathered together into a constructive, positive bank of information. This will help signpost tinnitus people onto the road to recovery. We need to listen to what has worked and how people have got better. This is what matters both in science and inside people's nervous systems. One of the problems is that positive case histories resulting from successful therapy are locked away behind a wall of confidentiality, inside filing cabinets. We can't see this, which gives a skewed view. However, on-line, ready to traumatise anyone at length in the comfort of their own homes, are the endless horror stories of people who are still stuck in tinnitus and not getting anywhere. The internet presents a dreadful picture. Many of my clients have become deeply disturbed by what they have exposed their minds to on-line. The people who have got better just move on naturally, so all the positive stories are largely hidden, giving the impression that they do not exist.

I am very happy to say that You Tube has created a way around this problem. I started putting out videos on how to help tinnitus, because I believe this kind of information is worth sharing and should be freely available. The videos have proved to be quite popular and at the time of writing this book have just topped one million viewings. The best thing about this is that people are sharing their own experiences with each other. They are reporting how Craniosacral Therapy and Yoga and Tai Chi have helped them make a good recovery. This is brilliant because the message is getting stronger and is becoming harder to ignore. The more evidence there is to show that tinnitus is just a temporary state that can be radically improved with therapy, the more the people in authority will be further encouraged to signpost people down this road to recovery.

All of us health practitioners need to refer to each other to work in a more integrated way. With tinnitus people, most people need to be directed to therapists to settle the nervous system and learn how to take their minds off the noise with low-cost and easily accessible body-based practices such as yoga or tai chi. It often helps to have hearing tests and it can be helpful to fit a hearing aid. Rarely there may be a need for an MRI scan or deeper investigation. I believe that standard practice should point tinnitus people down the therapeutic route, which could save a lot of money in healthcare.

It is my aim with this book and my You Tube channel to provide health practitioners with more information so that they can think twice before doling out negative messages. This condition would be improved massively overnight if the authorities could put out positive constructive advice that would have a beneficial trickle-down effect. I hope the message gets through on my You Tube channel.

Please read what tinnitus people have said for themselves. I often encourage my clients to write to their GPs and ENTs when they have got better informing them what helped let go of tinnitus. In this way they can learn and help more people with tinnitus get the right kind of advice. We need to map out the path to recovery more clearly. In this age of information the greatest problem with tinnitus is getting rid of the negative messages on the net that can take root in people's minds.

So my request to ENTs and GPS is please signpost tinnitus people towards body-based therapists who can help bring them out of fight or flight, and process trauma. Please inform tinnitus people that yoga or tai chi not only takes the mind off the ringing like listening to music does, but also settles and deactivates the nervous system, which, in turn causes the sound to pipe down. This is a steady path to recovery and takes a couple of months. Please encourage tinnitus people to take responsibility for learning to soothe themselves and setting up the right kind of help.

I wrote to my ENT and told him I had made a full recovery. I asked him to consider the consequences of the messages he was giving people. He wrote a very pleasant letter back thanking me for the information and told me he no longer worked in ENT but appreciated my comments.

I once met a trainer in a salsa class who teaches people about tinnitus at an ENT hospital. When I found out where he worked, we quickly started chatting.

"So you help people with tinnitus do you?"
"Yes. I get quite good results. Some of my clients go on to make a complete recovery with no noise in a quiet room, and many find their symptoms going very quiet."
"What do you mean, you help their tinnitus go away?" he said, starring back at me blankly.
"Yes. Its tremendously satisfying. You seem surprised."
"Gosh it must be," he said looking almost shocked. "But how do you do that? How is that possible?"
"Well, hands on work calms the nervous system down and helps release the buzzy

charge in the temporal area, which often causes the sound to go down. It is not a quick fix, but gradually helps the alarm bells stop ringing. I bring people out of fight or flight and help settle the charge. I also teach them body-based focussing techniques that help take the mind off tinnitus."

"Is that so? Well if that were true, surely you would have a queue a mile long outside your door!"

"Well I am quite busy actually, but it doesn't work like that. A lot of people are looking for a quick fix or a pill to pop. This approach involves a bit of commitment and working on oneself and not everyone is prepared to do that. People need to be committed to treatment and keep coming. When push comes to shove, not everyone is prepared to take responsibility for their own recovery and do this kind of work on themselves."

The trainer looked at me a bit blankly.

"What is it you said you did, again?" he asked politely.

"Craniosacral Therapy."

"I see.... I haven't heard of that."

I started explaining some of the basic principles of cranial work but watched him stare off into space. This man, who helps educate ENTs about tinnitus, amongst other things, and helps an army of consultants go out and disseminate potentially suicide-inducing messages of doom, knocked back his pint and smiled back apologetically.

"Look I think I'm going to have to make tracks."

"Listen, I would be very happy to give you a demonstration so that you can experience the work for itself. Would you be interested?"

"Look, really, it has been a pleasure talking to you, but I'm going to have to go now."

"Here's my card if you are interested. Craniosacral Therapy is very relaxing and de-stressing."

He took the card and then took off rather hastily. I felt a bit foolish like I had been bashing my head up against the brick wall of the old school, selling myself cheaply. But then I had to admit to myself that it took me years to get my own head around Craniosacral Therapy and how it works, so why should I expect anyone else to get it in just one conversation? But at least I could go back to work and enjoy dropping people into stillness again. That always feels immensely satisfying. I felt like I was one of the lucky ones that enjoyed getting good results most of the time.

I tell people to find a practitioner to switch them off and drop them into a deep state of calm once a week, and to take up one body-based practice like Yoga or Tai Chi to relax and take the mind off things. Those that follow this advice tend to make a gradual or steady recovery.

I am very grateful to my own tinnitus for leading me to excellent Craniosacral Therapists, who helped me discover internal well-being, Psychotherapists who helped me work through my issues and addictions, and Buddhist teachers that have provided me with a means of relating to the big, big stillness that is here right before our eyes, and not freak out about it.

In retrospect, Craniosacral Therapy was largely responsible for curing my tinnitus. The work carried me deeper and deeper into the Long Tide where stillness washed over me again and again, until I could see that it is here and has been here all the time. It was the Long Tide easing me gently into stillness, that helped me reached the end of my journey, and come back to silence.

May all people with tinnitus find the path that helps them let go of the ringing in their ears. May we all find peace.

My father, the late Ian James Cowan Hill was the first person to show me this great silence when he took me to the end of the road in the Saudi Arabian desert. I remember that experience with him vividly like it was yesterday. It was his way of showing me the big mind. He wanted me to hear, feel and experience the big silence and emptiness that only a magnificent desert can show you. When we both stood there, in that empty space of rock and sky, and let the awareness soak into our little bodies from out of the vastness of the heat and the sky, it is wrong to say nothing happened. There was something immeasurable, powerful, and yet quiet as a mouse hanging out there in the stillness, something empty and timeless, that was constantly presenting itself anew. The big mind was just there exuding an emptying kind of emptiness: the kind of emptying that leaves you feeling more and more liberated the more you give into it. Dad showed me how small and insignificant we are for the brief period of time that we walk on this earth in human form.

Thanks Dad for all the wonderful experiences you have given me. Thanks for driving me in my pyjamas at a hundred miles per hour in the Jensen down the motorway to get Chinese food. Thanks for sneaking up the Empire State building with me after it had shut. Thanks for taking me flying in that incredible Jet Provost high up into the afterglow of that summer night over Lincolnshire. Thanks for watching a square moon rise over the Greenland ice-cap with me. Thanks for sending me to one of the best schools in England. Thanks for playing the Pink Panther on the saxophone and for recording your radio programme: "Smooth and Sentimental," with me. Thanks for opening my life up to Agua Amarga and the brilliant light of Andalucia. Thanks for our differences and counterpoint, as this helped me find myself. May we forgive each other and let go. May we all appreciate what we have left of this precious life. May you rest in peace Ian James Cowan Hill.

At the last you vanished, gone to the Unseen.
Strange the path you took out of this world.
Strange how your beating wings demolished the cage,
And you flew away to the world of the soul.

You were some old woman's favourite falcon,
But when you heard the falcon drum,
You escaped to the placeless.

You were a drunken nightingale among owls,
But when the scent of the rose-garden reached you,
You were gone.

The bitter wine you drank with us left its headache,
But at last you entered a timeless tavern.
Like an arrow you went straight for the target of bliss,
Straight to the mark like an arrow from a bow.

Like a ghoul, the world tried to deceive you with its false clues,

But you refused the clues,
And went straight to that which had no clue.

Now that you are the sun, what good is a crown?
And how do you tie your belt,
Now that you've vanished from the middle?

Rumi
That Which Has No Clue

Acknowledgements

I'd like to say a big thank-you to the following people:

Sue Newport for suggesting Craniosacral Therapy to help my tinnitus. You possibly saved my life!

Lin Coghlan for inspiring me to write my own story in the first place.

Kate Horsley-Parker for sharing her enthusiasm, excellent editing skills and providing invaluable feedback on the writing.

Thomas Atlee, the Director of the College of Craniosacral Therapy, for helping ease me into this wonderful profession.

Maura Sills, Founder of the Karuna Institute for helping me find my ground in the world, teaching me the value of letting be and waiting to see what emerges, and for connecting me directly with Buddhist compassion.

Franklyn Sills, Head of the Craniosacral Therapy training at Karuna, for sharing his great insight and awareness, and providing me with great holding and safety.

All my fantastic therapists, who for boundary reasons shall remain surnameless: Angela, Peter, Joshua, Andrew, Erwin, Alastair, Rosie, Susan, thanks for holding me together through thick and thin and for connecting me directly with an embodied sense of safety.

All my fascinating clients/teachers who have taught me so much about tinnitus.

The wider Craniosacral Therapy community for sharing the wisdom of the body, and the Core Process Psychotherapy community for teaching me the value of relating being to being, and stopping doing.

All the yoga and tai chi teachers for helping me relax and connect.

The monks, nuns and teachers of Hosshinji and Miotsuji monasteries for sharing your inspiring and precious way of living and presence.

Namkhai Norbu Rinpoche and his Sangha for connecting me to the great Dzogchen teaching.

Chogyam Trungpa Rinpoche for your books that changed my life.

Thich Nhat Hahn for your heart-warming teachings.

James Low for your deep understanding of the Dzogchen path, for showing me what really matters in life and for connecting me to a priceless teaching.

My mother for being there for me, for being positive and for believing in me when the going got tough.

Andrew Whitley and Rafael Ramos Garcia for being such good quality people with great hearts. Thanks for being part of my family and for providing great support.

Further resources:

Craniosacral Therapy Association of the UK
http://www.craniosacral.co.uk/

To find a Craniosacral practitioner in UK and Europe please go to:
http://www.craniosacral.co.uk/practitioner-directory

To find a Craniosacral practitioner in North America please go to:
https://www.craniosacraltherapy.org/practitioner-referral

College of Craniosacral Therapy – London UK
https://www.ccst.co.uk/

Craniosacral Therapy Education Trust – London UK
http://www.cranio.co.uk/

Resonance Trainings – Gloucestershire UK
http://www.resonance.org.uk/

The Karuna Institute – Devon UK
https://www.karuna-institute.co.uk/
Offers Kum Nye retreats, Craniosacral and Psychotherapy Trainings

Brief Bibliography

After the Ecstasy, the Laundry
Jack Kornfield, Bantam Books 2000

A Path With Heart: A Guide through the Perils and Promises of Spiritual Life
Jack Kornfield, Bantam Books 1993

Buddha's Brain: the Practical Neuroscience of Happiness, Love and Wisdom
Rick Hanson, New Harbinger Publications Ltd 2009

Candida Albicans: A User's Guide to Treatment and Recovery
Gill Jacobs, Optima, 1990

Cutting Through Spiritual Materialism
Chogyam Tungpa, Shambala 1987

Feeling Safe: How to be Strong and Positive in a Changing World
William Bloom, Piatkus, 2002

Lick The Sugar Habit
Nancy Appleton, Avery 1996

Life in Motion: the Osteopathic Vision of Rollin E Becker
Rachel Brooks, Stillness Press 1997

Money, Sex, War Karma: Notes for a Buddhist Revolution
David Loy, Wisdom Publications, 2008

Rumi: Bridge to the Soul: Journeys into the Music and Silence of the Heart
Coleman Barks, Harper One 2007

Simply Being: Texts in the Dzogchen Tradition
James Low, Antony Rowe Publishing 2010

Tao Te Ching
Addiss & Lombardo, Shambala 2007

The Body Remembers
Babette Rothschild, Norton & Company, 2003

The Crystal and the Way of Light: Sutra, Tantra and Dzogchen
Namkhai Norbu, Snow Lion Publications 1986

The Embodied Mind: Cognitive Science and Human Experience
Francisco Varela, The MIT Press 1991

The Heart of the Buddha's Teaching
Thich Nhat Hanh, Rider Books 1998

The Heart of Listening: A Visionary Approach to Craniosacral Work
Hugh Milne, North Atlantic Books 1995

The Miracle of Mindfulness: a Manual on Meditation
Thich Nhat Hanh, Rider Books 1991

The Nation's Favourite Poems of Love
Daisy Goodwin, BBC Books 2004

The Pocket Rumi
Kabir Helminski, Shambala 2001

The Psychology of Awakening
Gay Watson, Stephen Batchelor & Guy Claxton, Rider Books 1999

The Sanity we are Born With
Chogyam Trungpa, Shambala 2005

The Rumi Collection
Kabir Helminski, Shambala 2000

The Scapegoat Complex: Toward a Mythology of Shadow and Guilt
Sylvia Brinton Perera, Inner City Books 1986

Tinnitus: A Self-Management Guide for the Ringing in Your Ears
Henry & Wilson, Allyn & Bacon 2002

Waking the Tiger: Healing Trauma
Peter Levine, North Atlantic Books 1997

Why Zebras Don't Get Ulcers
Robert Sapolsky, Holt Paperbacks 2004

Working on Yourself Alone
Arnold Mindell, Arkana 1990

Wisdom in the Body: the Craniosacral Approach to Essential Health
Michael Kern, Thorsons 2001

Made in the USA
San Bernardino, CA
11 May 2018